We Were Strangers

The Story of Magda Preiss

Magda Riederman Schloss

Edited by
Aaron Greenberg, PhD
AJ Greenberg

D0912468

BIOGRAPH LLC

Published by bioGraph
Chicago, IL
bioGraphbook.com

First bioGraph trade paperback edition January 2020

For information about discounts for bulk purchases,
please contact info@bioGraphbook.com

Designed by bioGraph
Manufactured in the United States of America
3 4 5 6 7 8 9 10

Printed on 90gsm acid-free paper

Library of Congress Control Number: 2019919653

ISBN: 978-1-951946-00-5 (paperback)
ISBN: 978-1-951946-01-2 (eBook)

A portion of proceeds from this book will be donated to
Holocaust remembrance and advocacy for refugees

To those who lost their
lives in the Holocaust and those with the
courage to tell their story.

Every instinct within me rebelled against being launched into eternity. I loved life. I was going to live. The nightmarish months began and ended as we went through the motions of living. So long as I believed I could not be destroyed, so long would I live. And even if they killed me, I would not die.

Magda Preiss

Table of Contents

The Story Behind The Story

Foreword by Bill Schloss

The rebirth of Magda's story began at Kol Nidre services on September 18, 2018 when I ran into my former neighbor, AJ Greenberg. He and his brother Aaron had recently started a storytelling and publishing business called bioGraph. I mentioned that my mother had written her story after the Holocaust and it was saved, precariously, on my cousin's virus-ridden computer. Intrigued, they requested a copy. Despite a sad comedy of technological glitches, we successfully retrieved the story: a 328-page PDF, each page a JPEG of the original typewritten manuscript. The yellowed pages were torn and wrinkled, yet Aaron and AJ were awestruck by the story and its relevance today. They urged me to preserve Magda's words in a book. The project unfolded, and we all realized our obligation to share this story with a wider audience.

"Do you want to know how this book came about?" asks Aunt Vivian at a meeting at my home on March

31, 2019, just under a century after my mother Magda was born. Aunt Vivian is my mother's youngest sister, and while contemplating the publication of my mother's story, I needed Aunt Vivian's perspective.

Vivian reminisces about her older sister playing wonderful Hungarian folk tunes on the family's baby grand piano in Uzhhorod (also known as Ungvár) before World War Two. She'd play piano and sing with the windows open and people would gather outside to hear. As you'll read, my mother was the only member of our family trapped in Europe during the war.

My mother's family in America spoke of Magda constantly and never gave up hope that she would survive. Until one Sunday morning, soon after the war, a letter came from her husband with a devastatingly brief message: he had not found Magda. Now the family was scared and prepared for the worst.

Before long, my other aunt, Susan, had a dream. She woke up in the morning and said to my grandma, "I dreamt that Magda is still alive."

"No!" my grandma wailed. "There's no way she could have survived."

But that very day, a policeman knocked on the door and asked, "Do you have a daughter named Magda Riederman?"

"Yes," my grandmother replied.

"Well," the policeman cleared his throat. "She's alive!"

After surviving the horrors of the Holocaust, my mother reunited with her family in Rock Island, Illinois. She had this great need to tell her story, and so my grandmother took my mother to Pioneer Women and Hadassah, where they listened to her tale between the songs she sang at the piano. At home, Magda would tell her story to whomever would listen. It got to the point where she needed to write a book. It was an outlet for her. She tried to publish at a few places but dropped it after being rejected. This was in the late 1940s.

There are too many similarities between the Holocaust and events in the world today. My mom always said, "Billy, just remember. This can happen again and probably will." Anti-Semitism, or any form of hatred, is too dangerous to ignore. People ignored Hitler and look what happened. We must take the warning signs seriously.

Everything happened gradually for my mother. First, she couldn't wear a fur coat, then she had to wear a yellow star, and the next day she had to surrender her jewelry and travel with a special permit. Before you know it, people are dragged out of their homes and forced to sign away all possessions. "It was all so legal and strictly within the law," my mother coldly reflected. It was a gradual erosion of human rights. By the time you realize what's happening, it's too late.

My wife Leslie has read many Holocaust books, but she insists that this book is "a whole different way of telling the story." My mother was kind of a romantic, and this book is a love story. But don't get me wrong—my mother was really tough. She wouldn't have survived otherwise, I would never have been born, and this story never told.

This book is addressed to future generations. By having the courage to read and share Magda's story, you are preserving the legacy of the Holocaust and helping to create a better world where all people can live free from fear and free to love.

We Were Strangers

The Story of Magda Preiss

A True Story

*"You shall not oppress a stranger,
for you know the feelings of the
stranger, having yourselves been
strangers in the land of Egypt."*

Exodus 23:9

Luftmensch

Sweet slumber, beloved; come, close your dear eyes,
The sun in its journey e'en now leaves yon skies;
Sweet dreams, my adored one, God keep you all night,
While under your cradle stands a kid, snowy white;
The kid leaves for trade marts to seek his fortune,
But my son studies Torah as his rightful portion;
When you are a man, and I am a grandma,
Around you will glow a rabbinical aura
And you will be learned in the Talmud and Torah.
Sweet dreams, my dear namesake, toys and sweets for surprise,
You will find in the morning when you open your eyes.

I think this lullaby sung by Mama to my brother, Mythieu, expresses the keynote of the fairyland that was my home and my childhood. It was a beautiful world of color and love and adoring parents, and sweet storybook Grandma, really our great grandmother, who always seemed to have a sweet or toy in her pocket and a blessing on her lips. It was a wonderful adventurous world of trips to relatives in Hungary, my own Petrof concert grand piano, and a home of costly and luxurious furnishings. It was a leisurely world, where there was always an abundance of time for Mama to work on petit point, and give lavish teas served on intricately embroidered, handmade lace cloths. It was an exciting world of poetry, music, and shopping expeditions to Prague and Budapest. It is only now that I appreciate the beauty of Dresden and Meissen, and the paintings and objets d'art in our home.

Mama is a woman of great charm and beauty and was highly regarded in Uzhhorod as a hostess without peer. Mama is tall and slim, with huge brown eyes, cameo-fine features and an "air." Suzi has Mama's length of limb, and is a lady to her fingertips, something which, alas, I fear I shall never be. But Suzi has flaming red hair, so I have hopes for her.

Vivian is the baby of the family and her moods range from Charlotte Brontë to Eleonora Duse. She is a tall blue-eyed sylph, and can do the csarda like a flaming gypsy. Upon the slightest provocation and without encouragement whatsoever, Vivian becomes the most fascinating coquette who ever allured. Du Barry, Recamier, Pompadour: their spirits seem to take over her body and soul, and she is no longer Vivian but the character she is playing. You might call it self-hypnosis. Lord help us if she ever portrays de' Medici.

Papa is a man of substance and prestige. The substance comes from his crystal, china and stained glass window business; the prestige from his own innate dignity and position as president of the Asa Chassid Synagogue. Papa idolized his offspring, but the antics of his high-spirited darlings left him in a state of perpetual bewilderment.

One day he would find his living room transformed into the Black Forest of Hansel and Gretel. That would be Vivian and Mythieu. A childhood friend, Magda Herskovitz was always given evil sinister roles because she was fat. Needless to say, she was the witch. Mama's curio cabinet was the ginger house. I invariably insisted on playing the musical background, unless it was the star role like Mozart being found in the middle of the night up in the attic playing the piano. To add realism we opened the windows even though it might be the dead of winter and a storm raging outside.

Mythieu, having been born in the United States, loyally insisted that every performance begin and end with the "Star-Spangled Banner." He would never play the wolf in Prokofieff's *Peter and the Wolf*. Oddly enough Vivian was ecstatic with joy if given the chance. She said it was a good meaty role into which she could sink her teeth. Speaking of wolves, we loved *Little Riding Hood*, and of course Magda Herskovitz was the grandmother. Suzi and Vivian were more accomplished and convincing actresses than I, but I had the voice and so I played Mimi, Lucia di Lammermoor,

Gilda, Lola and all the tearful heroines who sang themselves to death. But the part I really loved was Delilah.

I was born in 1920 in Uzhhorod, Ruthenia, which was in the eastern part of Czechoslovakia. The Republic was created November 14, 1918, out of what had been part of the old Austro-Hungarian Empire. It consisted originally of our states—Bohemia, Moravia, Slovakia and Ruthenia. Ruthenia is sometimes referred to as Carpatho-Russia.

The Republic owed its existence largely to the efforts of the late Dr. Thomas G. Masaryk, its first president. With the collapse of the Austro-Hungarian Empire in 1918, Slovakia and Ruthenia voted to join with the Czechs in the new Czechoslovak Republic. And on May 8, 1919, a joint session of the National Councils in Ruthenia proclaimed their union with the Czechoslovak Republic. Ruthenians are a branch of the Ukrainian race, some speaking Ukrainian, some Russian, and some local dialects. Thus, although Mama and I were born in Uzhhorod, Mama was born a Hungarian and I a Czechoslovakian.

When I was just beginning to walk, Papa who is a veteran of World War I with four years service in the Austro-Hungarian army, sold his crystal and stained glass window business to the city, along with the stately brick home I was too young to remember. Then we crossed the ocean to visit Mama's father who lived in Sharon, Pennsylvania, and still does. And this is how Mythieu was born in America. Although when Mythieu is asked about how he came to be born in America, he always answers, "the usual way."

Papa always says it was only my tender years that prevented me from disrupting the entire ship and standing it on end. But he adds, I almost succeeded. Grandfather urged Mama and Papa to remain in America, but Papa says they went back because he was certain the Gendarmerie would personally escort me to New York Harbor and put me aboard a ship.

Seriously, they loved Uzhhorod. It was their home. Though they had formerly thought of themselves as loyal Hungarians despite the rampant anti-Semitism, now they had high hopes that inasmuch as Uzhhorod was in Czechoslovakia, and part of a liberal and democratic government, for them and their children there would be a measure of security. For them, returning to Uzhhorod was the course of least resistance. Had they faced facts fearlessly and without self-delusion, they would have known they were sleeping on a volcano. Since when have boundaries and statutes changed human nature for the better?

We bid Grandfather farewell and crossed the ocean again, but now we were four. Papa established himself in Uzhhorod where Mama had a sizeable network of relatives and a dearly beloved brother, Uncle Desidur.

Amidst all this radiant happiness there were three piano lessons weekly. I marvel now at the patience of my teacher. Remonstrating I should never become a genius, no, not even a virtuoso, Mama's determination nevertheless won this battle. She said, "Young ladies must be accomplished if they wish to marry well." By this she meant not material wealth but culture, dignity, and prestige, which she called "yichus."

And speaking of yichus, I must tell you about Papa being the president of Asa Chassid Synagogue. This was a distinction of almost regal stature. Only a man who could ornament his office with majesty and bring glory and honor to it was ever elected. And Papa was always conscious of his dignification. Morning and evening with faithful regularity he went to the Synagogue for Shachris, Minchah, and Mairov (daily prayer services). But on the High Holy Days, Papa was radiant.

On these solemn occasions he left early for the synagogue, attired in Prince Albert coat, striped trousers and high hat. Solomon in all his glory could not aspire to Papa's incandescence. As it was forbidden for Jews to labor on Holy Days, which prohibition included striking matches to light a fire, and I, having a consuming curiosity about the inexorable laws of nature, on several occasions lit matches just to see if the heavens would fall. They didn't.

In winter I loved skating on the Uz. In my imagination I was Maria Theresa fleeing for my life to Nevicke, a half-hour train ride from Uzhhorod, with the breath of my arch enemy, Frederick, hot on my neck, and the stork bringing one of my sixteen children, only a flap of the wing behind. Or I might be Columbus sailing over the edge of the world. Oh, to go winging along like a bird, like a soul released, on a long silver ribbon and never, never having to stop.

Some days I was Eliza, tightly clutching my child to my bosom and running from the bloodhounds in *Uncle Tom's Cabin*. But always at four o'clock I was once more Magda Riederman. For one whole hour, for I must be home at five, I strolled up and down Galago Strasse, casting what I hoped were amorous and flirtatious glances at Bela Yaklowski across the street.

The grandest residences were on Galago Strasse, mostly occupied by Czechoslovak government representatives who had come in after Czechoslovak autonomy was established. If Bela had crossed the street to greet me, I should have fled in terrified delight, for Bela was not a Jew.

Bela was the only non-Jew in the Maccabees, a Zionist Youth athletic club to which I belonged, chiefly for the purpose of wearing a very fetching uniform. It consisted of light blue shorts and blouse with white collar and a white Star of David over the heart.

We Were Strangers

While strolling up and down Galago Strasse, Magda Herskovitz and I munched on pretzels we bought from poor children who wore tattered clothing, torn shoes, and a lean and ravenous look. It was a source of wonder to me they didn't eat the pretzels themselves. Occasionally I returned a few but they never ate them.

I played tennis at Fuzes, and Mama dressed me in the whitest of white shorts. Then there were dancing lessons. Ah, the dancing. Knowing I should never be a Pavlova, Mama nevertheless insisted, saying, "Young ladies learn how to walk and sit properly if they study dancing." But, O, the wild abandon of the csarda; and the rapture of dancing until the blood pounded madly through my veins and I was on fire, intoxicated with motion and emotion. Who cares about walking and sitting? Give me the csarda.

At school we were taught German, Czech, and Russian. At home we spoke Hungarian, Mama's native tongue. Walking home our Christian schoolmates ridiculed us and sang:

> Jew, Jew, you Wandering Jew,
> May one thousand worms crawl over you;
> Jew, Jew, you stinking Jew with roots in sand,
> What seek you here in *our* fair land?
> May the Devil take your mother's Lord,
> And all Jews perish by the Christian sword.

What did they mean "*our* fair land?" Was this not

my land, too? Had not I also been born on the soil of the Czechoslovak Republic?

One day when I was about twelve, I caught Volcha Sadowski by the collar, she who had just recently come from Poland.

"You, Volcha, this is *not* your land. You are a Pole. It is *my* land. I am a Czech."

"No. No. You are only a stinking Jew nobody. You have no homeland. I have Poland, but you have nothing. You are a *Luftmensch*, one wafted hither and yon by the air."

"You are crazy. I *am* a Czech, and you are not."

"I am so a Czech if I want to be, because I have my own land, Poland. But you have no land, no Jew land. You have a home no place. So you are a *Luftmensch*. Everyone fears you, you ghost, you corpse."

Was I a ghost? Was I a corpse? I pinched my arm. It hurt. This was incredible. Was this the explanation of why Mama and Papa were invited to Jewish homes only? Why their guests were only Jews?

"A ghost, am I? A corpse, am I? You will see what kind of ghost I am."

And with that I rained blow after blow on her head and face until blood spurted from her nose and mouth, and she fell in a heap. Horror gripped me—perhaps I killed Volcha. Screaming and with tears streaming down my face, I dashed for home running wildly all the way.

Now Mama loves a game of cards. She played afternoons with the Three Upturned Noses, as we referred to them in the bosom of the family. Each one fondly imagined the sun revolved about her august person. Each one believed herself to be the social leader, the bellwether of the Jewish community. Truthfully, with their silly affectations and pretenses, they were three shallow, superficial, empty shells, one more boring than the other.

Myra Wolfson looked like a crow, scrawny and sallow with dark circles under black beady eyes. She always whined about the state of her health and lived in terror lest her friends suspect she had enjoyed just one day free of illness. After a conversation with her, Mama always said, "I feel as if I've had a trip through Myra Wolfson's bowels."

Hannah Rabinsky was of a fatness and form that can only be described as Gargantuan. Her mammoth breasts and derriere heaved and swayed as she walked. She never sat down. She collapsed on a chair; usually the smallest and daintiest. And her quivering fat flowed over the sides and dangled. Invariably she wolfed almost all of the cakes, strudel, and bonbons Mama served, saying, "I usually eat less than a bird. I don't know what keeps me alive. Dear Aronka, your goodies tempt me. Just this one time I think I'll nibble." And with one nibble then another she nibbled everything but the design from the plate. Hannah was a "nosher," one addicted to overeating, especially sweets. She fondly imagined herself an intellectual because her father had been a Hebrew teacher and her brother was a doctor in Paris.

Minnie Braun surpassed them all. A widow, "sexually frustrated," I heard Mama whisper to Papa once when they didn't know I was listening. For Minnie, life was one great and endless battle to protect her virtue from the besieging assaults of potent and importuning gentlemen whose wives were incapable of arousing their interest—she said.

And then added, "You know I am a passionate woman. After all, I'm only in my thirties. But how can I even think of marriage. No, Latzi was the one man in my life, may his soul rest in peace. How can I think of robbing another woman of her husband. I pray for strength to resist temptation."

Papa said, "What Minnie needs is a good dose of the town bull." And Mama said, "She is fifty, if she's a day."

One thing the Three Upturned Noses all had in common: in their own eyes they were the queens of the universe, and the most intellectual and cultivated females that ever lived on the face of the earth, or at least upon the face of Uzhhorod.

Mama and the Three Upturned Noses usually played

cards in the sitting room. Our parlor was too formal for every day entertaining. The sitting room was lovely; dainty French gold furniture upholstered in pale yellow satin with an overall pattern of gold fleur de lis, and a gold colored Chinese rug on the floor.

As they were commencing their first game, in I flew screaming, "I have killed Volcha Sadowski! I have killed her!" Then I dashed into my bedroom and slammed the door with such violence that a Dresden figure toppled from the French onyx pedestal and crashed to the floor. The crash was soothing to my nerves.

I learned later Mama rose from her chair, turned to her guests and said, "Ladies, I am sorry but there will be no game today." They departed in a huff, their noses all but touching our ceiling.

Mama came in and sat on the bed where I'd flung myself. Between sobs I poured out my story. Mama said, quietly, "It states in our prayer book, 'Help me to be meek when others wrong me that I may readily forgive them.'"

"But Mama, am I a homeless *Luftmensch*? Am I a ghost or a corpse that people are afraid of?"

And then Mama told me about Theodor Herzl and the Balfour Declaration and the Palestine Mandate.

"And before you are my age there will be a Jewish State in Palestine. Then Czech Jews will be equals with Czech

Christians, and French Jews will be equals with French Christians, and the Volchas of the world will not be able to call you a homeless nobody and hate and fear you. Jewish homelessness—the cause of their fear and hatred, which actually does make a corpse and a ghost of the Jewish people, floating about as they do, a soul without a body—will have been eliminated. If we wish to cure the Volchas of the disease of Jew-hatred, we must take care to remove the cause of the disease: Jewish homelessness."

"Mama, how can you be so sure?"

"Because, my child, the honor of fifty-two nations, including the great and honorable United States of America, is involved. They are all signatories of the Palestine Mandate. And if the great nations of the world do not honor their pledged and plighted word, then there can be no peace—for them or for us."

Since Mama was the highest living authority, I was at peace.

Die or Be an Old Maid

L earning to chat with boys is an accomplishment you must acquire when you are fifteen or forever remain a spinster, thought I. And so at the beach, I dove in, literally and figuratively. The water was fine. No longer a bothersome youngster beneath their mature and lofty notice, I began to attract swains on my own.

Tibor Klein was the first to recognize my undeniable charm, and it was he who ushered me into the magic circle. One day he asked, "Magda, may I present my friend who is eager to meet you?" I agreed casually enough but my feelings were anything but casual. Of course I had noticed the tall newcomer with the piercing gray eyes, olive skin, and silky black hair.

"How do you do," I asked, and we were off to a stimulating if not lengthy friendship. It ended too soon and too disastrously.

He was Vas Karcsi, the son of a lawyer, and I liked him. This group of Czechoslovakian youth fondly imagined themselves communists. They discussed Stalin, communism, free love, Lenin, Trotsky, and free love. If any other political ideology had offered free love they would have been for it. They considered themselves men of the world, although the eldest, Vas Karcsi was not yet eighteen.

Mama was delighted that her darling was dating the son of a wealthy lawyer, a young man who would himself be a lawyer one day. Mama would have swooned had she known they considered themselves communists and were all agog about free love. Being vague about their "scholarly" discussions, and interested only in associating with a young, exciting, laughing group, I tried to appear understanding and sympathetic. This was easily achieved by remaining silent. So Magda was wonderful and Mama was happy.

One smiling, sunny day Vas Karcsi and I walked the length of Galago Strasse, and beyond where the houses are few and far between. Sprawled on the grass he placed his hand over mine and said, "Magda, I love you."

I was on fire. I was the Sleeping Beauty being kissed by Prince Charming. Striking a languorous pose I gazed into his eyes. He leaned toward me.

"Magda, be my inamorata?"

The meaning was all too clear. Jumping to my feet, I ran all the way home. This was the end of all joy, the end of life itself. Love's young dream, a hideously shattered illusion.

Now, as I said, Mama loves a game of cards. Just as she and the Three Upturned Noses were about to begin their first game, in I flew screaming, "I have been betrayed, I have been betrayed," dashed into my bedroom and slammed the door with such violence that a Meissen vase toppled from the French onyx pedestal and crashed to the floor. The crash was soothing to my nerves. I was to learn Mama rose from her chair, turned to her guests and said, "Ladies, I am sorry but there will be no game today." They departed in a huff, their noses all but touching our ceiling. Mama should have been completely scared out of her wit, but she wasn't.

Quietly entering my bedroom she let me sob out the whole sorry story on her breast. Vas Karcsi was the first and last love of my life. And he had dared to suggest...

"I want to die. I want to die. Let me die. My heart is broken. My life is at an end."

The atmosphere of the Riederman home was heavy with grief. I cried from morning to night. Poor Mama and Papa were beside themselves. Mama insisted that I go out among my friends, but this was one battle she lost. My heart wasn't in it. There was room in my heart only for Vas Karcsi, and him I had imperiously sent away for all eternity.

At the precise moment when the whole family was about to have a nervous breakdown from my weeping and moaning, although it never affected my appetite for

Mama's strudel and cheese kuchen, Mama said, "Magda, you must go away for a visit or all this crying and grieving will make you sick and ugly."

"I don't want to go away. I shall remain here and die or be an old maid."

"Papa is getting a passport for you and you will soon be on your way to Uncle Lajos."

Uncle Lajos was Papa's brother and he lived in Satu Mare, Romania, a distance of several hours by train.

Elizabeth Weisberger made me eight dresses. One was pale yellow with tiny sprigs of flowers, and a black velvet sash. Another was white brilliantine trimmed with pearl buttons. And there was a brown challis with a dainty white and green figure, a blue dotted swiss with insertions of white swiss lace, and a blue challis. They were all attractive and flattering thanks to Elizabeth, who now lives in New York.

My shoes came from Uncle Desidur's store on Masaryk Street and my hats, coats and lingerie from Prague. Mama took me as far as Czop where Uncle Lajos met us. Kissing Mama good-bye, Uncle Lajos and I proceeded to Satu Mare. You might say they were people of modest means, for Uncle Lajos was a small restaurateur. But he had six tall sons, one handsomer than the other. Life was becoming rosy again. The problem was which son to choose.

Cousin Earnest's unconcealed devotion was more than cousinly. We went walking, played tennis, strolled to the sugar baker for ice cream, and danced. How we danced! When he held me in his arms, I floated. Mysteriously, I fractured the law of gravity. I swear my feet never touched the floor. Life was rapturous and I sang and sang in Russian, in Hungarian, in Polish, in Slovakish, and in Czech. I wrote Mama, "I am so happy my heart isn't big enough to contain all my joy. I am in love."

Two days later Mama was in Satu Mare and I was packed and on my way home. Mama was like a volcano on the point of erupting. I could see she was holding back until we boarded the train. After all Uncle Lajos was Papa's brother and restraint was indicated. But once on the train the volcano erupted and the lava enveloped me.

"What do you mean by falling in love with Earnest? Have you gone mad? You know he is only a poor working boy without prospects, and not even properly educated. And a cousin…What future does he have?"

"But Mama, we are in love."

"Enough. The discussion is finished."

Earnest followed me to Uzhhorod, ostensibly to visit his sister, Sari, who was delighted at the prospect of the marriage. I was indifferent. What was the matter? "Am I fickle?" I asked myself. First Vas Karcsi, and now

Earnest. I wouldn't cross the street to say hello to either one of them. I went to parties and dances with Susan Katz, Vera Kovich and Agnes Vayda. Dancing partners were numerous, eager and willing. And Mama brought me a fur coat from Budapest.

Cousin Earnest was destined to die on the field of battle, a victim of German "heroism." When the Russian armies retreated they protected their rear by mining roads and fields to slow down the oncoming Germans. In front of the German army marched tens of thousands of helpless Jews right across the mined areas. The mines exploded, the roads were pronounced safe, and the brave Germans thundered on over Cousin Earnest's dead body. This was the "future" Mama had scolded about that long ago day back in Satu Mare.

Holy Day Queen

F riday evenings, Erev Sabbath, was always festive in our home. Mama blessed the Sabbath candles and we were all comforted in their golden glow. Friday and Saturday evenings and Saturday noon our home was open to all poor strangers in the community. Usually emaciated Polish Jews whose clothes hung upon them like scarecrows in the wheat fields. Their hunger was awesome and pathetic.

I think open house on Passover was the peak of Mama's entertaining. Then the tables were loaded with roast goose, roast chicken, wines, liquors, chremzil, fruit, honey kuchen, macaroon torten filled with orange and chocolate fillings, and an endless variety of delicacies. For this occasion a cateress and staff came from Prague. Only one other lady, the banker's wife, imported a cateress. However, being the president of Asa Chassid Synagogue outranked any banker, so our open house was the pinnacle.

The High Holy Days were something else. Preparations for Rosh Hashanah were complex and arduous. A third servant girl usually reinforced our Agi and Mari. Mama, like Napoleon planning the Battle of Waterloo, based her strategy on the weather and number of guests expected; she strove mightily so only those relatives presently congenial would be under her roof at the same time. She dreamed up potential romances for those of marriageable age, even going so far as to name the first born of couples who had not yet become acquainted. But it was Grandma who actually carried out Mama's strategy and tactics, hustling and bustling, fluttering and sputtering, hastening and chastening for days on end.

Suddenly all at once there was a hush. The Holy Day Queen was descending. It was Erev Rosh Hashanah in the home of William Riederman, president of Asa Chassid Synagogue. A sweet and hushed solemnity pervaded our home. Papa came home early, donned his Prince Albert coat, striped trousers and high hat. Before leaving for the synagogue he placed his hand on our heads and blessed us in the order of our ages: I, Mythieu, Suzi, and Vivian.

Faithfully, Erev Sabbath and Erev Yom Tov, at the setting of the sun before the Sabbath and before a Holy Day, Papa gathered us in his arms, and looking up at the petit point sampler made by Mama, he read, "They labor in vain who build the house, except the Lord build it." It was in Hebrew and we repeated it after him. Then he kissed Mama and Grandmother and departed, prayer book and prayer shawl in hand.

The Holy Day Queen reigned. I close my eyes and see

our dining room. The crystal chandelier aglow in all its brilliant splendor. It consisted of hundreds of crystal prisms, intricate and gossamer crystal flowers. At the moment the sun set, Mama ushered in the Holy Days by kindling the candles and whispering a prayer: "May our home be consecrated, O God by Thy Light. May it shine upon us all in blessing as the light of love and truth, the light of peace and good will. Amen."

Mama's silver candelabra had thirteen branches and I imagined each candle was a beautiful girl angel. The walls of our dining room were covered with a celestial blue satin damask Papa had imported from France. On the floor was a rose Persian rug and the chairs were tufted in pink satin. At the windows which extended almost to the floor hung French lace curtains. The draperies were made of pink satin with large blue flowers worked in trapunto. On the serving table proudly glittered Mama's silver tea service. On the credenza two large and spreading Dresden candelabra, all cherubs and flowers, guarded the thirteen-branched silver candelabra which for this night shed its golden glow between them.

Returning from Divine Services, Papa brought the male guests with him. The ladies came early. Always there was Aunt Bella, wife of Uncle Desidur. She was to die as a German slave laborer. Their son, Imre, met the same fate. The remaining son, Latzi, became a displaced person in Frankfurt. Last I heard, he was still awaiting an American visa.

At the dinner table Papa lifted up the wine cup and prayed: "Let us praise God with this symbol of joy, and thank Him for the Blessings of the past week, for life, health, and strength, for home, love and friendship, for the discipline of our trials and temptations, for the happiness that has come to us out of our labors. Thou hast ennobled us, O God, by the blessings of work, and in love and kindness Thou hast sanctified us by the blessings of rest through the commandment: 'Six days shall thou labor and do all the work, but the seventh day is the Sabbath hallowed unto the Lord, thy God;' Praised be Thou, O Lord our God, King of the Universe, who has created the fruit of the vine."

Then Papa cut off the end of a loaf of Challa (white bread baked especially for the Sabbath and Holy Days) which was covered with a napkin and said, "Praised be Thou, O Lord our God, King of the Universe, who causest the earth to yield for all." Papa placed his hand on the head of each child and blessed us.

For this night we were one with God to the depths of our souls. A New Year was being ushered in. This was a time for self-communion. Papa who had read the Jewish philosophers explained this was a time for self-searching, for prayer, a solemn season of self-judgment; that tomorrow we shall hear the ram's horn in the synagogue, and listen in solemn awe, stirred to our very souls not only by its notes but by its meaning; that the ram's horn is Israel's call to repentance and self-renewal, meaning "Awake ye sleepers; be not of those who miss realities in their hunt for shadows. Consider your deeds. Purify your hearts. There is an eye that seeth all. There is an ear that heareth all things. There is a heavenly judge with whom is no unrighteousness, or forgetfulness, nor respect of persons."

Mama told us children confidentially that she thought Papa was somewhat vain of his Hebrew learnings.

Then we had dinner, a dinner that was the consummation of Mama's generalship and Grandma's Herculean efforts. Roast chicken and goose, sweet and sour tongue, gefilte fish, noodle soup, strudel, and an alluring variety of compotes, pastries, fruits and delicacies. For this festive occasion Mama took down her best china dinnerware, usually kept for security reasons in the upper regions of a tall black ebony cabinet. It had been Papa's gift on their tenth anniversary. Of Rosenthal make, it was decorated with a two- inch cobalt blue bank, bordered on each side with a bracelet of gold. Each piece was emblazoned with a blue and gold letter R. The table was breathlessly lovely and from the center smiled a colorful floral decoration.

We Were Strangers

My parents had a passionate love for their religion and they revered all that was beautiful and true and moral. We children studied Hebrew and it was fondly hoped Mythieu would be a rabbi. It was at such moments that I resolved to be a little lady like Suzi. Then I should not have to be apprehensive of the Seeing Eye and the Hearing Ear; but alas for my resolutions.

When morning came Papa left early for the Synagogue. After breakfast Mama took us children there, all shining with an inner glow, and complete new outfits from Budapest. Mythieu and I walked ahead and Mama held Vivian and Suzi by the hand.

The interior of Asa Chassid always overwhelmed me, and it was the only thing that did. Mythieu sat with Papa. The women being segregated by a partition, I was obliged to remain with Mama, but this did not prevent my peeking through the openings in the latticed partition.

In the very center was the Almemor, the Court of Honor, on which stood the dignified, venerable, upright, and aged. The altar was a white and gold magnificence and hanging above it an Eternal Light which I fondly imagined was of solid gold. The elders wore snowy white robes, white satin yarmulkes (praying hats), and long white beards. In the eyes of an impressionable child they were elderly angels; the rabbi was Abraham, and the cantor was David. At least for this day. On the morrow they would resume their normal names and stations. The cantor instead of being David singing the Song of Songs would again be Avrom Reichfeld. But for today, how his voice rang out, strong and clear and sweet as he sang.

Love Laughs at Mothers

I n 1938 the handwriting on the wall was becoming clear. The birds of ill omen in German uniforms were hovering like vultures over Europe. Even the most optimistic among us realized our destiny was hanging by a thread and our very lives trembling in the balance.

Our family was more fortunate than most. Mythieu, having been born in America, could claim citizenship and return to the land of his birth. This was the fulfillment of a lifetime wish. Grandfather Klein sent the necessary affidavits and Papa and Mythieu sailed early in 1938. This was the moment when the Germans were starting the trouble in the Sudetenland which was to set off the chain reaction that was to be World War Two.

Papa took $4,000 with him, planning to return to Uzhhorod, sell the business, properties and holdings, and take us all to America. Poor Papa. He invested in a bakery in New York which was a failure, and then in a fruit shop which completely wiped out his capital. But Papa had his pride. Now a pauper living from day to day on whatever pittance he could scrape together, he nevertheless sent us cheerful reports, not daring to discourage us from coming. This was the time of the Anschluss and Italy's invasion of Albania.

Papa was no fool. He knew the Four Horsemen were shodding their steeds. Papa is eighty generations from the destruction of the Temple, but in which generations have Jews not been the scapegoat?

Mama started to sell the furnishings of our home. When she sold my Petrof concert grand piano a part of my life went with it. It had been friend and companion since my eighth birthday. To it I had brought my joys and woes, my tempestuous and my amorous moods. Fortunately the home was not to be dismantled until after our departure.

The business we sold to Cousin Emil, Papa's assistant. Like Earnest, Emil also was destined to die making a mined Russian road safe for "brave" German warriors. The buildings on Masaryk Street were never sold and to this day title has not been surrendered. Uncle Desidur writes they are all standing; the iron foundry, shoe factory, apothecary, grocery store; the "traffic" store which was a government operated business selling tobacco, newspapers, and stamps; the barber shop and the Singer Sewing Machine Agency. They are all there. I might add they are Russian-occupied as Ruthenia is now incorporated in the Ukraine.

When one is not yet eighteen, life has its own enchant-ments and raptures, and political machinations seem vague and unreal. Life was intriguing and soon I would be in America. Life was indeed a bed of roses for the Riedermans, for we would sail in only a few weeks.

One day feeling mellow and at peace with myself, I walked into Magda Herskovitz's father's restaurant. And then my heart stood still. For there was the man, the only man in the whole world for me. Here was my heart of hearts, my paradise. I was floating on pink clouds. Suddenly anger swept over me like a storm. What right had Magda Herskovitz to be laughing and bantering with him just because it was her father's restaurant? I'd show her.

"Who is he, Magda," I asked in what I hoped was an indifferent tone of voice.

"Why, don't you know? He is the new pharmacist at Donath's Drug Store. He is charming and I've met his father and he dines here every day."

I interrupted, "Perhaps you will introduce me?"

"Well, if you insist."

I stamped my foot and tossed my head.

"Who's insisting? I am merely trying to be polite to a stranger in our midst."

"But really, you are too young. He is twenty-five and certainly not interested in chicks your age. He rooms at

Susan Katz's home and I know he is going to the theater Friday evening."

That was all I needed to know. Friday evening Mama and I were at the theater. During intermission I casually strolled over to my girlfriends. They were hovering about my one and only, and gushing and fawning as if they owned him. It was disgusting.

Gustave Preiss was tall, handsome, well-groomed, dignified and quite as nonchalant as I. He had thick brown hair, a wavy lock of which fell over his eyes and which he was constantly pushing back. His eyes were brown and sympathetic, his face long and lean, with a narrow nose and a sweet mouth. Well, I for one would neither gush nor fawn. Two could play at this game of indifference.

For several days I walked up and down Main Street, hoping to meet him, but in vain. I shopped at Donath's but all I got for my trouble was cool indifference from Mr. Gustave Preiss. And a supply of toiletries I didn't want.

Then it happened. Susan Katz invited me to her birthday party and Gustave was there. This was March of 1938 and just prior to my eighteenth birthday. I ignored him. Someone asked me to sing. I sat at the piano and started to play and sing the Pola Negri "Mazurka."

> I feel in me, I feel in you,
>> The same wild blood.

Conscious that Gustave was standing at the piano, I was afraid to raise my eyes to his. I was suffocating.

"You play and sing well, Magda. May I have this dance?"

It was a Strauss waltz, perfect for lovers. He waltzed me into the cozy sitting room, and we sat on the chaise longue. Blushing and tremulous I tried to avoid his burning eyes. Suddenly he drew me into his arms and kissed me. I was transported to an enchanted world where dreams are spun. It was the moment for which I was born: pure, unalloyed ecstasy. It was the happiest moment I have known before or since. Just then Susan entered, took in the situation at a glance, and announced supper was being served.

"May I take you home, Magda? And may I have the pleasure of seeing you tomorrow?"

"Yes…I don't know…Call me tomorrow."

Now, again, Mama loves a game of cards. This evening she was playing with the Three Upturned Noses. I walked through the sitting room like a somnambulist, looking neither to the right nor left. I saw no one. I floated as in a trance. Closing the door gently, I sat on the bed. What was wrong? What was missing? Opening the door quietly, I picked up the Meissen bird group on the French onyx pedestal and crashed it to the floor. The crash was soothing to my nerves. I was to learn later, Mama rose and said, "Ladies, I am sorry there will be no more playing this evening."

They departed in a huff, their noses all but touching our ceiling. Mama came and sat on the bed.

"Magda, what has happened?"

"Nothing, Mama."

"Yes…Your eyes are sparkling. You are too quiet. What is it?"

"O, Mama, I am so very much in love. I am so happy. He is the one. He is the real love of my life. I am swooning."

Scornfully but relieved she said, "Oh, is that all? I thought perhaps you were ill. Ho-hum, you will have other loves, I am sure. You are going to America in a few weeks and America is full of charming young men."

"No, Mama. I feel I am not going to America. I have a feeling I am going to remain here with this man. He is my destiny."

"Goodnight, Little One. Sweet dreams."

"But, Mama, may I go out walking with him tomorrow evening?"

"With whom?"

"With my love. With Gustave Preiss."

"You may if you still wish to by tomorrow."

The following evening found us strolling along Galago Strasse. Gustave pledged his undying love and asked me to marry him.

"How do you *know* you love me in so short a time? To

how many other girls have you pledged your love?"

"Don't tease me. You are the only one I have asked to be my wife."

"In a few weeks I shall be on my way to America."

"I will never let you go."

Mama wouldn't hear of it.

"Are you crazy? I will certainly not leave you here, a girl not yet eighteen."

But love laughs at mothers.

"I shall be eighteen in a few weeks and you cannot stop me."

"Listen, my child. I want your happiness above everything. You know the Germans are lusting for war. They will be satisfied with nothing less than a bloodbath and the enslavement of Europe. I cannot let you remain. Even now they are starting in the Sudetenland. You know Germany intends to expel or enslave all Czechs, as explained in *Mein Kampf*."

"I cannot give him up. I will marry Gustave and we, too, can go to America and be safe and free."

Honeymoon

W e were straws in a sucking whirlpool. Being in love, I regarded the approaching whirlpool with detached indifference. The Anschluss of Austria was no concern of mine and I gave my friends bothered ear when they went into throes of anguish over it. True, it was forbidden by the Treaty of St. Germain and Versailles. Nevertheless it was consummated March 13, 1938.

German troops marched in on the invitation of the Austrian government and took possession, greeted by hysterically joyous demonstrations. Two days later when Hitler announced formal incorporation of Austria to Great Germany to a vast throng in Vienna's Square of Heroes, it meant nothing to me. What cared I that, as foretold in *Mein Kampf*, Austria resumed her medieval status as the Ostmark, outpost of the Germanic peoples against the Slav races? What cared I about Germany's historic love for penetration to the East?

Papa being away, Uncle Desidur assumed the responsibility of passing judgment on Gustave, and making the momentous decision. On my birthday, March 20, I received a bouquet of eighteen roses. On the attached card Gustave had written, "Much luck and happiness to you. G.P."

Susan Katz fetched his gift, a silver compact. Mama was furious.

"You cannot accept a gift from a stranger."

Susan took it back reluctantly. Before long she dashed into our home, panting and breathless.

"Magda, Gustave says if you do not accept his gift he will throw it into the Uz."

Mama relented. "Passover is coming, and you will return a gift to him."

On a soft spring Sunday evening Gustave came to dinner. Mama introduced him to Aunt Bella and Uncle Desidur. I was painfully self-conscious. Vivian and Suzi giggled. The blushes which stained my throat and face were too red for beauty against my red hair. Gustave's embarrassment was revealed by the trembling of his voice. It was only with the greatest effort that I restrained my natural impulse to break dishes over the heads of Suzi and Vivian.

After dinner Uncle Desidur and Gustave had a lengthy conversation in the privacy of the sitting room. About ten, after gravely shaking hands all around, Gustave left. I could no longer contain myself. It was only with great difficulty that I'd remained silent up to this point.

"Magda, he is not for you. I do not give my consent."

"*You* don't consent? I don't care for your consent

anyhow. I *will* marry him. I love Gustave. I love him…
I love him."

I was shaking my fists wildly, my eyes filled with tears
of frustration, my voice choked. Uncle Desidur put his
arms around me.

"Quiet, child, quiet. I was only testing your love. You
have my blessing. He is a fine young man."

For a few minutes we laughed and cried together. I sat
down at the piano and played and sang until long past midnight. Uncle Desidur, Aunt Bella, Mama, Vivian, and Suzi
danced and sang with me. It was a lovely evening.

Gustave wrote Papa for my hand about the time of the
plebiscite in Austria, April 10, 1938. The matter for the Austrian people to decide was, "Do you agree with the reunifi-
cation of Austria with the German Reich that was enacted
on March 13 1938 and do you vote for the list of our Führer
Adolf Hitler?"

The Austrian people voted "yes" by 99.73%. It was a
stunning revelation even to me. An influential factor in the
response of the Austrian voters was the statement issued
prior to the plebiscite by Cardinal Innitzer and the Austrian Roman Catholic bishops. They declared that they had
"freely and joyfully decided to vote 'yes' as a national duty
and that they expected all good Austrian Catholics to do
the same." It was read from all Austrian pulpits.

When Mama and her friends discussed it, stark terror gripped them. For which helpless nation would the clock strike next? Helpless Albania was invaded by Italy, her manpower savagely attacked, her women ravaged. The Italians were nothing but common horse thieves. They stole King Zog's prize Arabian stallions. And King Zog and Queen Geraldine, who had just been delivered of a son, fled for their lives.

Gustave's parents came for the engagement dinner on May 20. Discreet investigation revealed they were fine and honorable people residing in Mikuláš, Slovakia. Gustave's mother gave me her engagement ring. It was lovely, in the form of a crown set with rubies and diamonds. Papa wrote he was trying to get a visa for Gustave. Mama generously offered to let us live in her home.

"The rents from our properties will provide well for you," she said. "Now that the Germans are absorbing the Sudeten—"

Gustave and I were married on August 20, at the Hotel Korona. The chuppah, or bridal canopy, was covered with white flowers and set up in the middle of a blooming, colorful garden. In the background, brightly garbed gypsies played as only Hungarian gypsies can play; the dreams, hopes, and innermost secret passions of a young bride.

My dress was sheer white net, and the rose point veil

and train were Mama's. Vivian and Suzi were little angels in rose and blue floor-length taffeta. The morning was spent in prayer, meditation, and fasting—and also much fussing with my hair and gown.

About noon we left for the hotel. Mama bore up gallantly but she must have missed Papa terribly. Only a mother can know the pain of marrying off one's first born precious treasure.

The rabbi placed a white satin band over my eyes and blessed me. Aunt Bella and Gustave's mother led me at the head of the bridal procession to the chuppah. Gustave, very grave and very handsome, awaited me. He wore a formal cutaway coat, striped trousers, and high hat. A snowy white kittel (prayer robe) enveloped him.

I was Venus, the goddess of love. And though enraptured and bewitched by the flames of passion and adoration, there was tenderness and sweetness in my love for my husband-to-be. In a few dazed minutes the consecration and benediction were pronounced and the traditional glass broken.

The blue skies, the golden sun, the throbbing, sensuous gypsy music, Gustave's kiss, Mama's tears, and the felicitations of relatives and friends shall always be fresh in my memory. The dinner, enjoyed by two hundred guests was delicious. I know because I didn't miss a course.

Gustave wished to go to Budapest, his birthplace, for our honeymoon. Unable to obtain visas, we went to Prague. On the train in a dream world of our own, we met a number of Gustave's friends, who were in uniform. They had been drafted as soldiers of the first mobilization on May 21, 1938.

"We wish you luck, Gustave, but soon you will be in uniform, too." How true. How prophetic. Our two weeks in Prague were idyllic. We had no thought of the black clouds which were gathering.

One week after our return to Uzhhorod, Gustave was called into the Czech army. The German beast was on a rampage, panting to murder, rob, rape, and ruthlessly destroy for the mere gratification of bloodlust as she had been doing for one thousand years. Mama was in a quandary.

"How can I leave you now that your husband is away?"

She postponed her departure from day to day. Is there need now to describe the ruthless and deceitful propaganda which preceded Munich? The fear, the self-deception and treachery which led France and Britain to desert the stronghold of democracy in Central Europe, at the moment of the heaviest attack on it?

The Czechoslovak people knew well the flood of German conquest would engulf all Europe if their nation were surrendered, and yet they were powerless to stop it. They were astounded and grieved to see the weasel diplomacy of Runciman followed by Chamberlain flying with his umbrella in one hand and a knife for the throat of Czechoslovakia in the other, to offer Germany whole areas of their territory.

For one thing that territory had never in all history been part of Germany; in the second place, it was not Chamberlain's and Daladier's to give away.

The Czechs were stunned when the British and French ambassadors, Messrs. Newton and Lacroix, awoke President Beneš on September 21 to tell him that if his government did not accede to the German demands, Czechoslovakia would be adjudged alone responsible for war which would follow.

On the heart of every loyal Czech are slashed the written words of Chamberlain to Germany: "I feel that you can get all the essentials without war and without delay."

Any government on the face of the globe would be incompetent fools not to realize that just as His Majesty's government betrayed the Czechoslovak Republic they would betray any government—and have.

On September 30, 1938, at half past twelve, European democracy received an almost mortal blow. The people of Uzhhorod refused to believe their ears. There was consternation, incredulity, anger, and fright—ever increasing, horrible fright.

At that black moment, four "great" powers, England, France, Germany and Italy signed a pact in Munich. Russia was ignored. With a few strokes of the pen, the Czechoslovak Republic was declared open territory for the thieving German nation.

Are the memories of man so short that this foul deed, Great Britain and France giving away the independence and territorial integrity of Czechoslovakia, can be forgotten? Let man forget at his own peril.

It was destined that more blows were to fall each more crushing than the one preceding. On November 2, the arbitrary First Vienna Award announced by the German and Italian foreign ministers gave Hungary about 4,600 square miles of territory in southern Slovakia and Ruthenia, with a population of 869,299. This included Uzhhorod.

It meant the Hungarians were coming in. Mama took it more philosophically than I, for she was born Hungarian. For me, this invasion portended evil. It meant for one thing that Gustave would be in Czechoslovakia and I in Hungary. Only a European can truly understand the importance placed on borders, and how jealously and suspiciously, yes, hatefully, those separated by borders regard one another.

I shall never forget the day the Hungarians entered Uzhhorod. It was around the 7th or 8th of November.

Mama's pleasurable anticipation puzzled me. How could I know she was concealing fear? The populace was ordered to line the streets and greet our "liberators" with proper deference, and obsequiousness, and make an enthusiastic demonstration of loyalty.

Poor Mama, how she tried to quiet my fears. Lining the streets, there we stood. Each one afraid to show any emotion but joy. There is something about authority in European countries that seems to paralyze the soul. Of real freedom, freedom from fear, they know nothing. Since living in America and drinking deeply of the wine of freedom and liberty, I know for the first time in my life what it really means to be free.

And then they came, these German-influenced Hungarians. Evil things in the forms of men. Once Papa took me to the zoo, and the sight of tigers and lions sickened me. Realizing instinctively they were the killers of the animal world, I felt a million crawling things between my skin and flesh and retched and vomited all over Papa.

The same emotion overpowered me. Now I knew these arrogant Germanized Hungarian monsters were the killers of the human race; wild beasts, vultures, butchers crazily lusting for human blood.

Suddenly I was crying—screaming. Mama almost died. She pinched my arm fiercely.

"Can't you see you will get us all killed? Raise your arm; cheer them."

That evening all Jewish stores were broken into and robbed. What they didn't want, they destroyed. Jewish youths accused of being communists were beaten and murdered. Many were arrested and sent to Budapest, never to be heard of again. The Dominion of Arrogance was upon us. How very convenient the accusation "communist" was for those who used it to cloak their natural homicidal mania, their lust for raping and looting.

Mama hoped the Christian clergy would make an outcry, but she hoped in vain. I asked her, "Mama, what are you hoping for? The clergy remained silent when Italy invaded Albania. The clergy remained silent when Italy invaded Ethopia and bombed and gassed helpless human beings. What can you expect now?"

The Czech army was demobilized but Gustave could not come to me. He was in Czechoslovakia, and I was in Hungary. Whichever one crossed the border forfeited the right to return. Out of loyalty to Czechoslovakia, he refused to enter Hungary. Czechoslovakia was his country. Proudly he had worn her uniform and fought under her flag. It had been home and homeland since infancy. No, the only solution was that I go to him. Mama left the decision to me. I made it.

"What happens to my husband, happens to me."

How would I enter Czechoslovakia? That was the puzzler. The border ran right through Uzhhorod but no one could obtain a military permit to cross. No one but Mama. Businessmen were unable to reach their offices and stores downtown, and those who happened to be in their business establishments when the border was officially set could not reach their homes. That is what happens when a border runs right through a city. Mama, a seasoned campaigner, conceived the idea of taking me to the Hungarian military commandant. Her intrepid persistence achieved the impossible: an interview with the commandant. My plight, the young bride separated from her adoring husband, must have intrigued his fancy. We got the permit.

Mama and I walked to the border. There stood my Gustave. My heart leapt for joy. We kissed across the border. A Hungarian soldier pushed between us. I shrank back in terror. Mama triumphantly waved the permit right under his nose. Suspicious and annoyed, he let us talk.

Gustave pleaded, "Magda, dearest, stay here with me. I want you so."

"But, Gustave, I have nothing with me; no clothes, no toiletries. How can I stay?"

"Mama can bring your clothes tomorrow. Then we shall go to my parents in Mikuláš."

Mama was strong. She agreed to bring my things on the morrow. I stepped across the border and we went to a hotel. It was primitive and dirty, especially the bed clothes which were unbelievably filthy. But Gustave and I were in each others arms and the realities of little concern.

During the night we were rudely disturbed by loud pounding on the door. A Czech soldier strode in. Ashamed, I cowered under the covers trying to hide myself. He pulled back the covers.

"Who is this woman and what is she doing here?"

"She is my wife."

"Bah! Do you expect me to believe that story? She is a spy. Get up, you red one."

And saying that he began hauling me out of bed. Gustave flung himself on the intruder and shouted, "Here are my identification papers. Here is my uniform. You see, I, too, am a Czech soldier. She is my wife, not a spy."

"Your wife...likely story. Report to headquarters in the morning."

There was no sleep for us that night, but Gustave held me in his arms and the world was mine. In the morning Gustave proved our identities.

No one but Mama could have commandeered a horse, a wagon, and a driver. Down the street creaked an ancient wagon, drawn by an ancient, bony horse, driven by an ancient, bony, creaking driver. The wagon was loaded perilously high with my belongings; luggage, leather beds, pillows, bed clothes, and all the lovely linens, laces, and embroidered tablecloths and bedspreads of my voluminous trousseau. Mama took me in her arms.

"Be strong. Be brave. Be true."

She kissed me farewell. When shall we meet again? Mama was going to America, I to Slovakia.

Edicts

The train to Mikuláš was overflowing with men in uniform, mostly Czechs and Hungarians. All was confusion. Sitting on our luggage for the entire trip, we arrived in Mikuláš at midnight. Gustave's mother embraced me and said, "You have come to a mother, not a mother-in-law. Don't be afraid, my child. I shall be a real mother."

She spoke German in the home, elsewhere Slovakish. Her welcome was genuine and loving. How I must have tried her patience in the months ahead. I was especially inept and inexperienced in the household arts. Gustave's father was sweet and pathetically happy with his new daughter.

One day to our great astonishment we received a telegram stating that Mama was coming. Only a strategist like Mama could have conceived the plan and had the daring to carry it out. Obtaining permission to visit her "sick cousin" in Sobrance, which was close to the most recently established border, Mama remained on the train past her designated stop and in the morning was in Mikuláš. This took courage. Had she been discovered, not only would she be refused permission to return, but she might have been arrested as a spy. And what would have happened to Suzi and Vivian?

"I am leaving my child," Mama cried, "she who I did not permit to put her hand in cold water, and now I am leaving her to the mercies of a mother-in-law."

She made the return trip safely, packed her bags, and left with Suzi and Vivian for America.

Mama's letters were joyful: Papa and Mythieu were delighted, and they were all happy and comfortable. Actually Papa and Mythieu were unemployed, Suzi was sewing doll's dresses, and Mama was making ties from which they eked a substandard existence. This was early in 1939. I, too, had problems to face.

Agitation by pro-German leaders in Slovakia, namely Monsignor Hlinka and Monsignor Jozef Tiso, later hanged by a war crimes tribunal for cooperation with Germany, brought about the dissolution of the Slovakian government and its seizure by Germany.

The Hlinka Guard, named for Monsignor Andrej Hlinka, were activated. The Hlinka Guard resembled the German Storm Troops. Anti-Semitism started in earnest. Life was to be lived from one Hlinka edict to the next.

As Jews could no longer be employed as druggists, it was impossible for Gustave to obtain employment. Then Papa Preiss lost his position. In the beginning we lived on the old gentleman's life savings. They were meager to start with. Soon it became necessary to sell his property which consisted of a farm. We lived on the principal. When this was just about gone, his old-age pension commenced. It saved us from destitution.

Life was hard. Financially we were ruined, root and branch. Gustave, frustrated and thwarted, felt the ground had crumbled under his feet. He said, "I can no longer accept Papa's bounty. I am taking the bread from out of his mouth." But we lived on love and I was happy. My letters to Mama were embroidered with glowing accounts of my life of pleasure and ease. When Gustave's irritability reached the boiling point, Mama Preiss suggested he join her cousins, the Haas brothers, owners of an extensive leather manufacturing business. And so not without reluctance, Gustave began to learn the buying, tanning, processing, designing, and production of leather goods. Soon his amiability and diligence won for him the respect and affection of his co-workers and the brothers Haas. We were happy, as happy as we dared be under Monsignor Tiso and his German-controlled Slovakia.

About this time there began the series of edicts for Jews which were to culminate in the decree for their total extermination. I shall never forget the day an edict was issued forbidding the employment of Christian housemaids by Jews. Our Elka became hysterical and threw herself on the floor in a paroxysm of grief.

"What is to become of me? I have no home. No one has ever treated me so kindly; no one cares for me but you, and now I must go."

Mama Preiss cried as if she were bidding farewell to a dear child. If heretofore her attempts to teach me how to run a home were met with ill-concealed resentment, what was to happen now? It was not until much later that it dawned on me she was trying to help a handless and unappreciative girl become a resilient woman. How many times I have hung my head in shame at the memory of my mulish stubbornness not to yield an inch, not to learn one thing about cooking and housework. Mama always said, "Magda shall never put her hands in cold water."

With Elka's departure came a change. Determined that Father Tiso or no, Gustave was going to have a comfortable, clean home and palatable meals, I put my heart into it. Zestfully I scrubbed floors, washed clothes by hand, and did the thousand and one menial chores a home requires. Suddenly they were not menial chores. They were loving deeds of making a home and a life for my darling Gustave. I sang and sang, and inwardly defied Father Tiso.

Then came the edict ordering every employed Jew to prove that his services were necessary, and that his monthly salary must not exceed five hundred crowns. In addition, every Jew was taxed five hundred crowns for the privilege of working. Gustave had no difficulty in securing his "proof." But again we were bankrupt. Once more we lived on Papa's pension and a wealth of love.

Gustave's brother Pauli, who was to meet his death at the hands of the Germans, was employed by a Mr. Kroll, brother-in-law of Minister Shamumach. Mr. Kroll assured Pauli he was safe and did not require the "proof." For this generous protection all Pauli's salary was turned over to Mr. Kroll.

Then came an edict forbidding Jews to be employers or proprietors. All titles must be transferred to Christian ownership. And this, too, was done.

Why did Christians dress up this wholesale grand larceny with a flimsy cloak of legality? I wondered at the time; now I know. It was a legalistic device to guard against the enforced return of stolen wealth, should the unforeseen occur, and one Jew survive to demand the return of his property or business establishment.

Maybe they hated Jews because we gave the world the Ten Commandments. Maybe Father Hlinka and Father Tiso and the Germans didn't like the Ten Commandments, especially "thou shalt not kill" and "thou shalt not steal." Perhaps they deluded their inner souls, "We are not stealing. Are not the Jews transferring the titles to us willingly?

And what have we to do with the Jew Moses and the Ten Commandments and the Jewish God who gave them to Moses and the Jewish tribes as a way of life?"

In due time the Haas Brothers plant was transferred to a Christian. It was "Aryanized." The new owner, a teacher, knew nothing of the leather business, but he was a Christian and that was sufficient. Henceforth, all the profits were his even though he had not invested a crown.

The next edict ordered every man who did not have a work permit card (which thousands were unable to obtain and as a result were unemployed) to report for three months of service in a labor camp. Poor Pauli. Mr. Kroll laughed in his face and mocked him for his credulity.

Off they marched, these Jewish men, ranging in age from nineteen to forty-two, never to be heard of again. Has Pauli, I wonder, become a cake of soap? The Germans made thousands of tons of soap from human carcasses. Is Pauli fertilizer enriching a German cabbage field? The Germans made thousands of tons of fertilizer from human carcasses. Was Pauli skinned alive to make lamp shades for a German officer's lady? Or was the lifeblood drawn from his body for a German blood bank? Maybe Pauli went up the chimney at Auschwitz, those chimneys which nightly belched forth volumes of red fire and black smoke. Poor Pauli. I wonder what God thinks of the British, the self-righteous British, the proud British, with their inflexible caste systems and their mouthing of the word "democracy." I wonder what God thinks of Churchill who said, "When a great nation breaks its word, it breaks the hearts of men."

But I, Magda Preiss, say, "When a great nation breaks its word, it breaks its own back."

At the precise moment when it became apparent that the murder of millions of European Jews was being planned and about to be executed, the British government issued the infamous White Paper of 1939, proposing to limit Jewish immigration from Europe to Palestine.

At that moment Pauli and Kathi, his wife, were aboard a ship, if you can call it that, in Bratislava, destination Palestine. It was a ship that was destined not to sail, thanks to the British. So Pauli marched away, head erect, and was never heard of again.

The next edict ordered all girls over sixteen years of age to the slave labor camps. No one questioned. The guards of Monsignor Hlinka were the law of the land. And so the girls marched away and were never heard of again. Mothers could only weep and pray that their daughters meet death quickly and without too much suffering.

Knowing that before long all Jews must go to slave labor camps, Gustave prepared stout shoes and leather knapsacks. From day to day, we awaited our fate.

One afternoon Gustave came home early. His distress was evident. He had been accused of black marketing American dollars which Papa Riederman had intended to send to Papa Preiss. The shock was too great for me. I was with child and became ill. Gustave barely had time to rush me to the hospital before being taken to Rosenberg by the Hlinka Guard. This was a prison for criminals in which was also located the High Court.

Papa Preiss walked into my hospital room the following afternoon as I was crying for the baby I would never hold to my breast. Yes, Gustave was in prison. No, of course there had been no trial.

"Gustave said they'll release him on payment of ten thousand crowns."

"Ten thousand crowns? Where can we find ten thousand crowns?"

"It doesn't matter. Gustave told them he wouldn't pay it if he had the money as he is innocent."

On the fourth day they reduced their demands to five thousand crowns and on the eighth day to one thousand crowns. On that day Papa and Mama Preiss sold their jewelry and Mama Preiss' fur coat. The one thousand crowns were handed to the court, Gustave came home from prison, and I from the hospital.

Gustave applied himself and rendered loyal and

devoted service to the new "owner" of the Haas Brothers plant, the Christian teacher. The products, leather boots, and knapsacks went to the Germans.

It seems there was a new edict every day. Jews possessing fur coats or furs of any kind must surrender them. I had a handsome Russian broadtail coat Gustave bought on our honeymoon. I delighted in its beauty and elegance. It was taken from me. Only a woman who loves elegance and style can understand my vexation. Shortly before Haas Brothers was "Aryanized," Gustave designed a fine leather coat for himself. One day he was accosted by a Christian.

"Listen, Jew. I like your coat. It is a long, warm one. Give it to me."

Without a word Gustave took it off and handed it over. Had he refused he might have found himself in Rosenberg charged with a major crime, perhaps murder. It was not uncommon. I could not wear a hat, only a shawl, as I should certainly have been approached by a Christian lady who would either snatch it from my head or demand it from me in vile and insulting language.

But what to do for a coat? Hidden in a chest was a length of fine camel hair cloth Mama gave me in happier days. Secretly I carried it to a tailor. That poor man, yearning to create an elegant garment, must have put his whole heart into my coat. It was a creation, British style. Smuggling it home, I posed in front of the mirror holding it this way and that. When Gustave saw it he fumed.

"You must not wear that coat."

"Why can't I? It is mine and it isn't fur."

"Because you are a Jew, and you cannot wear a coat as good as this."

"I will wear it. I will. I will. You cannot take it from me."

In the morning while I slept he took it from the closet and gave it to a young Christian lady who worked in his office.

Two weeks passed before I could bring myself to talk to him. He pleaded, "Magda, darling, I am sorry. I am so sorry."

Gustave was right. Had I worn it, it would certainly have been torn from me. Moreover, Gustave might have been accosted and "asked" for at least one thousand crowns from the government.

Next came an edict ordering all Jews to wear a large yellow Star of David. Jews having work permits had to wear small ones. We complied. Father Hlinka's guards saw to that. Woe betide the Jew who didn't. The guards watched us every moment of the day and night. Jews were forbidden to talk with Christians. Jews were forbidden to enter Christian homes. The guards spied beneath windows to learn if Jews were tuned in to English or Russian broadcasts. This was really a pretext to accuse

Jews of listening to verboten programs and "appropriating" their radios.

One day there was an edict ordering Jews to surrender all their jewelry. Hlinka's guards came to our home and stole what they wished; linens, down pillows and feather beds, silverware, objets d'art, anything they wanted. They even tore the engagement ring from my finger. All other jewelry had been sacrificed to raise one thousand crowns for Gustave's release from Rosenberg. In all the land it was forbidden for a Jew to own gold or precious jewelry.

After Pauli was taken from us, Papa Preiss seemed to lose the will to live. Too weak to rise from his bed, he lay there, uncomplaining, the sweetest, dearest old gentleman in Mikuláš. Our love was mutual. It was forbidden for Jews to enter Christian markets to buy food. The doctor prescribed butter for Papa. I determined he was going to have butter.

"Mama, I am going out on the streets to look around. Perhaps I can find someone who will sell me butter."

With tears streaming down her cheeks she pleaded with me not to do this rash thing. Standing in a doorway with a shawl over my head, I watched and waited. A woman carrying a basket walked by.

"You are going to market? Perhaps you have butter?"

"Yes, I have butter."

"Quick. Into the doorway."

But, alas. In my anxiety I had not noticed a Hlinka guard in civilian clothing watching me. Bounding into the doorway, he took in the situation at a glance. He thundered, "Jew, don't you know it is verboten for Jews to buy from Christians?"

"Yes, I know that. But my father-in-law is ill and I need butter for him."

This was serious. To be caught by a guard in the act of violating a Hlinka edict could and often did mean death. The guards were coarse and brutal.

"Jew, what is your name?"

"Magda Preiss."

"The wife of Preiss who works in Haas Brothers factory?"

Writing my name and address in his notebook, he left, threatening to return soon and take me to jail.

Mama Preiss was hysterical, terrified out of her senses.

"My unfortunate child, the grave is closing over you."

Not over me, thought I. Picking up my shawl, I ran all the way to the factory and sobbed out the story to Gustave. I know now they were tears of anger and frustration, not fear of consequences. We Jews were beyond fear. Gustave phoned the guard who promptly came over and betrayed Monsignor Jozef Tiso for two pairs of shoes. The incident was closed.

How shameless they were. How they lusted for cruelty and thievery, these guardians of the law who had the authority of the Protected Government of Slovakia to back them up.

One sport they indulged in with great zest was hunting at railroad stations for unwary victims, travelers who usually had with them all their worldly wealth. These unfortunates, easily distinguishable by the Star of David, were beaten, robbed, and left for dead. It always puzzled me that the primitive instincts of the Christian guards were so close to the surface, that the veneer of religion and civilization was so very thin. What had kept these murderous instincts on a leash until Father Hlinka came into power? Was fear of punishment the only deterrent?

One edict forbade Jews to travel without a special permit. When I wished to visit my aunt in Michalovce, I couldn't get one. One edict banned Jews from theaters, concerts, coffee houses, and any place of recreation. Wherever you looked there were signs: "Jews and dogs forbidden." Even Jesus of Nazareth could not have been served a cup of coffee in Father Tiso's Slovakia.

But the nights... Then the guards broke into homes and dragged the heads of families to Guard Headquarters, where beaten and bleeding they were forced to sign away all their possessions, including their homes. It was all so legal and strictly within the law. The victim could neither refuse nor object. He considered himself lucky to reach the bosom of his family alive. By this method all Jewish homes and business establishments were transferred to Christian ownership.

All these months having no radio or other source of information, we were ignorant of what was happening in the world. We only knew that World War Two was being fought and that the United States and Russia were allies. When Jews were beaten and murdered on the streets, we inferred that Germany was having setbacks.

Then came an edict ordering all Jews to leave their homes. They were to be occupied by Christian families. It was perfectly legal, even when the Jewish owners had guns pointed at their heads as they signed away their homes. Jewish families were ordered to move into crude, poor, primitive homes, places without water, bathrooms, toilets, electric lights, or gas; just four walls and a roof.

We were assigned two rooms. But we had each other, and in those two rooms there was love and loyalty and faith in God, and there was hope.

"When the war is over, we shall return to our lovely home, and we shall get back our own furnishings."

When a few days passed without street murders, we

felt the war was going well for the Germans.

Then an overwhelming blow fell. An edict ordered all Jews to be at the synagogue with twenty-five kilograms of food packed in knapsacks. So we cooked and baked and prepared for the trip. Edicts or no edicts, and despite my first unfortunate encounter with the guard, I bought food from Christians. For the most part they were cooperative; perhaps the fact that we paid them double the market price was a factor.

We Jews had agreed among ourselves not to cry, not to show fear, but to walk our road cloaked in dignity as we have walked for two thousand years. Came the fatal morning. Our knapsacks were packed. The guards came at dawn.

"Are you ready, Jews? You are going to labor camps. You will soon learn the meaning of work and hardship, Jew."

"Yes," we said calmly, "we are ready."

We were four families in that house, and we decided to walk together. Yanchi Weinstock, only six years of age, began to cry.

"Mama, I don't want to go to a labor camp. I know we will never come back."

An old hag hobbled into our rooms and croaked, "Dirty Jews, I am going to live in your house. You are going to die, and everything will be mine."

She was so dirty even the wrinkles of her face were

filled with filth. Anger welled up in me like a mighty torrent. I screamed, "You will not live in my house. I *will* come back. And Tiso and the whole German army cannot stop me." I shook my fist in her vile face. The others blanched.

Mama Preiss pleaded, "For God's sake, Magda, I beg you. Hush. Lower your voice. The guards are outside. They will beat you with the gummi knueppel (rubber whip)."

It was a bright Sunday morning. Overhead the skies were blue and the sun made golden the streets of Mikuláš. We marched in formation. As agreed, we held our heads high looking neither to the right nor the left. The ladies and gentlemen who had just come from church lined the curbs. I think the entire population turned out for the fun. They were in fine fettle. Laughing, ridiculing, cursing, shouting words of satisfaction and derision, there they stood. They were animals. I pitied them.

At the synagogue was a silent crowd of hundreds of Jews. Men and women, young and old, rich and poor, sick and well, babes in arms and the very aged who also had to be carried.

The guards formed us into groups of sixty and marched us through the town to the railroad station. European freight cars are considerably smaller than American. Sixty to a wagon was the arrangement. As the first groups were climbing in (there were no steps), a telegram was received ordering all men having work permits to return to their jobs. Their families were permitted to remain with them.

Thus we and the Weinstocks were saved for the day. Our neighbors, the Loffs, and Mama Preiss's brother and his wife and sixteen-year-old son had to leave. I see him now, a handsome manly lad. Ergon was his name.

"I don't want to go to a labor camp," he pleaded with his parents. "I'd rather try to smuggle myself into Hungary."

Thousands had stolen across the border in the dead of the night.

"Mama, please let me try to make my way into Hungary. It is not too late. I can try. I don't want to die. Mama, let me."

"No, Ergon, I cannot live without you. You will have to go where we go. Whatever is in store for us, we will face together."

And so hundreds of human beings climbed into the wagons and were never heard of again. Who cared? They were only Jews. Jews, people of the book, people whose only crime was that their ancestors gave to the world the Holy Bible and the Golden Rule, the Ten Commandments and the Sabbath.

Among them were dozens of our relatives and close friends, and Kathi, wife of Pauli. We begged her: "Kathi, don't go. Why don't you try for Hungary? Maybe it's still possible to steal the border."

"No, I am going after Pauli. I must find him. I will find him."

The anguish of those poor souls was terrible. The Hlinka Guard deliberately separated families; they could not even die together. Small children were torn from their mothers' arms, husbands were separated from wives, and sister from sister. What possible pleasure the vile, loathsome guards could derive from this added suffering, I don't know. Then they were sealed in wagons, and for them it was the seal of doom.

Walking back I said, "Gustave, the one satisfaction I have is that the foul old woman will not have our home." The first one I saw when I returned home was she. I shook my fist under her nose.

"Well, here I am. I told you I was coming home. Get out."

I glared at her and she ran away in fright. We put Papa to bed for he was on the verge of collapse. And then we cried for Kathi and Pauli, and all our relatives and friends who were in the transport. Mama said, "One more edict and we shall be launched into eternity."

Every instinct within me rebelled against being launched into eternity. I loved life. I was going to live. I was going to outlive Father Tiso and all his edicts. The nightmarish months began and ended as we went through the motions of living.

One day I received a postal card from Kathi. "I am well. Send money." The address was Lubartów, Poland, near Lublin. This is how we knew she was in an abattoir. A few weeks later came another request for money, and that was all. Thus ended the story of Pauli and Kathi, two ardent Zionists.

They had met at a Zionist gathering, fell in love, and with a true pioneer spirit planned to go to Palestine and build a life for themselves. They yearned to go to a carcass of a land, to hot desert sands, a land on which for two thousand years no loving hand had been laid. By their own blood and sweat they wanted to transmute it into land, alive and life-giving. They wanted to wrest this land back from nature and make it once again a viable country flowing with milk and honey. Who but Jews could love the land of Israel so profoundly, so passionately? They yearned to go home to the brown breast of Mother Eretz Yisrael.

Mama cried gently, "And with his life savings, Pauli signed up for passage on a ship which was to sail from Bratislava. On a Friday morning came word the ship was to sail on Sunday. Pauli and Kathi were married within the hour. But, alas, for their plans. After waiting on that tramp ship for two weeks, they were told she would not sail. The British White Paper..."

They came back for a year of happiness together, ever aware their lives hung by a thread. Well, now the thread was snapped.

When it came it was almost a relief, this drastic edict that every Jew must register. Thus was struck the death knell of Slovakian Jewry. We were all to be shipped to labor camps. Friday evening Gustave said, "Magda, you know every Jew must register on Monday."

"Yes, I know. I read it in the Ústredna Židov."

"Dear, I prefer that your name not appear on this list."

"But why?" His suggestion puzzled me. "If your name is on the list, I want to be listed also."

"No, never. It is my duty to keep you off. I promised your mother I would take care of you and protect you. It is my duty to take such action as I think is wisest."

"What do you want to do with me?"

"Our friends, the Fishers, are going to steal the Hungarian border early Sunday morning, and I wish you to go with them."

"What shall I do in Hungary? What is to become of me?"

"I will arrange Christian identification papers for you. Thousands have them. You'll have your mother's family and the income from your father's property.

Uzhhorod is now in Hungary so you'll have no difficulty collecting them. You will be amply provided for. If conditions worsen here, I'll come to you. If the war ends in a few months, which seems likely, then you can return to Mikuláš. Don't breathe a word to Mama or Papa until you leave Sunday morning."

Dejected, I spent Saturday afternoon with a dear friend, Valerie Becher. A cripple chained to a wheel chair since infancy, she had known much of torment.

"Why are you so sad, so spiritless? It isn't like you at all, Magda."

"It is only a mood, Valerie. Goodbye, for now."

I knew I should never see her again. Little did she dream it was the last time she would see me.

Saturday evening I wept in the privacy of my room. They were not tears of fear. I was crying because of the awful loneliness that was already clutching me in its grip, the hunger and longing for Gustave. How was I going to live without my husband, he who was my dearest friend and companion? The prospect of tramping for hours through ice and snow on a bitter January night seemed trivial enough. Physical discomforts were irrelevant. Gustave was the breath of my life.

A gentle tapping on the door and there stood Mama Preiss. When I'd told her, she said, "Perhaps my son is right.

You are young. You must make every effort to save yourself. Please spare Papa."

All through the night Gustave held me in his arms and whispered words of comfort and love.

"Do not cry, darling. I promise to come for you in a few weeks."

"Are you sending me away because you really wish to save my life or because you have found someone else?"

He looked at me so hurt I would have given anything to take back those cruel words. His only answer was to turn out the light. Not another word was spoken but each knew the other was not asleep.

Dominion of Arrogance

Morning had not yet dawned. At four, I dressed: three undershirts, three panties, three pairs of stockings, two dresses, and the coat without fur lining. I loved that coat. It had been a gift from Gustave, a protective cloak of love. Outside in the half light the snow was falling like clouds of feathers from a feather bed sky. Tiptoeing into Papa's room which was also the living room and kitchen, I said cheerfully, "Papa, dear, goodbye. I am going to Hungary."

"To Hungary? Are you crazy? Why do you alarm me so?"

"Gustave wants me to go for a few weeks."

Papa was gasping for breath. He had angina pectoris, I think. Only the previous day water had been drained from him. Suddenly there was the sound of a horn.

"I shall see you soon, Papa. Goodbye for a while."

Holding my hands he said, "My own sweet child, I think I shall never see you again." Mama Preiss kissed me convulsively. With tears streaming down my cheeks, I dashed out to the car. Gustave got in and we were off.

We Were Strangers

In the car were the engineer Lajos Fisher and his wife. Mrs. Fisher was as fat as Hannah Rabinsky, Mama's card playing friend in Uzhhorod. Her size was awe-inspiring and one wondered about her private life. Of her three children, two had been shipped to Auschwitz never to be heard of again. Her third was with her, almost concealed by his mother's bulk. They were fleeing for Mr. Fisher's life. It seems the Christian gentleman now holding title to Mr. Fisher's business had informed the guards he was black marketing. For the consideration of all the Fisher household furnishings, a well disposed guard had warned him to flee for his life. He was to be found guilty and executed, even though it was nothing more than a plot.

After a half hour's ride Gustave left us. He held me tightly in his arms and said, "Darling, be strong, be brave, be true." Mama's words. I don't know how he returned, but he probably walked. The Fishers having promised to take care of me, I was at ease. Not realizing what was ahead, I was neither deeply moved nor distraught.

The driver was a member of an illegal smuggling organization which every day smuggled hundreds of Jews into Hungary at six thousand crowns per head. I don't know where Gustave got the money.

Entering Prešov, a town on the Czech border, the driver conducted us to a small restaurant. It was overflowing with confused and bewildered Jews of all ages. Crying children, forlorn youths, haunted elders. I marvel now at their self-control. Perhaps after eighty generations, Jews had become inured to their suffering.

Soon after darkness fell, a car came for us. Poor Mrs. Fisher probably lacerated her flesh squeezing through the door. Huge snow drifts blocked the ice-rutted roads and driving was hazardous. The car slid and slithered sickeningly. The cold was bitter. In about three hours the car came to a stop. Stepping out gingerly and stiff with cold, we saw we were in a forest. Our guides, three uncouth peasants, came out of the shadows.

"Where are you taking us," asked Mr. Fisher.

"When you have passed through the forest you will be in Hungary."

It was all so mysterious; the dark night, the tall trees, the howling wind, the fugitive nature of our trip. The snow was above my knees. Walking would have been difficult under any circumstances, but the need for haste and my agitation tore the breath from my lungs. Soon Mrs. Fisher collapsed.

"Leave me here. I cannot take another step. Go on without me."

The peasants, strong as oxen, pulled us through. We walked for about four hours coming to a town the name of which I cannot recall. Luck was with us. However, much to my chagrin the peasants gave me five pengoes. I knew I should have been given five hundred as arranged by Gustave.

"Five pengoes are enough for your railroad ticket. You will be given the balance in Košice."

They vanished into the night. We were alone. Entering the small, dingy, poorly-lit depot, Mr. Fisher, in Hungarian which he speaks like a native, asked for four tickets. The agent made no comment as he gave us the tickets. We were really in luck. The train was dark. Passengers were sleeping. Neither the Fishers nor I had identification papers. No one asked for them. Providence was watching over us that night. Sitting on wooden benches, I think we held our breath for the whole hour it took to reach Košice. It was still dark when we arrived. But what now?

Standing on the platform, uncertain and confused, we were approached by a gaunt Jew.

"Are you from Prešov?" We dared not tell him.

"Don't be afraid. I am expecting you. Come with me and in the morning you may go where you wish. You are free." Free?

His home was a small hovel, frightfully untidy. Soiled clothes and about ten children were strewn all over the place. Poor souls, they were making every effort to help their fellow Jews. They had nothing to give but themselves. The bed clothes were so soiled we preferred sleeping on the floor.

"I appreciate your kindness but I don't want to sleep here," I said. "My husband's uncle lives here in Košice. If we can get word to him perhaps he will take me into his home. We've never met but if he learns Gustave's wife is here, I feel sure he will give me shelter. His name is Aladar Preiss."

"Oh, yes. I know Aladar Preiss. He is a man of means."

And without another word he put on his coat and went out into the cold night. Why were the prosperous Jews sleeping snug and warm in their clean beds while beggars like my host were willing to suffer any discomfort; even risking the safety of themselves and families for the sake of helping utter strangers. This was a question that would take much deliberation. But not in the middle of the night.

Though we had never met, Uncle Aladar's fatherly embrace reassured me.

"So you are Gustave's wife. Don't be afraid, child. You are going to live in my home and have nothing to fear."

After a hot meal and bath, I fell into a clean bed, soft as a white cloud, and slept until evening.

What transpired while I slept I shall never know. I suppose self-preservation is the first law of nature. In the cold light of day Uncle Aladar's impulse to befriend me withered on the vine.

"I am sorry, Magda, but you cannot remain in my house. You do not have identification papers. If you are discovered in my home not only you but I shall be in serious trouble. Either you must have Christian identification papers stating you are not a Jew, or papers under your maiden name, Magda Riederman, residence Uzhhorod. Uzhhorod is in Hungary now and you can manage." I had no choice but to agree.

"I shall phone Uncle Desidur in Uzhhorod and ask him to come here and make the arrangements. I don't wish to be a burden to you."

I phoned. Aunt Bella told me Uncle had gone to Budapest to meet me at Gustave's wired request. She said Uncle had phoned to tell her that after waiting forty-eight hours in the Budapest railroad station he feared I had vanished into thin air. Aunt Bella wired him and the next day he was in Košice.

We hadn't seen each other for five years but he kissed me with a world of affection and we cried like babies.

"Don't cry, sweet. I promised your mother I'd look after you. I'll stop at nothing to help you."

Uncle returned to Uzhhorod to buy identification papers under my maiden name. It seems one could buy anything for money. Waiting for his return was a strain. Uncle Aladar was terrified out of his wits. He was paralyzed with fear. A knock on the door and I dashed for the bathroom or hid under the bed. Uncle Aladar's dearest friends were not to be trusted. Who could be loyal at such a time? Who could be trusted? It seems no one.

Four days passed. Uncle Desidur returned. He had identification papers for Magda Riederman, yes, but said, "I'm sorry, Magda, but you cannot return to Uzhhorod. It seems everyone knows you are in Hungary. There is the danger someone will report you to the Hungarian Military, and you'll be arrested. If you wish to remain in Hungary you must live in a large city where you are not known. Tonight we leave for Budapest."

Who was the guilty one in Uzhhorod who talked? And why? Was it really concern for me that prompted Uncle Desidur to take me to Budapest, or was it fear for his own skin?

Grateful as I was to Uncle Aladar for giving me asylum, I still believe him to be a craven coward. He must have sighed with relief when I left his home.

Uncle Desidur was frightened, too. He warned me, "On the train, try to sit near me, but do not talk. Pretend we are strangers."

Trying to shrink within myself, I scarcely dared breathe. In thundered three Gendarmes; tall, coarse, wearing high feathered hats. When I saw them, I thought my blood would freeze. "Relax," my uncle whispered.

"Everyone must identify himself," they roared.

It was obvious they were looking for illegal immigrants. With trembling hands I showed them my papers.

"Why are you going to Budapest?"

"I am going to visit my cousins."

Lucky for me I speak Hungarian like a native.

"Very well. You pass."

The train roared through the night. At one of the stops the conductor announced Nyíregyháza. This had been the home of Mama's grandparents. Across my memory flashed the recollections of happier days. In this town as an adored child, I spent long and happy summers. Everyone loved and cherished me. When my tonsils were removed, Grandmother fetched me ice cream...

And here I was, a weary fugitive seeking haven, separated from my loved ones, my future doubtful. What am I to do in a big city among strangers? All alone. Who would love and cherish me now? Who would take me in? Not Uncle Desidur. Not Uncle Aladar. The full impact of my predicament only now penetrated my mind. I thought of Gustave and his words of farewell. "Be strong. Be brave. Be true."

Very well. I will be strong. I will face whatever I have

to face. This I vowed: I will live. I will return to Gustave.

Budapest was swarming with men in uniform. Jews were not permitted to be soldiers, only army workers doing menial work. Their uniforms were unattractive and shoddy. The yellow arm band was a conspicuous means of identification. So, the air in Hungary was poisoned, too.

Uncle Desidur asked, "Where shall we go? To your mother's cousins or to your mother-in-law's sister? She being a woman of means and influence might be in a better position to help you."

And I added enthusiastically, "She is active in Jewish organizations, a clubwoman with many contacts. Let's appeal to her. She has everything."

She had everything but a heart. Looking back now I wonder. Should not Uncle Desidur have suggested my own Mama's cousins who were his cousins, too, and blood ties? After all my mother-in-law's sister was a stranger.

It was evident she had been informed of my coming and so was prepared. Her apparent alarm was almost comical.

"Don't be alarmed," I said. "I have not come here to burden or jeopardize you."

She laughed icily.

"Indeed, I am not alarmed. But in your own best interest you cannot hope to remain in Budapest under false identification. Wherever you go you will be questioned and as you are not Magda Riederman but Magda Preiss, you will only get yourself and me into trouble."

I had fondly but foolishly hoped she would give me shelter. She continued, her eyes darting from window to door as though Hitler himself were peeking in. "There are thousands of Jewish refugees in Budapest. From Germany, Poland, Czechoslovakia, and elsewhere. Jews without papers who were arrested on the streets." (But I had papers.) "For them we have established and maintained three camps. You need to remain there only three months. Uncle Desidur can then secure the services of an advocate and you will be free. In the meantime have Desidur send you the income from your father's properties."

The income from my Papa's property in Uzhhorod? I hadn't even thought of it. If I returned to Uzhhorod it would be all mine. She wished me luck. Little did she realize she was to need it more than I. A bomb killed her.

There was yet time for Uncle Desidur to advise me to appeal to Mama's cousins. It was at his suggestion I was in Budapest. I wonder what held him back.

Pava utca, formerly a home for the Jewish aged, was maintained by Hungarian Jewish organizations, and not by Gustave's aunt personally which was the impression she evidently wished to give. Large sums were paid to the Hungarian authorities for their "kindness" in not shipping the helpless Jews to Auschwitz and death. The Pava utca office was run by a Hungarian official. I explained my plight.

"And I am surrendering myself as I do not wish to be hunted and haunted."

Kissing me fondly, Uncle Desidur promised to send clothing, toiletries, and anything I wished. He was a man of his word in this regard.

After registration, the official led me into the women's quarters. The room was pleasant and spotlessly clean. He graciously introduced me to the others and assigned me to a second tier bunk. Without a moment's hesitation the women extended a cordial welcome and tried to allay my fears.

"Don't be depressed or forlorn. It is pleasant here. We play cards all day and once a week you have a few hours leave."

Breathing more freely, I was grateful for their considerateness. They vied with each other to raise my spirits.

A gray haired lady said, "I am your countrywoman. My home is Humena. I've been here three months. You see I am well. It is only a matter of time, and we shall all return to our families and homes. Do not despair."

And another said, "I am Mrs. Dr. Feldman from Vranov, Czechoslovakia. My bunk is above yours. I hope we shall become friends. Have courage, child. View things *en couleur de rose*. Don't be sad."

"But I have left my Gustave in Mikuláš. How can I live without him?"

And good souls that they were, they consoled me and quieted my fears. They were so buoyant, so debonair. Was this a mask to conceal their horror? A sort of self-preservation? Or was it self-delusion?

Breakfast consisted of black coffee and bread. No one complained. Certainly not I, for I discovered a piano. I played and sang in Czech, Hungarian, Polish, Slovakish, Russian, and German. My new friends were pathetically happy to hear songs of home, ballads in their native tongue. My spirits soared. Music is the sunshine of the heart.

From the beginning, Siegfried attached himself to me. Having lost his parents and six brothers in Vienna, everyone pitied him. He saved himself by fleeing to Hungary. All day he played his Hawaiian guitar. His very obvious devotion annoyed me but amused the others. When he tried to kiss me my temper flared. I looked at him in startled anger.

"Magda, don't be angry. I love you." He was so earnest.

"Siegfried, you are two years younger than I. To me you are a brother. So don't be silly."

Avoiding him was impossible. I tried being sisterly. Siegfried arranged to have the same free period as I. He always tagged along. I tried to imagine he was my brother, Mythieu.

Uncle Desidur's generosity was boundless. There was a constant stream of delicacies which I shared with Siegfried who had no one. Aunt Bella sent elegant dresses, handmade lingerie, silk stockings, toiletries and cosmetics. Materially I was well provided.

One Sunday morning, Ilonka, the daughter of Papa's sister Ava visited me. She lived in Uzhhorod. It was our first meeting in five years. She was quite casual and I instantly knew she hadn't come to Budapest for the purpose of visiting me.

"What brings you to Budapest, Ilonka, a shopping expedition?"

"Aunt Malvin is here in Budapest, in the Szabolcs utca. Lolka, her youngest child is with her."

"Aunt Malvin here with Lolka? But why—how?"

"She and Lolka were caught trying to steal their way into Hungary. They were arrested right on the border. Lolka is being released because she is a child and I have come to take her home with me." This was news indeed.

"Oh, Ilonka, I didn't know. I shall visit Aunt Malvin today."

Poor Aunt Malvin. She was never again to see Michalovce, her home.

Mama's Budapest cousins sent boxes of food. What

a fool I'd been not to appeal to them in the beginning. I wonder if they would have sheltered us. Gustave contrived to send letters through the underground. What happiness they brought me.

"Darling Magda: No words can describe my longing for you. Be strong and endure what you must. Soon, God willing, we will be together again. How could you have been so foolish as to make your presence known to the authorities? Thousands are living freely with false identification papers. You should have done the same. I question my Aunt Aranka's good faith. Why didn't you appeal to your mother's cousins? Why didn't you use your head?"

Gustave was right. In one weak, panicky moment, I let someone do my thinking for me. The lesson was well learned. Hereafter, I will stand or fall on my own judgment. Gustave sent my clothes. They never reached me.

When not playing the piano and singing, I played cards. Rummy and Preference were the favorite games.

The dietary laws were strictly observed. As the kosher practice of shechita was forbidden in Hungary, we had no meat. The meals consisted mainly of noodles and other starches. Before long my weight went from one hundred and twenty to one hundred and forty pounds. Friday evenings the women kindled and blessed the Sabbath candles. We yearned for divine services but the camp director and his wife were atheists and forbade them. They, too, were from Uzhhorod. Hence each one prayed silently for a half hour period set aside for meditation and devotion. The silent prayers were nourishment for the soul. On the Sabbath we sang Hebrew songs, recited Bialek's poetry and discussed the great souls of Israel. Sundays, Siegfried and I went to the theater, to visit my cousins, or just walk around the town.

Budapest is more than a city. Budapest, the Paris of Hungary is a beautiful enchantress with a thousand glittering facets to her personality and charm. Through the city runs the Danube like a sparkling circlet of diamonds spanning her slender waist. The theaters, the concert halls, the smartly dressed women radiating glamour and feminity; the adoration of artists, writers, musicians; the zest for life, the appreciation of the beautiful; this is Budapest. This magnificent, gorgeous, scintillating, superb Aphrodite, Budapest. I loved her.

The Kehillah, a Jewish service organization, sent matzah for Passover. This was the only observance. Where was the twentieth-century Moses who would lead us out of the land of bondage? In what form would a new tablet of the law appear? Would the peace table be our Mount Sinai? Would a Jewish State in Palestine be our liberation?

On Sedar night my thoughts went back to Sedar in the

home of William Riederman, president of the Asa Chassid Synagogue. I thought of Mama, and Mythieu, Vivian and Suzi. Did they know where I was? How could they? Was Mythieu a soldier? Later I learned he fought in the Pacific theater of war. They seemed so close to me. I could almost reach out and touch my loved ones.

From deep within me welled an awful anger. Why were Jews subjected to persecution and its attendant horrors? Why Auschwitz, and the fiery ovens, and the gas chambers? Who was this Father Jozef Tiso and this Father Andrej Hlinka? Who was this Hitler, and this Goebbels and this Goering?

Then the voice of reason made itself heard within me. It told me these men were not the seducers of their fellow countrymen. It was not they alone who had hatched these fiendish plans for the extermination of millions of Jews. Rather it was their countrymen, the German people, the Italian people, and the Hungarian people who had produced leaders to lead them in the paths they wished to follow. The people had chosen their leaders.

Well, they were not going to murder me. So long as I believed I could not be destroyed, so long would I live. And even if they killed me, I would not die.

The morning of March 20, 1944 (my birthday) dawned radiant and sunny. It was Monday. Siegfried and

I set out to visit Aunt Malvin. Noticing crowds of excited people milling about, I wondered about it. My uneasiness annoyed Siegfried.

"Why are you so agitated, Magda? You are in a big city. People are out strolling. I can see nothing unusual."

There was something in the air. You could almost touch it. A sense of foreboding and melancholy swept over me. What was this thing that made my blood run cold?

Aunt Malvin was sick. She had diabetes. Daily she gave herself insulin. Without it she could not live. She feared that when her supply was exhausted she would die.

"Perhaps I shall be taken to the Jewish hospital," she said. "If you do not find me here next Sunday come to the hospital."

We kissed goodbye.

Strolling along the main thoroughfares, through Danube Park and along the banks of the river was exhilarating. It was a delightful place. Walking about were theatrical stars, artists, writers, the elite of the professions; well dressed smiling people for the most part. Over all brightly shone a spring sun.

Why am I in a frenzy? Do I imagine people are darting about, hurrying here and there? Is this a creation of my brain?

"It is nothing, really just your imagination," scolded

Siegfried. "You are giving to nothing a name."

Lulled and quiescent because I wished to be, we walked slowly to Pava utca. The camp director stared in amazement. The others crowded about and cried, "You have come back to this place?"

"Why not? Has anything happened?"

"Don't you know? Didn't you see? The Germans occupied Hungary at ten this morning. The Gestapo is already rounding up Jews."

Now I knew. I appealed to the camp director.

"You are a Jew in equal jeopardy with us. Unlock the gates. Give us a chance for our lives; a chance to get home."

"I cannot unlock the gates," he gasped. "I am afraid. The Germans will kill me."

"They are going to kill you anyhow," I urged. "Be a man. Fight for your life. Even a rat will fight when it is cornered."

He was half dead already, from terror. The women wept. The men were grave. No one ate his dinner but I. I gorged myself until I was almost nauseous. Instinctively I was storing up energy.

About two in the afternoon the Hungarian overseer ordered us to pack. He was now a different man. Gone was his courteous amiability. Arrogant and domineering, abuse flowed from him. Was everyone a Dr. Jekyl and Mr. Hyde? Jammed into a bus, we were driven to the Rocksilard Palace

Hotel. There I found Aunt Malvin and hundreds of other refugees of the Szabolcs utca.

The Hungarian Jews were there also. This was their day of doom. Among the first to be rounded up were doctors, lawyers, engineers, rabbis, artists, professionals, and intellectuals. On this Lord's Day in the year 1944 began the Dominion of Arrogance in Hungary. About six thousand Hungarian Jews were imprisoned that day. What malevolent power had over night turned the Hungarian Gendarmes into bludgeoning savages? Had the comforting assurance of German backing given free rein to their natural desires?

The Dominion of Arrogance was indeed upon us. Herded forty to a room, we slept on the floor. When we went to the toilet, Hungarian police beat us with gummi knueppels and cursed us for attempting to escape. For three days and nights we were given no food. Those who had food shared it generously, but there was little of it. The gracious charm and compassion of those unfortunates, one for the other, was enough to melt the heart. The aged insisted on giving away all their food to the children. A little silver haired lady told me she taught piano for forty years in Budapest. She begged me to take her treasure, a jar of strawberry preserves. I gave it to a young expectant mother. A prominent obstetrician told me her son is a doctor in the American army. Many had blood ties to America and England. On Tuesday a Jewish doctor announced all healthy prisoners must go to labor camps. The sick were to be taken to hospitals. I kissed Aunt Malvin goodbye—and that was the end of her. We now numbered about eight thousand. Everyone not possessing Christian identification papers was arrested on the streets.

Wednesday morning we were ordered to pack our belongings. We formed long lines five to a row. The Hungarian police stuck us indiscriminately with their gummi knueppels—men, women and children, the aged and the new-born. They had gone mad.

"You stinking Jews, we will teach you what life is. You won't be doctors and lawyers and businessmen now. You are going to be work slaves."

And they whipped and whipped and all reason was gone from them and they were monsters, *things*. Laden with knapsacks and bundles, we walked through the streets of Budapest to the railroad station, perhaps a distance of several miles. Lining the curbs and screaming with insane joy were the Christian ladies and gentlemen. They hurled old shoes, stones, and trash.

How many had been brought into the world by Jewish doctors? How many had been extricated from trouble by Jewish lawyers? How many had been gainfully employed by Jews? To how many had Jews extended a helping hand in time of need? How many could trace their family's residence to Hungary as far back as many of these Jews now walking as slaves through the streets of Budapest, Hungary, in the year 1944?

Missiles were flying. The contents of a slop pot splashed in my face. Scooping up a handful of horse manure I darted out of line. With all my strength I rubbed it in the face of the thrower, a fat pig. I could give as well as take.

At the railroad tracks we saw only cattle cars and wagons. After my Mikuláš experience I knew they were for us. The Hungarian Jews were stunned.

"Surely we are going to travel in coaches," they said. "The authorities wouldn't dream of packing us into wagons."

They could and they did; sixty to a wagon, regardless of age or sex. Those unable to climb in quickly were beaten and manhandled. As I hesitated a moment to wipe off the filth thrown on me en route, a Gendarme whipped me across the face. I saw red.

"You devil," I screamed shaking my fist at him. "I am coming back. I heard President Beneš promise to come back, and I promise you I am coming back to your destruction. Neither you nor the Germans nor the whole world can destroy me. I am coming back, and I will bear a son and call him Yisrael Chai—Israel lives."

The whip came down on my head and I knew no more.

Gates of Hell

"Who shall ascend into the mountain of the Lord and who shall stand in His holy place? He that hath clean hands, and a pure heart; who hath not taken My name in vain, and hath not sworn deceitfully. He shall receive a blessing from the Lord, and righteousness from God of his salvation. Such is the generation of them that seek Thee; that seek Thy presence, O God of Jacob."

The motion of the train had brought me back to consciousness. Where was I? In Papa's synagogue? The prayers and conversation droned in my ears from a distance.

"Lift up your heads, O ye gates, and ye lifted up, ye everlasting doors, that the King of Glory may come in. Who is the King of Glory? The Lord of hosts; He is the King of Glory."

"Sh'ma Yisrael Adonai Eloheinu Adonai Ehad"

"Mama I am hungry."

"Water. I want water."

"The law of the Lord is perfect, restoring the soul."

"Don't cry children, God is with us."

"Water. I want water."

"The testimony of the Lord makes wise the simple."

"God will help us."

"Water. I am dying of thirst."

"The precepts of the Lord are right, rejoicing the heart."

"Children, have faith in the God of Israel."

"Mama, I want water."

"The fear of the Lord is clean, enduring forever."

"The slop pail is overflowing."

"Dump it through the bars."

"Behold, a good doctrine has been given unto you; forsake it not."

Painfully I opened my eyes. Around me were huddled sixty men, women, and children wedged so tightly that they had to sit with their knees under their chins. Through bars near the top of the wagon I could see the darkening sky. An old bearded Jew in prayer shawl and skull cap was praying. Hunger cut like a knife. I had eaten only a few morsels since Sunday dinner. This was Wednesday night. Whimpering cries of children and babies brought tears to my eyes. The slop pail was the only means provided to take care of our natural needs; no privacy. The stench was revolting. Unable to stretch my legs, I was numb.

"If only I could have my Gustave," I thought. "Dear God, what is happening in an insane world? Has the whole world become a jungle of crazed tigers and venomous snakes?"

"I know what you are thinking. You are thinking how heavenly it would be to be in your own clean bed, and you are thinking of your husband or sweetheart."

This was my introduction to Klari Czetel.

"I, too, am thinking of my sweetheart," she ran on. "Today we had lunch at the home of my future mother-in-law and made wedding plans. My mother is home expecting me. She doesn't know where I am. Frank was leaving for Miskolcz on a business trip. He is in the jewelry business."

She showed me her engagement ring. It was a magnificent diamond.

"After lunch I went to the railroad station with him and we were both made prisoners. I think he, too, is in a wagon."

In the deepening gloom the elegance of her gown and Persian fur coat were not lost on me.

"I hope this is a mistake and we can return home in a few days. My wedding date has been set. And, anyhow, I have no clothing or toiletries with me."

She was really lovely. Tiny and dainty as a Dresden figurine, blue eyes fringed with long black lashes, olive skin, black lustrous hair, and an impish smile: this was Klari.

"Come now. Let us forget we are here," she said. "I shall tell you all about myself, my life in Budapest, and my romances."

Klari had no inhibitions. She told all. Ordinarily I should have found her risqué accounts very titillating. I gave her a bothered ear. My thoughts were of Mikuláš and my family in America. I thanked God they were spared this. Klari talked through the night. The lucky ones fell asleep.

With the coming of morning everyone stirred and tried to stretch. To do this we all stood up together and tried to get the stiffness out of our aching bodies. A faint light flickered through the bars. Up went the slop pail, much of its contents splashing on us as it struck the bars. The stench was overpowering. Many became ill. Later we were to take care of our natural needs in the presence of anyone as indifferently as drinking a glass of water. This morning I was ashamed unto death.

In the morning light I found Mrs. Dr. Feldman, Alice, and Inga Mulberg, an accomplished and educated young woman from Vienna. I presented Klari and we were drawn together in a bond of fellowship. Then another day and another night of horror. When Friday morning dawned we'd had no food or water since being sealed in Wednesday. Actually no food had been given us since Sunday. The little food given me in Rocksilard by fellow prisoners, I had not the heart to eat. Most of it I gave to the children and pregnant women.

As the tallest looked through the bars they cried in relief, "We are still in Hungary, our own beloved Hungary. We are safe. This can't be Poland." The train stopped. This was it.

"Open the wagons!"

This was barked in German. When the doors were opened, I saw a small shack, the depot, with a sign that said "Auschwitz." On the platform in addition to the Gestapo were about fifty creatures in horrible striped pajama-like drill uniforms. The children of Israel in bondage.

They dragged us out for we were too weak and stiff to move. It was hot and I was dying for water. The twenty dead in our wagon, I counted them, were thrown on the ground and left there. Among them was the aged rabbi who said, "Have faith, God will help you." Maybe God had helped him.

"Form lines in rows of five," barked the German officer. "Women and children in one group, women in a second group, and men in a third."

Jewish slaves took our bundles and tossed them into trucks. At the risk of their lives a few tried to warn us.

"Do you speak Polish?"

"Yes," I whispered.

"Tell mothers with young children to give them to old women. Mothers with young children are killed at once."

I gave the alarm.

"Attention," barked an officer. "Attention. Stand up. You will walk a few miles to camp. Do not be afraid. No harm will come to you. Your belongings will be returned. You did not come here to rest. You are going to work. Räder müssen rollen für den Sieg. Arbeit macht frei. (Wheels turn for victory. Work makes one free)."

I looked about at thousands of my fellow Jews, hungry and miserable. Free? An hour passed. We waited. A Red Cross ambulance drove up. Out stepped a German officer.

"Anyone unable to walk may ride in the ambulance. Step in. You will be driven to camp."

I doubted my own ears. Such gallantry was startling. Approaching Mrs. Dr. Feldman, he said in a voice dripping with honey, "Madam, you are older than others. Perhaps you are tired and wish to ride?"

"Indeed, Sir. I am very tired. Thank you."

In she stepped and that was the end of her.

"You wish to ride also?" he asked of Alice who had gray hair.

"May I? You are very kind, Sir. My feet bother me."

"Sir, my feet hurt, too," said Inga. "I have an infection. May I ride?"

"Of course. You are welcome to ride."

I marveled at his courtesy. Were Germans human after all? Riding is better than walking, thought I. I walked over to him.

"My feet hurt, too, and I am tired and thirsty," I pleaded. "I should like to ride."

He looked at me in surprise, gave a hard punch in the side which threw me to the ground, and turned away. The ambulance drove off—and that was the end of all of them.

Now we were two, Klari and I. A slave loading bundles whispered in Polish, "Be happy you aren't in that car. The aged and the ill are put to death immediately."

Now I knew.

"I beg you to tell young mothers to give their children to older women," he repeated. "Young mothers with children are put to death without delay. The older women are, too. If young mothers give up their children before reaching camp, they can at least save their own lives—for the time being."

His eyes darted about in fear.

"This is the town, Auschwitz," he said. "The camp Birkenau is a few miles from here. They have crematoria. They burn all but the young and the strong. Only those able to work are permitted to live. I've been here two years. They murdered my wife and child. Never again shall I be free."

He slunk away. I looked at Klari. Klari looked at me. She was crying. I was choking with rage. The light was beginning to dawn. Klari sobbed.

"Now that we are alone, Magda, be a sister to me and I shall be a sister to you."

We clasped each other's hands and swore the fidelity of true sisters.

Marching to camp in the usual rows of five was not difficult. It was a warm sunny day. We passed what seemed like miles of barbed wire about ten feet in height. Every ten feet stood a concrete pillar topped with a powerful searchlight. Although it was daylight, about 4pm, the searchlights were lit.

We marched up to the gates of hell. Out from a wooden gatehouse came about ten guards, men and women.

"Remain standing."

They counted us, five in a row. One, Fraulein Drexler, swaggered in her guard uniform and deliberately whipped us for the pleasure it afforded her.

"Enter, five at a time."

And in we marched, right into a large building which we were to learn was a crematory. In a huge barracks-like hall, Jewish slaves in uniforms, just boys and girls, ordered us to undress. Moving about among us, guards forbade conversation. We were about three thousand women. I writhed in agony when a man looked at my nakedness. I was menstruating. Hunger had passed, but my thirst was burning. After several hours of standing naked the Germans permitted us to sit on the warm cement floor. Utterly exhausted as I was, the warm floor seemed comfortable and I fell sound asleep. Had I known thousands of living human beings were fuel for the fires which warmed the floor, could I have slept so soundly?

Sudden outcries roused me. Guards were running among us swinging their gummi knueppels on bare flesh and stepping on bare bodies.

"Stand up. Stand up. As soon as you have bathed you will be given food," they barked.

It was now late Friday evening. Not a drop of water or a crumb of food had passed my lips since Wednesday morning.

"Form lines, five to a row, for tattooing."

Jewish girls were the tattooers.

"Hurry. Hurry," shouted excited and impatient guards. "Tomorrow we expect new transports."

My tattooer jabbed viciously.

"You are hurting me."

"Shut up. Be glad you are getting this number. It means you will not be put to death at once."

I looked at my arm: 80314. More than eighty thousand slaves had entered these gates of hell before me and most of them had gone up the chimney in smoke. And this was only the beginning. And this was just *one* German murder factory. The Germans had others.

Then a row of five to the barber, a Jewish girl, who cut off my lovely red hair. I knew I could endure what I had to endure; hunger, thirst, standing for hours naked with blood running down my legs, being tattooed, all these I could bear. But when they shaved my head and all the hair on my body, it was a dagger in my breast. Such is the vanity of women.

"I am menstruating," I said. "Will you help me?"

"Help you? Bah. Don't be simple. Next month you'll not menstruate. Your belly will become as large as mine. I haven't menstruated in two years. If I can stand it, so can you."

Horror was upon me. These were Jewish girls who had themselves become brutalized by their sadistic, diabolical masters.

In a large cement room were about one hundred showers, four girls to a shower. Having neither soap nor wash clothes, we ran our hands over arms and legs. Guards came in and licentiously looked us over. If a girl was especially pretty, they slapped her breasts and buttocks.

"Come here," they called to another. "Come look at this pretty Jewess."

No one stopped to notice their presence but inwardly we cringed, especially the teenagers. Herded into the drying room, we were told to dry ourselves by running around. This, instead of towels. Armpits and groins were sprayed with antiseptic; typhus precautions, I think.

My "outfit" consisted of brown shoes, one with a French heel and the other heelless, a brown dress that swept the floor and could go around me three times, and a slip which had once been white. Garments were deloused, never washed. A patch of drill was sewn across the back of every dress for identification. Passing through a narrow door which was the entrance to the camp proper, a Jewish girl painted a red cross on every drill patch. A woman guard barked, "Form lines, five to a row."

Each detail was carried out with precision. After waiting for what seemed hours we were assigned to a Block. Klari and I were to be in Block One.

"Go to your Block," the woman guard continued. You must obey your Block Elsterer (Block Leader). You must behave, you must conduct yourselves properly, and you must take orders from her. If you are obedient you will have a fine time here and all will go well with you."

Fine time indeed, thought I. Klari and I looked at each other and burst out laughing. Stripped of her Budapest finery, and with her shaven head, she was ludicrous, and I told her so. I laughed until I was weak.

"You laugh at me?" she flared. "If you could only see

yourself. Your head is big and grotesque without your red curls."

"Klari," I soothed her, "Your fiancé isn't here, and my husband isn't here, so what does it matter how we look?"

The barracks which was to be our home was crudely built, and about eighty feet in length and forty in width. Wooden partitions divided it into four sections, or Stuben, with a central hall extending through from front to rear. Each Block had a Block Elsterer and four house maids, or Stuben Dienst. The position of Stuben Dienst carried with it power and authority. The Block Elsterer had practically divine and dynastic rights over us. Along the walls were rows of wooden shelves or bunks called Koyan, three tiers high. The Koyan were partitioned into sections, ten women to a section. Each section was provided with one straw sack and one cover. We were so cramped for space that if one wished to turn the other nine had to turn with her. Lying on our sides was the only way ten women could squeeze into that limited space.

It was now past midnight, really Saturday morning. They fed us. Our meal, which was the first morsel since being sealed in the wagon Wednesday morning, consisted of black "bread" and a cup of coffee, black and unsweetened. The coffee was hot and reviving.

"It's bitter and has an acrid odor," the women complained.

But we were ravening and swallowed it anyhow. I soon learned it had been drugged to keep us docile and to stop the menstrual flow. All was silent. We were too spent to talk, just satisfied to have a place on which to lie down.

"You will save your bread for tomorrow," said the Block Elsterer. "There must be no conversation. Each room has a night watcher who is stationed at the door by the slop pots. She will report all conversations."

Who could talk? I was almost too weak to breathe. I fell into a deep sleep, but not for long. About 4am the Stuben Dienst ran about pulling off the covers and screaming, "Alle Aufstehen für Zählappell (Everyone get up for roll call)."

No miser counted and recounted his treasures with greater zeal and thoroughness than the Germans daily inventoried us. Usually out of sheer bestiality they made us stand hours before taking Zählappell. And we weren't treasures. We were slaves.

I climbed down from the Koya. Having slept in my dress, I was ready to go. It was dark and cold and a few hours of sleep had not restored me. The unlucky ones near the door were ordered to carry out the slop pots. They hesitated and fell back crying, "We don't want to. It is sickening."

"Aha. So? You don't want to carry out the slop pots?"

The Stuben Dienst was screaming at them, and her stout cane rained blow after blow on defenseless heads.

"I'll show you," she screamed. "You are not home. You are slaves and must do what I tell you. You are lucky to have a Koya to sleep on. When I came here two years ago I slept in the snow while we were building the barracks."

She beat them as if they personally were to blame for her misfortune.

"Klari," I said, "you see how it is. Tomorrow morning let us be the last to leave else we may have to carry the slop pots."

Out we filed, one thousand from our Block, and formed lines, five to a row.

The whole camp, about twenty thousand slaves, was standing attention for Zählappell. Camp A, women; Camp B, me; Camp C, families (in the beginning families were permitted to remain together for a few weeks); Camp D, new transports to be shipped elsewhere for labor; and the Gypsy Camp. A few miles away in Auschwitz there were about five thousand men. Our Block Elsterer blew a whistle for attention.

"When I say 'Achtung' you must stand as still as statues," she warned us. "You must not even move your heads. If you are seen moving by a guard, you might pay with your life."

Looking at each other in amazement we asked, "What does she mean? Perhaps she is only trying to scare us into obedience."

"You will soon learn that what I tell you is the truth. You think I am your enemy? I came here in 1942 and I suffered more than you. There was no one to advise me how to conduct myself, how to keep out of harm's way. I was beaten like a dog. My friends have all been killed or have died. I am one of the few lucky ones who survived. I helped build these barracks. Now, you have shelter and a place to sleep. I slept on the ground in the snow and rain. You have shoes and dresses. I had no shoes. I tell you these things only because I wish to help you. I am not your enemy. If you wish to live, even if only from day to day, pay heed. Do not ask questions. Obey me. Obey the Stuben Dienst, the woman guard and the woman overseer. Obey quickly. You are aware that from this place no one ever goes free. Perhaps you have seen the chimneys? They are on the crematoria. I have warned you. Your duty is to obey me. My duty is to obey the guards. Otherwise we pay with our lives."

She snapped. "Achtung!" We became as marble statues.

Toward us swaggered a tall, overbearing, well-nourished, thick-thighed, bleached blonde with a coarse swarthy complexion. Her uniform consisted of gray green culottes, high black boots, green blouse and jacket, a Death's Head on her left arm, and another on the bill of her military cap.

So *this* was a woman of superior race? She was a swine—a careless incubator of bastards. Where were her forebears when mine were writing the Holy Bible, both the Old Testament and the New? Where were her ancestors when mine were giving the world the Ten Commandments, the Golden Rule, and the Lord's Prayer? Where were her forebears when mine were teaching the 23rd Psalm, and "thou shalt not take vengeance nor bear any grudge, but thou shalt love thy neighbor as thyself"? What were her forebears doing when mine were giving the Sabbath, the only day of rest in seven, to the world? I am of the seed of Moses and Isaiah, Amos and Jeremiah, Abraham and Jesus. Whence came she? When my forebears were prophets, priests, and kings, hers were brute savages in animal skins practicing animism and fetishism; lewd primitives indulging in mass sex orgies in the open fields to assure a good harvest. I despised her, this tigress with a gummi knueppel, this "superior" German woman. Yet I did not fear her.

Extending the whip, she began to count: five, ten, fifteen, twenty... She noticed a young girl standing silent and rigid, tears trickling down her cheeks. Flaming into a rage, she strode over and with all of her strength smashed the gummi knueppel across her face, twice.

"Why are you crying?" she thundered. "So? You don't

answer? Now you have something to cry about. You know there is to be no crying, only 'Arbeit macht frei.' And now because of you, you stinking Jew, I must count again."

When she was out of earshot the Block Elsterer said, "Did I not warn you to be quiet or else you would be beaten? Remain in line and you will be served breakfast."

In a nearby kitchen German women guards counted and dealt out tubs of black coffee. Four Stuben Diensten carried the quota of coffee for the one thousand women in Block One. Coffee was served in metal bowls holding about two and one-half pints, the allowance for five women. I was starving. I placed the bowl to my lips. Others counted to the count of ten and it was snatched from my hands. Each one quaffed to the count of ten. This count on the coffee bowl was our food ration for the day. Water was never available.

"There will be no food served during the day, not until this evening," said the Block Elsterer. "Do not enter the Block. Stay outdoors. This afternoon the guards will assign your work. Keep away from the administration buildings. Stay away from the crematoria."

Who wanted to go near the crematoria? Did they have to arouse us from sleep at 4am to tell us that?

This was Saturday. Klari and I strolled about. I ran into my mother's cousin, Leah Mittleman of Michalovce. She was about twenty-one years of age and had been a slave since 1942. She was now a Stuben Dienst

"Leah, is that you?"

"Magda, is that really you?"

"Yes."

"What are you doing here?"

"I'm here for a rest cure and the mineral baths."

"The same Magda. You haven't changed."

"Seriously, Leah, I was caught in Budapest last Sunday. I wonder how our relatives have made out? Have you news of Aunt Lenka? Is it true the Germans have enslaved her?"

Aunt Lenka's home was in Michalovce and if anyone knew it would be Leah.

"Your Aunt Lenka and her four daughters came in 1942, shortly after I. Lenka was burned almost at once as she was an older woman; Lili, as soon as they noticed she was pregnant; Manci died of typhus, and Dusi died only recently. Starvation, I think."

My mind could not accept it, especially about Lili, a young bride.

"It is true," she told me with emphasis. "Pregnant women are burned as they are unable to do hard work. We shall never be free. For us, there is no hope. If you still wish to live, work hard and be obedient. If not, touch the charged fence and you are mercifully finished. For myself, I want to live. Be strong and try to survive."

Would I survive? I would.

"Leah, I don't want to die. I do believe those who survive will be free. The Germans are starving us. I am ravenous. You are a Stuben Dienst and have bread and potatoes. Will you give me food?"

With evident reluctance she fetched a bowl of cold boiled potatoes. I grabbed.

"You cannot have the bowl," she cautioned, drawing back. "They are counted. Carry the potatoes in your dress. Go quickly. I don't want to be caught."

Sitting on the ground, away from prying eyes, Klari and I feasted on manna from heaven. I divided them equally and we swallowed them, skins and all.

About 2pm we stood for Zählappell. Standing rigid and silent, the one thousand women in Block One were accounted for.

Approaching us was a tall, handsome German officer in a beautifully tailored uniform. He was Commandant Kramer, later to be found guilty and executed by the War Crimes Commission. He addressed us.

"You are going to work," he said. "It is hard work. You are going to build a railroad. It is imperative you complete the railroad from Auschwitz to Birkenau in three weeks. It is more than a mile. If you work diligently you will earn easier tasks for yourselves in the future. Every day brings new transports of Jews and the road must be finished. The complete evacuation of Hungarian Jews is going to commence in three weeks. You are the first Hungarian transport. Now to work. That is all."

The woman by his side was Irma Grese, she who had counted us that morning and smashed her gummi knueppel across the face of the crying girl. She, too, was found guilty and hanged by the War Crimes Commission.

By 6pm we were mad ravenous wolves. The aroma of cooking was agony and delight. The Stuben Dienst selected ten girls to carry the bread, ten loaves to a girl. To be one of the ten was a stroke of good fortune as crumbs remained in the carrier's skirts. We all begged for the honor. Each loaf was cut in six portions. Later as the Hungarian transports arrived, our portions dwindled to a thin slice daily. The bread was hard, brown, tasteless and difficult to chew. As time passed, we relished it.

"You will eat your supper indoors, each one in her Koya," said the Block Elsterer.

In came the Stuben Dienst and her assistant with a large tub of soup. It was thick and hot. We were forbidden to talk or move, but two hundred and fifty pairs of eyes followed every movement. Again we were five women to a bowl for the count of ten. Those she favored or those who helped with the cleaning had their bowls filled. Others received half bowls.

"You haven't given me my full portion," cried a girl who a month later was to be burned alive when her pregnant condition became known.

"Shut up or I won't give you any," snarled the Stuben Dienst, and she threw the contents of the bowl in her face. This Jewish girl had been brutalized by her internment, which brought out the worst in her.

The thick hot soup tasted and smelled bitter. The women complained to the Block Elsterer.

"Eat it. It's good for you. You won't menstruate while you are prisoners."

Later we learned it, too, contained a drug that kept us docile.

"Save your bread, girls," she warned us. "Tomorrow morning you get only black coffee. You are going to work twelve hour shifts and won't be fed until evening. Now go to sleep. You are to be called at midnight."

Now I knew what my daily food ration was to be: a few swallows of black coffee in the early morning and a slice of bread and a few swallows of soup in the evening.

The Block was dark. How could we do heavy manual work? Some fell asleep. From a nearby Koya came singing. The voices of an Italian Jewess and a Greek Jewess floated through the darkness. They were singing in Italian, "Mamma, son tanto felice."

If we didn't understand the words, we understood the meaning. It was a plaintive melody. Tears came to my eyes. I was thinking of my family and Gustave. In my heart was a deep feeling of contentment and gratitude that they were in their homes, safe in comfortable beds and not starving. I lay on my side because there was not enough room to lie on my back. With tears in my eyes and a prayer in my heart, I fell asleep.

At midnight someone pounded against my feet. It was the night watcher crying, "Zählappell! Get up, make your bed, and get outside! Roll call!" A cold rain was pouring down. We huddled together for warmth, dreading to step outdoors.

"Heraus! Heraus," screamed the Block Elsterer, beating us with a stout cane, and into the cold wet night we stumbled. The rain beat a merciless tattoo on our shaven heads. My only protection was the dress in which I slept. The count of ten on the coffee gave me life.

German was the chief language and woe betide anyone who did not understand orders. They learned quickly. Among ourselves we conversed in Czech, Slovakish, and Hungarian. Speaking them all fluently, I had no difficulty. The Italian, French, and Greek Jews were drawn together by a common knowledge of Spanish. My Stuben Dienst was a Czech from Žilina, not far from Mikuláš. Liking me because I spoke her language, our Koya was one of the few which received full bowls of soup.

When the starving women begged her for their full quota and asked what she was going to do with the half tub of soup she was holding out on them, she flew into a tantrum.

"That is none of your business," she barked. "I can do what I wish."

I found out she took it to the pantry and traded it with girls from other Blocks for lingerie, potatoes, and carrots. The vegetables were brought in by slaves who worked on private farms outside the camp.

My Kapo, or overseer, was a Polish Christian girl, herself a prisoner of the Germans. Having fought with the Polish underground, one would expect Genia to have some feeling for her fellow slaves. Surprisingly, her hatred of Jews was insanely malevolent. It was a personal, venomous hatred. Her hatred was a psychic disorder that had been transmitted from mother to daughter for two thousand years. By contrast, the cruelty and virulent inhumanity of the German women guards was impersonal. It was merely an expression of the German nature to inflict pain and spill blood in order to prove one's superiority.

The German nature adores the heel that crushes it if that heel be in uniform; and if in turn they have helpless victims whom they can grind under their heels.

Genia was attractive, well nourished and warmly clad. She flaunted a raincoat, gloves, a warm dress, and over-shoes. Having been in Auschwitz for two years, she had contacts. My shoes, especially the high heeled one, were frequently sucked in by the ankle deep mud in which we marched. Genia swung her gummi knueppel across my back with exultant zest when I bent down to retrieve it. We reached the railroad in about one hour. It was quitting time for the men's shift.

"You will pick up where the men left off," Genia informed us. "Climb up on the cars. Shovel the gravel between the ties and level it off."

The shovels were unbearably heavy, and my strength was ebbing away. Genia played a tempo of whip lashes across our faces, legs, and backs if we worked at less than fe-verish speed. My hands were swollen and blistered. I could stand that. It was being whipped that almost paralyzed me.

"You dirty, bloody Jew dogs, because of you there is a war. Because of you I am here," Genia screamed. "Thank God, the Germans are going to kill all the Jews; all the Jews in the world. Do you hear that, Jew dogs?"

Fumbling in her bosom she brought to light the crucifix she wore on a chain and kissed it fervently.

The latrine was a hole in the ground having a board with openings placed across it. Used alike by men and women at the same time, privacy was impossible. When Genia wasn't looking we nibbled on the slice of bread saved from the night before.

At long last we saw lines of men in striped uniforms approaching. The twelve hours were up.

"Throw down the shovels. Form lines five to a row and march home."

Home? Yes, it was home and I was happy at the thought of just crawling into the Koya. Klari, although small and dainty, was stronger than I. Many unable to walk because of the whipping had to be dragged. For a week or two if someone pleaded, "I am tired. I cannot walk. Please help me," we helped her. Later, becoming hardened, we said, "You cannot walk? Then sit down." The battle for survival had begun in earnest.

Back at the Block we were given the usual slice of bread and a count of ten on the soup bowl. Days passed. Days without water. No toilet tissue, no showers, no toothpaste, no toothbrush, no water. When it rained, we folded our dresses and slept on them. My shoes were my pillow. Had I left them on the floor they would have been stolen and traded for a potato or a carrot. My portion of bread

I hid in my armpit or between my legs, saving it for the morrow. These were the only safe hiding places while one slept. One advantage of such cramped quarters was that I couldn't move enough for the slice to dislodge.

Sundays we worked until noon. Strolling about on the camp streets were about twenty thousand slaves, creatures created in the image of God. In whose heads was the knowledge of science and medicine and law! Whose dirty, gnarled hands only a few months ago had held the surgeon's scalpel and the artist's brush! From whose lips had poured golden notes of liquid diamonds! Under whose chin had been tucked a virtuoso's violin! Whose feet had danced a brilliant ballet! Into whose heart had a pen dipped and a novel conceived! Whose hands had hewn a form of magnificent splendor from a block of stone! In whose soul had sublime music echoed, to be delivered on paper! Who were the Hebraists, and who were the jurists, and who were the rich, and who the poor! Who were the wise and who the simple! Who were the learned and who were the ignorant! Who were the leaders and who the followers! Death levels all, teaches our religion. So does German slavery.

I thought of the time Mama asked a social leader of Uzhhorod to join WIZO—Women's International Zionist Organization. After Mama had patiently explained WIZO's objectives, especially those stressing the establishment of

Palestine as a free and democratic commonwealth, she was quite indifferent and almost hostile.

"If I join, my dear Mrs. Riederman," she asked, "with what class of Jews shall I be associating?"

"In my opinion there are two classes of Jews: those who are Zionists and those who are not," answered Mama sweetly. "However, in the opinion of our enemies, there is only one class of Jews. And you, my dear, are in that one class."

After two weeks of railroad building, scores of women collapsed. They were taken to the Revir—the clinic—never to return. The Revir was a one-way street. Those who entered left the world behind. When in pain, I kept it to myself. I was dirty all over. My hands were literally black and itched maddeningly.

"Girls be on your guard," warned the Block Elsterer. "If an Aufseherin (woman overseer) sees you have the itch, you will be taken to the Revir and that is the end."

It started between my fingers, then my arms, and soon there were red blotches all over my body. The itching was excruciating. Klari had it mildly. The other three in my Koya were Anci, a lovely blue eyed blonde from Békéscsaba; Luyzi, a fine intelligent woman from Budapest, and her niece, Suzi, gentle as a dove. Luyzi was a mother to us. Unable to sleep, she guarded our slices of bread and doled them out a bit at a time.

"We must save it for later," she encouraged us.

"Luyzi, what can I do? I have the itch all over my body."

"Bathing and inspection will take place in a few days. If Dr. Mengele sees you, that is the end. Magda, I have an idea. I know a nurse in the Revir. Perhaps I can get salve from her. But you must pay for it with a slice of bread."

"Give up my bread," I shrieked in horror. "What will I live on? It's the only food I get besides my ten on the coffee and soup. I'd rather part with my right arm than that slice of bread."

"Well, she isn't a cannibal—not yet. And she won't give it to you without payment. If you want to live, you must have the salve. You cannot hope to pass Dr. Mengele's inspection with red blotches covering your body."

"How can I live without my daily portion of bread? Tell me that."

"Listen to me. I hold the bread belonging to Anci, Klari, and Suzi. From each portion, including my own, I shall break off a little piece for you. You must have the salve."

That evening, at the risk of her life, Luyzi stealthily crept into the Revir. The exchange was made. The salve was white and greasy. In the dark so no one would be the wiser, she smeared me from head to toe. The next day the itch subsided and in a few days, just in time for bathing and inspection the blotches were gone. Bathing and inspection took place once a month. This was my lucky day. The railroad was finished, the blotches gone, and I was to get a shower.

In the morning after Zählappell, Commandant Kramer addressed us.

"I am satisfied with your work," he said. "As a reward one hundred and fifty women are to be assigned to special duty. You will bathe and Dr. Mengele will select those in the healthiest condition."

In the "Sauna," the shower room, I was given a small piece of "soap." Hard as a stone, it didn't lather. The hot shower was sheer luxury. I could feel my hair beginning to grow. There were no mirrors and I tried to see my reflection in the window. No towels, of course. The windows were open and we ran around until dry. Lines formed. One thousand nude women awaited Dr. Mengele's inspection.

He was an Adonis, the handsomest, most gorgeous male on whom my eyes ever lighted. Shining dark blonde hair, tall, glowing with radiant health, amiable, gentlemanly, sauve: that was Dr. Mengele.

Luck was with me. Having been well nourished and full bodied when captured, I did not resemble a scarecrow. Yes, I had lost weight, but I had it to lose. When he saw my healthy unmarked body he said, "fähig."

Thus one hundred and fifty were selected, among them Klari and Luyzi. Poor Suzi and Anci, they had no luck. Suzi had brown birthmarks, and Anci, beautiful and healthy, happened to be standing in the rear. The selected one hundred and fifty remained; the eight hundred and fifty returned to the Block.

I should like to tell you about Dr. Mengele, the congenial, benevolent, gallant, charming, cultivated German doctor.

"I love children," he frequently said.

And so, he had a Block of twin children from newborn babes to adolescents. He experimented with them. He operated on them. A woman in my Block, a fine person from Maramaros, Hungary, told me her ten-year-old twin boys were in the twin Block. Every evening on receiving her slice of bread, she brought it to the twins. I don't know what she lived on.

"Mama, I don't know what Dr. Mengele is going to do to me," he cried to her one evening. "Today they pulled out my teeth. Last week they took my blood. Yesterday they cut off my ear. Mama, save me. Mama, I want you."

A few days later the twins were all gone as though they had never existed. Dr. Mengele, the gentlemanly German physician had tired of his experiments. Word came from the gas chamber and that is how we knew.

Standing nude in the shower room, we waited. Two girls brought our uniforms; blue and white striped dresses, stout shoes, black aprons, red bandanas, and drawers.

"How lucky you are. You don't realize what good fortune is in store for you," they bleated.

"What kind of good fortune," I asked. "Where are we going?"

"Oh, the best, the best—you are the luckiest ones here."

When we were told anything was "good" we already understood it meant raw agony. I was past believing. But I had a pair of shoes, a uniform, and a bandana for my head. I looked almost like a human being once more. And what I had to face, I would face.

When we returned to our Block the Elsterer stared at us in amazement. She actually smiled in a friendly fashion. I had forgotten what a smile looked like. I was no longer accustomed to being smiled at.

"Do you realize what your new Kommando is?" she asked. "You are going to work in Canada."

"Canada? I know Canada is in North America," I said to Klari. "Here I am in Poland, in Auschwitz. What does it mean?"

"It isn't Canada in North America, but it is as good a place," she explained. "You are going to have butter and milk and the best food anyone could wish for. Delicacies and marmalade. It is the best Kommando in all Auschwitz."

"Why are these luxuries available in Canada and here we are starving? Block Elsterer, you see women dying of starvation every day. It is difficult to understand," I said.

"Transports of Jews from all over Europe arrive in Canada," she explained. "Tomorrow the Hungarian transports will begin to arrive, now that you have finished the railroad. These hundreds of thousands will bring with them food, jewelry, fine clothes—everything. All their possessions will be taken away and brought to Canada for sorting. You will have all the food and cigarettes you want. Girls don't forget me. You know I'm your friend."

Canada

My new Kommando was not to start until the following afternoon at six. Klari and I spent the evening and the following day strolling about in a happy mood. A whole day free, clean clothes, delightful prospects: this was heaven.

Several Stuben Diensten fawned.

"You are going to work in Canada?" they asked. "How we envy you. You can organize and steal."

Organize and steal? This was new to me. Discreet questioning revealed the whole camp was "organized" on a basis of larceny, both petty and grand.

"We don't care if you organize and steal," several German women guards told us. "But don't get caught."

So that's how it is, thought I. When a guard observed our Block Elsterer had satin lingerie and fine sheets, she said nothing. It wasn't her concern whence and how they were come by. However, if she caught anyone in the act of stealing it was her duty to report the guilty one.

"Please bring me a pair of stockings and I'll give you margarine," begged a Stuben Dienst.

Marmalade? Margarine? It sounded fantastic. Was

there any left in the whole world? Others begged for sweaters and blouses, lingerie, and cigarettes.

"How can I bring you sweaters and blouses?" I asked them. "I haven't been there yet. How do I work it?"

"How? Watch how the others do it. It's easy."

Then it dawned on me: food! Oh, my God. What a Kommando I am going to have. When I'm hungry, I can eat. When my slip becomes soiled, I can discard it. I can have a clean slip every day.

Promptly at 5pm the chosen ones stood for Zählappell, and off we went on a new adventure. Our Kapo, Ria, was a German prostitute. Diseased German prostitutes were confined to camps. Ria was a low-type German. Ugly to behold, puss oozed from the pimples which covered her face. As we were passing through the main gate, Drexler, watchdog of the gate house stopped us.

"You know in what kind of Kommando you are going to work?" she barked. "The best in the whole camp. If you organize and steal and try to smuggle, remember I am here to search you every day. If you are caught, you pay with your life."

We marched in formation, five women to a row, thirty rows. Ria insisted we sing, and she taught us several songs. Marching songs, she called them. She had three favorites:

The first:

> In meiner Heimat, dort blühen die Rosen,
> In meiner Heimat, dort blüht das Glück.
> Ich möchte so gerne mein Heimat zu sehen,
> Ich möchte so gerne bei meiner Mütterlein sein.
> Oh Mädel weine nicht, wenn dir das Herz auch bricht,
> Gib mir nur einen Küss züm Abshied Grüss.

The second:

> Weit ist der Weg zurück ins Heimatland; so weit, so weit.
> Und die Wolken ziehn dahin daher und zurück,
> Sie ziehn wohl übers Meer, mit Sack und Pack,
> Der Mensch lebt nur einmal und dann nicht mehr...
> Fällt es uns auch noch so schwer, wir weichen nimmermehr.
> Ja, heut muß der Sieg wie immer unser sein, wir glauben dran.

The third:

> Wenn das mein Mutter wusste, ist ja wohl,
> Wie es mir in der fremde geht, ist ja wohl.
> Shuhe, Strumpe sind zerissen,
> Haare abgeeschnitten,
> durch die Hosen blazt der Wind,
> Ist ja wohl.

When we stopped singing for a moment to get our breath, she smashed with the gummi knueppel.

Auschwitz and Birkenau were once Polish towns. Now there wasn't a home or civilian building to be seen. Wherever I looked there were barracks like ours, prisoners and prisons. In the fields we saw men in drill uniforms, horrible gray and blue striped pajamas.

At the main entrance of Canada, we were greeted and welcomed by the Oberscharführer, the chief overseer.

"Girls, I welcome you," he said like an expansive host receiving honored guests. "If you will be good, I shall be good. What goes on here is our secret and not to be told to anyone beyond these walls. You will have an easy pleasant time—but silence. My position here depends on your silence. I shall do all in my power to make your lot an easy one."

With solicitous sincerity, he led us into a huge barrack.

I looked about. Heaped up in high piles were hundreds of thousands of garments and apparel of all kinds: dresses, suits, blouses, skirts, coats. Every kind and every type from the crudest to the finest were in those piles.

"You are going to start work now," said the Oberscharführer beaming at us. "Your chore is to put ten good garments in a bundle; ten blouses or ten dresses or ten of any one item. Then place the bundle on the next table for tying. The individual quota is forty bundles a night. If you have finished by midnight you may sleep until six in the morning. And I tell you another secret. You have only to step outside and you will see piles of food; sardines, marmalade, margarine, cigarettes and other delicacies. Take whatever you wish, but silence."

This food was taken from incoming prisoners and thrown on the ground. When it rained, great quantities of perishable food such as breads and cheeses were spoiled. Only a few miles away hundreds were dying of starvation. I hold Commandant Kramer personally responsible for this awful tragic waste.

"At midnight you will be given a hearty supper. Our cook is a Polish Jewish lad named Schepsel. He will serve you all you wish. He cooks the finest Jewish meals." If this be a dream, I thought, may I never awaken.

True enough at midnight we were served a delicious meal. Schepsel cooked and he sang. He sang Russian, Polish, and Yiddish songs. The guards enjoyed both the singing and the cooking, frequently joining in a chorus. Cholent, a thick soup made of barley, beans, and split peas was served every night.

We filled our quota of forty bundles long before midnight. The Oberscharführer counted the bundles, thanked us for our efforts and said, "Now, girls, your supper is ready. Eat all you wish. Then you may sleep until six in the morning when you will be called."

For the first time I had a bowl to myself, and a real spoon. Cholent was served and I, hungry as a ravening wolf, ate two full bowls. Only one who has been starving for weeks can fully understand the ecstasy of satiety.

We Were Strangers

There were thousands of blankets and each one made a bed for herself. Finding a handmade silk nightie, I took off my uniform and put it on. I found cosmetics in many pockets and made up for the night. It was verboten to use cosmetics but here I was safe, and it certainly boosted my morale. Before drifting off to sleep I observed a number of women who after undressing slinked off to the men's quarters. They were "old timers" in Canada. Most of them went to the quarters of their fellow slaves, but when a woman was called by a German she responded. Ria found a man, too, and all was well. Her nervousness and cruelty vanished and from that night she was friendly and pleasant.

The first night, Klari remained with me. She was in strange and unfamiliar territory. After a wonderful night's sleep, we were gently awakened. Outdoors was a small lavatory and showers. We had no privacy to take care of our natural needs but had become accustomed to the staring German men. The showers were cold but what a feeling of well-being it gave us to be clean. The soap was real as it had come from the pockets of new arrivals in the Hungarian transports. Guards walked among us as we showered, and laughingly slapped buttocks and breasts. I ignored them.

When one exclaimed, "Oh, here is a red one," I showed neither resentment nor alarm. I simply did not deign to notice. Breakfastless we formed rows of five and marched back to camp. Having been warned by experienced girls not to smuggle on the first day, our hearts were light as we reached the main gate guarded by Drexler. She tapped, and she patted, and she searched. To her obvious disappointment, she found nothing.

We were turned over to Edith, our new Block Elsterer. Edith was from Považská Bystrica. She's blonde and short and has a heavy strong voice. Like a bear, I thought. She directed us to our new quarters: B Lager, Block 12. It was a pleasant surprise to find a passable clean Block. We actually had blankets, and they were clean, and straw sacks that were not black. The Stuben Dienst brought coffee, but most of us being sated by our midnight feast refused it. Who wanted coffee? Were we not going to gorge ourselves on cholent, come midnight?

The women laughed and talked animatedly and were in high spirits. Taking off my uniform, I used it as a sheet. Outdoors the day was sunny and milky. Indoors all was quiet and peaceful. Only night workers, and they were all sleeping, were permitted in the Block.

At noon the Stuben Dienst politely, even unctuously, awoke us. She seemed apologetic. We were soon to realize this affability was merely a prelude to frequent requests for smuggled goods.

"Aufstehen, bitte, aufstehen. (Get up please, get

up)." Please? When had I last heard that word? Coming from a Stuben Dienst it was beyond belief. "Here is your soup."

Soup? This concoction was a mixture of green leaves and water. Through a window, I handed mine to a girl. Her happiness and gratitude were pathetic.

Quickly dressing and having an hour before Zählappell, I strolled about among the Blocks. Klari and I were told that about three hundred freight cars were in this transport, the second Hungarian one. Eighteen thousand Jewish souls. My God...

Tonight, and for many nights the German lust for blood would be fed. The chimneys of Auschwitz would belch forth volumes of black smoke and red flames. Into the flames they would march, these Jews, with a prayer on their lips: the Sh'ma Yisrael. These were no craven cowards. They sang their theme song, which had been composed in the camp especially for the occasion: "Es brennt, Bruder, es brennt. (It burns, brother, it burns)."

It was on the railroad I'd helped to build that this transport had come right up to the hungry mouths of the crematoria.

There they were: the high and the low. If a nation's greatest asset is the strength and intelligence and enterprise of its people, was not Hungary being impoverished? How

much capital and how many years does it require to produce a doctor or a lawyer, an artist or a scientist? And how
much courage and effort and how many years of driving
and striving does it take to become a successful business-
man or industrialist?

Did the Germans murder the intellectuals of the
occupied countries only because they were Jews? Was it
because these intellectuals opposed German Kultur? Or
did not the Germans murder the intellectuals first precisely
because they were intellectuals and thus a thorn in the
German consciousness? Was there not an uncontrollable
urge in the German character which made it imperative
that these leaders and intellectuals be wiped from the face
of the earth in order to make certain the superiority of
German intellectuals? I wondered then and I wonder now.

"Come, Klari, let us look. Perhaps we shall see relatives
or friends."

Prevented by the guards from approaching close
enough to identify anyone, I nevertheless witnessed the
world's shame and tragedy. From three hundred wagons
came pouring eighteen thousand human beings, mortal
people. The same pattern was followed: men separated
from women, the young from the old, mothers with
small children, pregnant women. The Germans were
playing at being God, I thought, just like in the prayers

on Yom Kippur.

"On the first day of the year it is inscribed and on the Day of Atonement it is sealed." I was back in the Asa Chassid Synagogue, peeking through the latticed partition.

> How many shall pass away and how many shall be born?
> Who shall live and who shall die?
> Who in the fullness of his days and who before his time?
> Who shall be tranquil and who shall be harassed?
> Who shall be brought low, and who shall be exalted…?

Sometimes it was difficult to understand God and his ways; but tonight, I would feast on cholent.

Edith, the Block Elsterer verified that this was the second Hungarian transport. In reply to Klari's worried question she assured her these Jews were not from Budapest, but from small towns. My heart stopped. Uzhhorod was now in Hungary. Shall I find someone? Edith blew the whistle for Zählappell. We stood two hours waiting for the Aufseherin to count us. Additional duties with the new arrivals had detained her.

She finally came, arrogant as always. Never a greeting, just "Alles in Ordnung." Then Ria counted and said, "Out." At the main gate Drexler counted. This was the third count.

Crossing a bridge, we came to Auschwitz proper. This was a Kommando for men. It included among other plants a sawmill which used about three thousand slaves. As we marched Polish boys called to us from behind charged barbed wires.

"Do you know Shifra Rubenstein? She is my mother."

"Have you seen Esther Bernstein? She is my sister."

Poor Jewish children. I was afraid to answer. Ria was in front and there was a guard on both sides of us.

One day a voice called, "Does anyone know Aggi Wolfe from Uzhhorod?" Uzhhorod! I asked, "who are you?"

"I am her father."

This shaven, dirty, cadaverous, ghastly thing, the elegant suave, blooming Mr. Wolfe? Never. I could not believe it. But he recognized me.

"You are Magda Riederman," he quavered, "the daughter of William."

So now I had to believe the unbelievable. This was indeed Mr. Wolfe, the jeweler. His store was near Papa's iron foundry.

"Oh, Magda, poor child you have changed so." I have changed? Good God in heaven, how about yourself, thought I.

"I would recognize you anywhere, Magda. For so many years I watched you grow and watched you play with my Aggi. Don't you know where Aggi is?"

"No, I don't, Mr. Wolfe. Be here when I pass tomorrow morning and perhaps I shall have food for you."

"Food? Please. I am so hungry." Later I was to find Aggi in Sweden.

At midnight we feasted on Schepsel's cholent, really the best I have ever eaten, and lay on a soft bed of blankets. This was our second night and Klari was restless.

"Magda, I am hungry," she said, "perhaps I can find something to eat?"

Something to eat? Had she not gorged herself on Schepsel's cholent only a few minutes earlier? Into the darkness she drifted, and I don't know what happened to her. I asked no questions. What was the point? On her finger she wore a massive gold ring. I smiled and shook my head. Who could have a gold ring in Canada? Only someone who has a lover.

"What are you going to do with your ring?" I asked. "Are you planning to smuggle it into camp?"

"No, that's too dangerous. I'd never get it past Drexler. I'll hide it here and wear it nights."

"Nights, Klari?" I asked sweetly. Hmm...maybe the numerous colorful romances Klari had tried to regale me with were true after all. I was too new in Canada to know where the cache of jewelry was hidden. Later I, too, got hold of gold rings and jewelry—but I found them in the pockets of the burned-up ones.

It amazes me that I was sexually indifferent during this

time, given my emotional temperament, yearning, and hunger. I do not claim a higher moral character. I simply was not tempted. I think my fierce and inexorable determination to survive was the paramount and dominant passion of my being. There is a French idiom that he who sleeps, dines. I would not fritter away precious sleep. I would not waste a moment of rest that might mean the difference between life and death. To me, this was a fight for life, a battle for survival, and I must guard my assets jealously. In this instance, my strength.

Thinking of my promise to Mr. Wolfe, I made up a small bundle of things I found on the ground; bread, cigars, marmalade, and a pair of stockings. I slipped it into my bosom and tried to make myself as small as possible. He was waiting. Glancing to the right and left and noting the guards were looking straight ahead, I flung it. The woman at my left gasped, "I have seen others shot for that."

"I know. I was careful and got away with it."

At the gate, Drexler searched again. Her frustration was almost droll.

In the Block excited women told me the new arrivals had been assigned to my old Block. Three crematoria burned the whole night through. Only those considered strong enough to work were spared. There were wagons from Munkács, Beregszász, and Uzhhorod. Uzhhorod?

My God. To whom had the Germans played God last night? Whom had they inscribed in the Book of Life and whom had they doomed to death by fire? This was my own flesh and blood. I had to see them.

I ran to the Block Elsterer, Edith. "My relatives and friends are among the new arrivals in A Lager, Block One," I pleaded. "I must see them. A common worker like I cannot enter another Lager. But you can. I beg you, take me there."

"Are you mad? I will not, I'm afraid." Then I begged her in Slovakish. She was startled to hear her native tongue.

"You speak Slovakish? Where is your home?"

"I am from Mikuláš. Perhaps you know my aunt who was from Považská Bystrica?"

"What is her name?"

"She no longer lives. Her maiden name was Valli Milch."

"Valli Milch. Of course, I knew her. There is a bond between us. I'll help you. Where do you want to go? What do you hope to do?"

I explained the situation. "And perhaps I shall find relatives and friends from Uzhhorod in Block One. Maybe I can help them to stay alive."

"Come, then. Should an Aufseherin ask where you are going, just say to the kitchen to help me." It was fortunate the kitchen was in A Lager.

It was now about 9 or 10am. There being no clocks, I could never be certain of the hour. No one stopped us.

"Go into Block One," said Edith. "There you will find the newcomers from the second transport."

I knew Block One! And I knew the Block Elsterer and the Stuben Dienst and they knew me. I asked them, "Are any here from Uzhhorod?"

"They're all here."

The first thing I noticed was that twenty women had been assigned to a Koya. When I was one of ten, we had been squeezed together on our sides. These poor sufferers were lying on their sides and on top of each other just like sardines in a tin. I called out in Hungarian. "Girls, is there anyone here from Uzhhorod?"

A chorus of excited voices shouted, "Magda, Magda, Magda!" I recognized one voice. It belonged to Aunt Bella, wife of Uncle Desidur. She was sobbing hysterically. I climbed up to her in the third tier. Great sobs racked her body.

"Oh, Magda, shall I ever see Uncle Desidur again? And Imri and Latzi?"

These were her first words. She must have known. We fell into each other's arms. She kissed me wildly and spasmodically sobbed and moaned. God, where were You that day? I tried to soothe her. "Of course, you'll see

141

them again, Aunt Bella. Now listen to me and I shall tell you something."

I, being the stronger had to encourage her, to breathe life into this terrified creature.

"Don't cry, darling. Be quiet. Let me look around and see who is here. Are any others of our family or friends here?"

Yes. Here was Iren Yuskovics. Iren's husband was a teacher of English. Her sister, Matyi Goodman was with her. Next, Mrs. Gluck whose husband owned a large and fashionable shoe store. She was lovely, a fine woman of great charm and a lady to her finger tips. Next, Mrs. Berman our neighbor, a woman of considerable means whose husband owned apartment houses. Next, my bosom friend and companion, Bozei Berman. Together we had gone to sewing school and the Maccabee Turein Club. It was her brother who had asked me to dance at my first party when I'd been sure I was going to be a wallflower. My confidante and confederate, Bozei. It was she with whom I had sneaked off to the pork butcher and bought ham and ate it where no one could see us. Then I found the two young daughters of Papa's cousin, Erna and Hannah. I also found Malvina Jacobowitz, a bride of a year and in her fourth month of pregnancy. Her condition was not yet too apparent. Otherwise she, too, would have been burned alive the previous night.

Crying and sobbing, they deluged me with questions.

"Magda, where is my mother?"

"Where is my husband?"

"Where is my child?"

"I don't know. I am going to tell you the truth. I don't know where the aged are, and I don't know what happened to the children. They probably were burned alive. But you are here. You are alive. I started exactly as you. My head was shaved. You see how my hair is growing out? So, will yours. I wore rags like you. Now I have a decent dress. So will you."

"But how is it that you have a good dress, shoes, and a head scarf?"

I tried to explain, and they listened attentively. One could almost see the change of character in their faces. Some were filled with despair and hopelessness. They would surely die. Others seemed to be charging themselves, like a storage battery. The fires of adversity were already tempering the steel. These would bend—but would not break. Aunt Bella was crying and kissing me as though I were the Angel of Liberation. Many cried, "I am hungry. I am cold."

"I know. I, too, was hungry and I, too, was freezing. That is why I am going to help you—somehow."

They told me they had been called for Zählappell at 4am, stood hungry and cold and miserable for six hours.

As they were not yet working there was no valid reason for this cruelty. This was simply an example of the German need for showing their authority, their "superiority." Yes, indeed, it certainly showed German superiority.

"Every day I shall bring you one sweater," I promised. "The first is for Aunt Bella."

Every woman in the Canada Kommando smuggled in one sweater a day.

"Arrange for one of you to be near the kitchen door every day and I shall give you my dinner, my ration of bread and soup."

Thus, I would be eating only once in twenty-four hours, at midnight. I felt I could do it safely as I slept most of the day. Also, I was swallowing all the pills and capsules I found in the pockets of garments, trusting to luck they were vitamins as I fondly imagined.

"I will try to smuggle in gold jewelry or something of value for your Block Elsterer," I said, "and she will see that you do not starve."

Then I kissed Aunt Bella, assuring her that I would return the next morning with food and a sweater. Approaching their Block Elsterer, I pleaded, "My aunt is a sick woman, please feed her. I will bring you gold from Canada." And thus, the deal was made; gold from Canada for food.

So began my trouble. In addition to my own trials and tribulations there was the gnawing distress and concern for Aunt Bella and the others.

Returning to my own quarters I appealed to the Block Elsterer. "I have located my Aunt Bella," I told her, "and many friends of my childhood. They are utterly helpless and suffer from cold and hunger. Out of the depths of their misery they look to me. I must help them. You have access to food. What do you want from Canada?"

"If you can bring me a piece of jewelry from time to time, I can promise you a few bowls of soup, marmalade, margarine, and bread every day. And I'll help you get it to them."

"How can it be arranged?"

"Every morning you will go with my Stuben Dienst to A Lager which is close to the kitchen. The rest is up to you." I was almost beside myself with joy.

Marching to Canada that evening I saw hundreds of newcomers, men from the second Hungarian transport. They had been assigned to the sawmill. When we halted for the day shift, a worker emerging from Canada recognized me. "Magda, Magda," a voice called.

It was Zigmund Halmos, the husband of Cousin Ilonka who had visited me in Pava utca in Budapest. He was a

Director of the National Bank in Uzhhorod.

"Oh, Magda, so you are here too? Have you seen Ilonka? Do you know where Aunt Rozei is?" Aunt Rozei was his sister.

"No, Zigmund, I haven't seen them. Perhaps they were sent to Germany. Have hope."

I well knew they had been burned alive. Again, the red flames had glowed and leapt all through the previous night.

"Don't worry, Zigmund. Perhaps they have it good. You must think of yourself and try to live. In the morning when I pass, I shall throw a package of food."

Awaiting me in the morning was a group of Uzhhorod men, Moskovics, the brick manufacturer, the little God, the richest Jew in the community. He was the one who scornfully refused to join the Zionist Organization. It was he who refused to contribute to Keren Kayemeth (Jewish National Fund) saying, "I am a Czech citizen. I am not interested in a Jewish State in Palestine."

If the terms of the Palestine Mandate had been honorably fulfilled, Palestine would now be a Jewish State, I thought, and the wealthy Moskovics would be manufacturing bricks there and not be a walking cadaver in a German slave labor camp. Next to him stood an old friend, Bandi Herskovics. He told me his wife and baby of six months were in the transport. He already knew that children were put to death and their mothers with them.

"Is it true," he sobbed convulsively. It was.

"I don't know, Bandi," was all I could say. "I haven't heard."

Poor Bandi. He sobbed great, racking sobs that went back eighty generations. The awful horror of it. Was there never to be an end to this maniacal lust for murder? Were not their bellies full after two thousand years? Poor Jesus. Poor gentle Jesus. I would not wish to be the soul of that well-meaning Jewish man.

Others asked, "Magda, don't you remember me? I lived in Masaryk Street near your home." Or, "Don't you remember skiing with me on the Uz?"

Every morning they waited. Waited for food to keep them alive. One day passed like another. I learned fast. Every day I smuggled packages of food and one sweater.

Klari had a kind, generous heart and was really enjoying life in Canada. Klari's emotional hunger was being well nourished. I was free from sex hunger. I seemed to have become neuter, I who had been so passionate, so sexually aggressive in my life with Gustave.

"Klari, help me. I have so many to feed. Give me your gold ring that I may bring it to my Block Elsterer."

She took the ring from her finger and without a word handed it to me. "If I find gold jewelry, Klari, I promise to repay you."

"How are you planning to get by Drexler's inspection? You know being caught with gold means death."

Putting the ring on my big toe, I prayed to God for a miracle as I had never prayed before. That morning of all mornings Drexler did not order us to remove our stockings, only our shoes. I had won the gamble.

Running happily to my Block Elsterer, I thrust the ring at her. "Here is a gold ring, here is the gold I promised you."

She turned up her nose disdainfully. "I don't want it. I have gold. I want a diamond ring."

"How can I give you a diamond ring if I don't have one? Take this and give me what you wish but I must have food. You know it is for the starving." She was reluctant but relented.

"For three days I shall give you a loaf of bread, a glass of marmalade and a koska (measure) margarine."

A koska margarine... Others paid a higher price as may be judged by the lyrics of a popular camp song, "Für eine Koska Margarine, eine halbe Stunde Liebe (for a measure of margarine, one half-hour of love)."

Man kennt am Gang,
Und an dem Haeren,
Was Hurren sind und Hurren waren.
Für ein Stück Kaiserbrot,
Da gibt man alles hin.
Und wen es darauf komt
Für ein choking
Da sing Ja nur die Capo Hurren
Die stehen am Draht zeigen Figuren
Die Hose hinunter,
Die Minchke zeigt
Da hatt der Capo schon alles erreicht.

This is not a matter for condescension. Hunger knows no morals. When Aunt Bella and the others saw a whole loaf of bread they laughed and cried. Starving had made them incoherent. Their twenty-four-hour ration was a small piece of bread, and the following twenty-four hours a mouthful of soup, but never bread and soup on any one day as they were not working. And here was a whole loaf of bread. Climbing into Aunt Bella's Koya, I took off a sweater, the second one. It was for Aunt Bella's sister. Giving the food to Aunt Bella I said, "You must divide it equally. Do not forget Malvine who is carrying a child." Aunt Malvine was Papa's sister and I visited her almost every summer.

"Any news of the outside, Magda?" they asked. "How long shall we be forced to remain here?"

"Not long. The Russians are getting close and the Swiss Red Cross is arranging to liberate us."

This was sheer fantasy, but it seemed to give them the will to hang on to life. The next day I told them I heard a rumor the Swiss Red Cross was planning to pay the Germans to free us.

"Magda, you are our life's blood. You are medicine for us." Their gratitude was overwhelming. They awaited me each morning as though I were a god. I contrived to visit them twice daily.

In Canada life was on another planet. The work was light, the atmosphere free and easy, the food plentiful and appetizing. There were no restrictions against carrying out food we found on the ground, or anything else we wished. Time and time again we were warned not to be caught. Occasionally like a mouse gnawing in my bosom was the fear I was becoming unsexed. Others were finding association with men a happy pastime. Why was I cold and disinterested? During my married life how different I had reacted.

I found gold rings, gold chains, and other jewelry but never diamonds. But the gold sufficed to buy enough food for my charges to keep the breath of life in their bodies. I brought them toilet soap smuggled in between my legs. In camp soap was worth more than diamonds. Whenever I found pills or capsules, I continued to swallow them, sometimes twenty at a time.

Two months passed. Every night the flames leapt high. Hungarian Jewry was going up in smoke. The stench was sickening. And every day Germans brought into Canada the clothes of the burned-up ones.

One morning running into A Lager with a loaf of bread I thought my heart would stop beating. The Block was empty. Dashing over to the Sauna where all must shower before leaving in transport, I saw the lines were already formed. I could not get close to Aunt Bella but she saw me and waved. I see her now. There she stood: filthy, torn dress, crying as if her heart was being slashed to bloody shreds. Well I knew this was the end of Aunt Bella. Before each transport was made up, Dr. Mengele made the "selections" of who shall live and who shall die. Later I learned, though not to my surprise, that Malvine, whose pregnancy was now evident, was put in a gas chamber. As usual this transport was being sent to Germany for slave labor, so the pregnant, the ill, and the weak were put to death. Dr. Mengele, the German doctor, was playing at being God.

For me it was a day of horror. I couldn't sleep. I could not shut out the sight of Aunt Bella from my mind's eye. Her devoted husband and her handsome sons adored her. How beautiful had been her life. She loved beauty and made her home a place of charm and loveliness. Her home was no showy place but a sanctuary for her friends and dear ones. Loneliness wrapped me in its icy clutches. I was alone, my relatives and friends gone. I had almost found forgetfulness in helping them. I was never to find anyone again although I watched many transports unloading.

Zigmund was still there and every morning I threw him a package of food and cigarettes. Then the inevitable happened. A guard saw the package fall and watched Zigmund pick it up. Not knowing who had thrown it he strode over to him. I thought now he would kill him. I had seen it happen. Opening the package and finding bread, stockings, and cigarettes, he handed them back to Zigmund. The morning packages continued.

Suddenly the transports stopped. Hungary was now Judenrein, free of Jews. About a half million Hungarian Jews were now no more. Their clothing had been sent to Germany. Their food we had eaten. I was back on the Block ration, a small piece of bread and a count of ten on the soup bowl each morning. That had to do for twenty-four hours. I decided to save the bread for my evening meal.

Zigmund was waiting by the fence. He saw the piece of bread in my hand. How could he know I was saving it for myself? He thought it was for him. He looked so pathetic I threw it to him.

Klari gasped, "Are you crazy?" What are *you* going to

eat tonight?"

"I don't care. I don't care. His hands were held out. I could not refuse him." My God, when I think of it. Zigmund, the Director of the National Bank of Uzhhorod.

That night hunger clawed my insides. Luyzi gave me half of her bread and made me promise never again to give mine away. There was no work for us and we knew our holiday in Canada was rapidly approaching its end. The Hungarian Jews had been eliminated, murdered in cold blood precisely and methodically after a plan. Our work was done.

The Oberscharführer addressed us. "Girls, I am sorry but there is no further work for you here. This Kommando must be liquidated. But I can promise you that soon we shall have large numbers of transports from Poland. The Lodz ghetto is scheduled to be brought here. I promise that you will come back."

With this cheerful prospect in view we burst into tears.

"Don't cry, girls. I promise that I shall ask Drexler to assign you to good Kommandos."

Hearing this, our lamentations were dirgeful and loud. Well we knew that when we returned from Canada our troubles would commence in earnest. Some of the women guards angered and enraged by our Canada vacation would wreak their wrath on our helpless heads. Our fellow slaves envious and maddened with jealously and frustration would take fiendish delight in seeing us assigned to hard and menial duties. Bidding the Oberscharführer a fond farewell, we thanked him for his kindness. Naturally we did not express the wish to return. Were not the Jews in the Lodz ghetto our blood brothers, and also created in the image of God?

Union

B ack in the Block we were stripped of everything. My uniform, shoes, the old-fashioned flannel open drawers which tied around the waist with a cord—everything. I was given a blue dress with brown sleeves and a red cross on the back for identification, and white shoes. This was autumn. The mornings and evenings were cold. All summer I sweated in heavy drill uniform with long sleeves, heavy shoes and flannel underwear. Now that winter was coming, I had white shoes and no underwear.

"You no longer belong in this Block," said the Elsterer. "Go to B Lager, Block 24." Twenty-four, the last Block was near the toilets, and this was an advantage.

The new Block Elsterer was an old Polish Jewish maid with a baritone voice and the devil's own disposition. She greeted us sarcastically. "Aha, the Mesdames from Canada. Into the Koyan, ladies."

Here we found Luyzi's niece Suzi, and Anci. Their animosity was bitter. "Oh, the fine Damen from Canada are honoring us with their presence. You will soon learn the taste of a good Kommando. You are going to work with us in the Scheisskommando." That's the shit Kommando.

155

We Were Strangers

Klari, Luyzi, and I looked at one another in shocked silence and said nothing.

But what does God do? The following morning a girl in the next Koya became ill. Her body was covered with red rashes and when I touched her, she was burning. Poor soul, she was taken to the Revir, and that was the end of her. For those who lay down in a bed in the Revir there was no returning.

An Aufseherin addressed us from the doorway. "The girl just removed has scarlet fever. You must remain in the Block for four weeks."

We were in quarantine. What good fortune. Our daily ration would be an absolute minimum, but we'd not be working. Tubs took care of our natural needs. There was no water for drinking or bathing. I was always thirsty, panting for moisture as my body dehydrated. I thought how heavenly it would be to have a glass of water. I had visions of water flowing from countless faucets. I had only to close my eyes to see rivers, lakes, and oceans. I pictured Niagara Falls and billions of gallons of water overflowing and my tongue seemed to strangle me. I was content to remain in the Block. We lay in the Koyan from morning till evening.

Hunger was torture. Hunger was gnawing, grinding, raw, throbbing, stabbing, agonizing, suffering. It destroyed the soul as well as the body. It was like a slow death, a little bit of you dying each day. A little piece of bread one day, a swallow of soup the next.

One thousand women, new faces every day, and each with a story, a tragedy of her own. One lady I shall never forget. She was a real lady, Mrs. Bardos from Budapest. When we cried, "Aunt Bardos, we are hungry. We can no longer endure this," she replied, "Today we shall discuss the great Hungarian writers. My daughter will recite the poetry of Endre Ady."

The daughter was like the mother, a young lady of charm, beauty, and genuine nobility. Another day we discussed Petofi. And she talked of world affairs, philosophy, history, music—anything to take our minds off the beast, hunger. Never was she bitter. If she hated Germans, she did not reveal it by word or gesture. She pitied them. "What a great waste of human material," she sighed.

One dark afternoon I heard moans of anguish from a nearby Koya. Sitting up, I observed the Stuben Dienst coming from the direction of the Revir with a woman in white. "Luyzi, let us look," I said. However, we were ordered to stand back.

After a short period, the patient was covered and the Stuben Dienst hurried past carrying a pail of bloody mass. Some said this baby had been still born. Others said the doctor aborted the baby to save the mother's life.

"But the doctor had no instruments and no medicine," I gasped.

"It is a common occurrence. She aborts expectant mothers with her bare hands. If the Germans learn of a pregnancy you know what happens, the crematorium for that one."

Now I was beginning to understand the mysterious happenings that had puzzled me; the contents of pails dumped into slop tubs. Later the Stuben Dienst told us that newborn live babies were put to death immediately and also dumped into toilets and tubs. After that, when I saw the doctor in the Block and the Stuben Dienst hurrying by with a pail, I knew. I understood. The mothers never received extra food, medicine or any care whatsoever. And if it happened in a work Kommando they kept on with the regular work schedule.

One morning when going to the toilets we saw a half dozen guards running after girls and dragging them into the Revir. With the others I ran into the toilets. Too late. They caught us. Into the Revir they marched us, and we knew not why. One thing was certain: it would be evil and sinister. About seventy-five girls waited in an outer room, and one at a time we were summoned.

One by one they staggered out, pale unto death. My lips silently formed the questions, "What is it?" They were past answering. Now it was my turn. They told me to sit down. Two rubber bands were put on my arm, one above the other. I felt the prick of a needle. I was afraid to cry out. The German vampires were sucking out my heart's blood.

"You may go now," I heard as from a great distance. "In the evening you will receive a loaf of bread."

I got up and staggered toward the door. I don't know how I made it. The world was spinning before my eyes. The ceiling was where the floor should have been, and the floor was above me. Somehow, I reached my Koya. I lay all day. True to German tradition, there was no loaf of bread that evening. My weakness bewildered me. I had always been so strong. I didn't cry like the others. I believed I could endure anything, like it was natural, like it was the regular order of things. I wasn't even angry. Couldn't talk. Others cried. How foolish. Crying only used up one's strength. I was lucky. The Germans left me enough blood to pump my heart. Others were not so fortunate.

Four weeks passed. The quarantine was lifted. Of the one thousand women in our Block, one hundred were assigned to the Kartoffelbunkers (potato ditches), seven hundred to dig out and level off a new Zählappell Platz (roll call plaza), and, alas, one hundred and fifty to the Scheisskommando (excrement work detail), including me.

We were given large shovels with long handles. Like

beasts of burden we hauled heavy wagons to the toilets. There we shoveled excrement of many thousands into the wagons and then hauled the loaded wagons about five miles out to the fields.

On the first day, the shovel of Agi Farkas from Kecskemét, Hungary collided with mine. I got the contents of both right in the face. The girls howled with mirth until they actually cried. And I cried and shrieked in rage. There were neither water nor soap nor towels. I could only try to wipe away the foul, stinking mess with my dirty sleeves. My eyes were full, my ears were full, and my mouth was full. It was not yet time for our monthly shower. For days my presence made others retch. The girls shrank from sleeping with me. I couldn't blame them. I shrank from myself. The shift was from 7am to 7pm but we were gotten out of our bunks at 4am to stand Zählappell.

The munitions factory was called Union. Why? I do not know. Thousands of slaves worked there. One day it was bombarded by the Russians. Only the windows were broken.

The crematoria were operated by Jewish boys. After a three-month period in the crematoria Kommando, they, too, were put to death. One group, knowing their time was approaching, secured explosives from the slaves in the Union. There was a tremendous explosion, a bombardment. Out from the crematoria ran about one hundred and fifty boys who knowing they were going to be murdered had nothing to lose. They dashed for the woods shouting in Hungarian, "Girls, run after us. Follow us."

How could we. We were behind barbed wire building the new Zählappell Platz. A woman guard with her huge dog, her gun, and her gummi knueppel watched us closely. And the fence was charged.

Instantly the guards sprang into action. They machine gunned the fleeing boys. They were mowed down like grass, the bodies dragged back and thrown alongside our fence. The Aufseherin barked, "Everyone into the Block!"

Through the windows I saw them drag the bodies to the Zählappell Platz and place them in regular rows. Drexler strode up and down shouting, "Do you see what has happened?" She shook her fist at us and screamed, "If any of you try running away you will look like this." And so saying, she kicked us and swaggered off.

The explosion did little damage. In a few days the crematoria were working at full capacity, burning up the ever-increasing thousands who walked into their fiery jaws.

Every month Dr. Mengele made the "selections" of who shall go to Germany, and who shall go into the gas chambers and the crematoria.

Germans are celebrated for their cleanliness, so I have been told. One day it was discovered the gypsies had lice.

That night thousands of them went up the chimney, and that was the end of the Gypsy Lager in Auschwitz.

One day I heard a rumor that a camp messenger had run away. The next day as I was working on the Zählappell Platz we were ordered to drop the shovels and form lines in rows of five. The Block Elsteren were talking among themselves. She had been caught they said. I pitied her. Then two guards appeared each holding her by one arm. She was from Belgium, a beautiful blonde who had been in Auschwitz for years. Her blond hair was streaked with mud, her face dirty and her clothes in rags. Behind them came Drexler looking as happy as I have ever seen her.

They halted. We hardly dared breathe. Drexler shouted, "Now you see how someone who runs away succeeds. And you are going to see how we hang her. You are going to see this with your own eyes."

Drexler smiled and looked at the poor girl with fiendish glee. While Drexler was talking, I noticed the girl fumbling with her skirt. I saw her draw her hands across her wrists; first one, then the other. Blood spurted out. My God, she had slashed her wrists.

Drawing herself to her full height she slowly walked the few steps toward Drexler and looking right into her eyes, said distinctly and clearly, "Mich wirst du nicht hangen (Me, you will not hang)." And with her last waning strength struck Drexler full across the face. She collapsed, her heart's blood spurting from her wrists.

Drexler screamed, "Take her away! Her blood's on my face!" Was it not also on the face of Germany?

In a few days it was forgotten. What was one life when all about us was death—up the chimney. The crematoria were going full blast day and night. If they weren't belching forth flames and smoke, we asked ourselves, "what's wrong? It's too quiet." Only when new transports were arriving was there respite. And it was a short one. A goodly supply of human fuel was soon available.

Each Block had its own night watcher. This was considered a sinecure. The lucky night watcher slept by day, received an extra food ration and had only to sit by the doors during the night hours. It was her duty to make certain the women used tubs to take care of their natural needs. Many had only the strength to crawl out of the Koyan. As a result the floors were an Augean stable. When the regular night watcher became ill, the Block Elsterer heaped this honor on me. She thought I was a Slovakian like herself and was trying to do me a favor.

It was a night to harrow the soul. Quiet reigned. The women slept. A whistle was the signal that no one was to leave the Block. The night was dark, mysterious, and very cold. Only in guards' quarters were there lights. The world was black and quiet. Occasionally a woman, crying and in pain, used the tubs. Suddenly there were lights and I saw long lines of shadows. Guards were shouting, "Ruhe, Schwein Juden! (Quiet, Jew pigs!)" And there was the sound of slashing whips against bare flesh, cries of pain, thundering profanity in German. Another orgasmic rapture was in store for the Germans that night. The shadows were thousands of Jewish men being herded into the crematoria.

I saw it. I saw the billowing volumes of red flames leaping into the sky. My ears heard screams. "Sh'ma Yisrael Adonai Eloheinu Adonai Ehad." Even in this hour, in the awful hour of their death by fire, they believed in God. God Himself could not pluck from their hearts their faith in Him. No cravens, they. They march into the flames like men.

My teeth chattered. My blood was icy cold. My flesh crawled. I was petrified with horror. "Mama, Mama, I want you. Mama, they are burning thousands and I can do nothing." Paralyzed, spasmed with fear, I was frightened out of my senses.

Then in my mind's eye I saw Mrs. Horowitch, the Hebrew teacher of my childhood. "If ever you are afraid and need God's help, wrap your arms about yourself and pray, Adonai lee v'lo ee-rah."

And there I was, rocking to and fro, crying out the prayer: Adonai lee v'lo ee-rah, Adonai lee v'lo ee-rah.

The screams, those petrifying screams crushed me.

The smell of burning flesh stang my throat and nostrils. I was sick unto death. I vomited and retched and retched and vomited. I was so afraid, so scared. Many times I had seen the red flames and the black smoke and heard the screams and smelled the living flesh, but never had I been all alone. And the night so black. For six hours leaping flames gorged themselves on the living fuel and then grudgingly subsided.

At 4am I aroused the Stuben Dienst, she called the Block Elsterer, and together they woke up the Block.

"Please, Block Elsterer. Will you get someone else to be night watcher? I cannot endure the screams and the flames and sickening smell."

"That is only because you aren't used to it. The crematoria are always burning, you know that. Soon you will become so accustomed to it you won't even notice what is happening. You don't seem to realize I have given you an easy job. You certainly don't seem very appreciative."

"I do appreciate what you tried to do for me. But I will never get used to it. I don't want to. Please get someone else."

"I will not compel you to keep this job but you will rue it. Sleep today and tomorrow you will start working in a new Kommando."

"What Kommando, Block Elsterer?"

"Oh, a really good one, the Kartoffelbunkers."

Inquiry revealed it was indeed a good Kommando. There was always the chance of being able to eat a potato when the guards weren't looking; a potato with the dirt and peeling, but nevertheless edible and nourishing. This was my first separation from Klari who was still in the Zählappell Platz Kommando. We still slept together.

The Kartoffelbunkers ran alongside the Auschwitz railroad I had helped to build. The potatoes arrived in freight cars. Girls standing atop the freight cars shoveled potatoes into troigles. A troigle is a large heavy wooden case with shafts fore and aft. When filled, two girls carried the troigle to a ditch and dumped the potatoes. There was mad tension in the air. We worked at feverish speed. It seems the Germans miscalculated when they anticipated remaining in Auschwitz for the winter. The Russians were coming and the potatoes had to be buried. The work was cruel and grueling. I was not in physical condition to continue hour after hour. When we put down the troigle for a moment, our Kapo, Hassa, a Polish Christian girl, beat us unmercifully with a thick wooden slat.

The Oberscharführer came to learn how the work was progressing.

"The potatoes must be buried in two days or they will fall into the hands of the Russians," he thundered.

"It cannot be done, Oberscharführer. Not unless we have more help," said the guards.

"Very well. I shall send men to help. But you must finish this job in two days."

Hope surged in my breast. Men were considerate and occasionally gave us a cigarette. A cigarette was wealth. For it I could get a half loaf of bread. For a potato I could get a slice of bread.

In the distance I saw a group of small boys. I asked a woman, "Are they the 'men'?" I was amazed, never having seen small children except those in the twin Block and they were for Dr. Mengele's experiments. The usual procedure was to burn children of tender years; they couldn't work.

The newcomers were small and awfully skinny, about twelve or thirteen years of age. The guards ordered them to carry troigles full of potatoes. I say here and now: this was one of the most shocking things I saw. Was this civilization? Have the Germans not even one human decent instinct?

In passing I asked a lad, "Where is your home? Do you speak Hungarian?"

"Hungary is my home. We are all from Hungary and were brought here about a month ago and separated from our parents. This is our first Kommando. We are starving."

"Eat a potato when no one is looking."

He tried but couldn't make them stay down. For myself, I relished raw potatoes. They were delicious, especially with a piece of bread.

Hassa marched up and down, up and down, striking indiscriminately with the slat, right and left, right and left.

"I cannot move another step," I said to my partner. "Let us stop for a moment."

I had been working for fourteen hours straight. I put down my end of the troigle, unaware that Hassa was pouncing upon me from the rear. With all her mighty strength she rained blow after blow on my spine. I collapsed. My partner helped me stand up. I could not move. But I had to. I could not cry. But there were tears in my eyes.

A slave digging a ditch raised his head and said, "You hear that distant rumbling? That is a bombardment. The Russians are coming. Es geht zu Nielah; vielleicht ist es auch unsere Nielah, aber…"

Nielah is the closing portion of the Yom Kippur service. The slave meant that the end is near; that perhaps it is our end, but at least it's the end of the Germans, too.

At long last darkness fell. Every moment was an agony. It was impossible to stand straight. I thought I would never reach the Block. They made us stand about four hours for Zählappell. And this after fourteen hours of torturous work. To us this was an indication the Germans were having military setbacks. No one could touch me for the pain.

When at last an Aufseherin came to count us the Block Elsterer said, "Aufseherin, the girls returned from work in tears. They say Hassa beats them unmercifully with a wooden stave and they are afraid to work in the Kartoffel-bunkers." The Aufseherin smiled sarcastically and said, "I shall tell Hassa exactly what you have told me."

I understood. Tomorrow someone will surely be beaten to death. And it was not going to be me. Klari and Luyzi dragged me into the Koya and I lay on my stomach. We held a council of war. We were not going to work tomorrow, no matter what happened.

They told me the woman guard removed the muzzle from her fierce dog, an animal which had been trained to bite, unleashed him, and laughingly ordered him to run after them. It was great fun for her. She was a real German sportswoman. The dog ran wildly among the slaves, biting, tearing off flesh and finally clamping his big jaws on the leg of Ibolya Weinstock.

Ibolya had been a cashier in Fileres Aruhaz, the largest department store in Budapest. She was engaged to a Christian and his family had reported her to the Gestapo. Her leg was cold and numb. She rubbed it and said there was no sensation or feeling.

And so the five us, Klari, Layzi, Suzi, Ibolya, and I were afraid to go to work on the morrow. There was no sleep that night. I trembled at the thought of tomorrow. My entire back was a mass of raised welts and blisters.

The plan was a simple one. When thousands swarmed out for Zählappell we unobtrusively sauntered to our pre-arranged hiding places. Three hid in toilets, one in the store room for empty food containers, and I hid in the tub which originally contained chloride. It was white, empty and dry. The die was cast. It didn't take long for our absence to be discovered, and a hue and cry to be raised.

"Es fehlt viele," barked the Block Elsterer to the Stuben Dienst. "Wie viele fehlt es?" How many were missing?

I crouched down in terror. The hunt was on. In stormed an Aufseherin. "It is late," she said to the Block Elsterer. "The women must go to work. You look for the missing girls. They must still be here in the Lager. They couldn't have gotten out alive."

I heard the thud of marching feet. All was quiet. Someone entered the storeroom. It must be the Stuben Dienst, Roozia. One by one she lifted covers. In the last one she found me.

"Here's the Hungarian cholera!" she screamed, striking blow after blow on my defenseless head. Another blow and another. I spoke the language so fluently she thought I was Hungarian.

Climbing out I defied her. "Yes, I am here. But I am not going to work anymore. You can kill me, but I am not going to work and you can't make me."

Again she struck me. I was in too much pain to strike back.

Later when I was coming to America I met her on the Gripsholm and it was with the greatest restraint that I did not hurl myself upon her. I was to meet her once more in the office of the Hebrew Immigrant Aid Society in Chicago.

Triumphantly Roozia summoned the Block Elsterer. The latter was calm and reasonable.

"Now listen here. Since you haven't gone out to work, you must work in the Block. Help Roozia with the cleaning."

All morning I scrubbed floors with chlorine. And then out of a clear sky the bell rang for Zählappell. This was unheard of. It was sensational. What does it mean? My four conspirators came out of hiding and joined me.

"I heard they are making up a transport," said Luyzi. "I don't know its destination but whoever wishes to go may do so."

"Girls," I said, "what it really means is another Lager. I am going to take the chance. If I remain here it means working in the Kartoffelbunkers. I understand transports are on the move constantly to Germany; the Russians are coming. Until this moment I did not believe it. C Lager is already empty. You know as well as I that the aged, the ill, the children, and the 'Muselman' (wasted, emaciated slaves) have been put to death. We are not yet so emaciated that we cannot pass Dr. Mengele's 'selection.' In a few weeks we too, shall be Muselmänner. In a few weeks we shall not be able to pass inspection. Then it is the crematorium for us." The girls wavered for a few minutes.

"Magda, where you go, we will go."

Without a backward glance at the Block we ran toward the Zählappell Platz. The bell was tolling as we formed in lines, five to a row. After a cold shower and a turn in the fresh air-drying room, one thousand five hundred nude women lined up for inspection.

While waiting for Dr. Mengele to decide who was to live and who was to die, I struck an acquaintance with newcomers from Slovakia. Among them was a girl from near Liptovský Mikuláš. She was in the last Slovakian transport and had been in camp only a few days.

"Please tell me about home," I begged her. "I have been away for ten months. What is going on in the world?"

"I don't know what is going on in the world. I can only tell you Monsignor Hlinka and Monsignor Tiso have seen to it that Slovakian Jewry is no more."

Her sorry story filled me with dread and foreboding.

Where was my darling Gustave? Later I learned he was hidden by Christian farmers.

The name of my new acquaintance was Dietelbaum, and with her were her sister and mother. The conversation revealed much to my delight that the Dietelbaums were related to Aunt Valli. Nearby was a young woman with whom I was to become as close as sisters. Her name was Pira Kraus.

The great Dr. Mengele arrived. We paraded past him, one by one. Of the approximately one thousand five hundred women, about one thousand passed inspection. The remainder were "selected" for death. Never shall I forget the screams of the two daughters when Mrs. Dietelbaum was "selected." They loved their mother.

"Don't cry," I said, trying to bring them a morsel of comfort. "She is coming in the next wagon with the older women." But I knew she had a rendezvous with the crematorium. Poor children, they believed me because they wanted to.

My new outfit consisted of a black dress, no underwear, torn shoes, no stockings, and a coat to protect me against the blasts of the coming winter. It was black and white striped georgette having neither lining nor buttons. I tied a rag around my waist.

At the door stood Commandant Kramer and Drexler.

The wagons were waiting.

"You are going on a long trip," said Drexler, "perhaps two or three days. Each one will receive a whole loaf of bread, three pats of margarine and one wurst."

It was about three in the afternoon and I had not yet eaten. I was unable to grasp the significance of this great good fortune. A whole loaf of bread in one piece? It was beyond my comprehension.

"Until I have it in my hands, I believe it will be only one portion," said Klari under her breath.

As we passed, Commandant Kramer counted us and ascertained that each had the identifying yellow triangle and tattooed number on the left arm. Whatever plans Germans executed was done with military exactness. To transport five thousand people or send them to the gas chambers was done with German efficiency, promptness, and dispatch.

Two guards were posted at each wagon. With great difficulty we pulled ourselves up and in. Added to the refrain of the guards—"Herein! Schnell! Hurry!"—was a steady tattoo of rifle beatings across our spines and buttocks. The interior was dark with only a small barred window near the roof. I huddled in a corner with my knees drawn up under my chin. There was no room to stretch out.

Luyzi was the guardian angel, the Mother. "You will

each give me your bread," she said. "I shall guard it for you. We don't know how long we shall be in here. I'll ration out the bread."

A sense of well-being pervaded my racked soul and body. It was dark and warm. Warm, because large numbers of bodies huddled together warmed one another. Peaceful, because for a moment no one was beating me.

"Luyzi, I don't care if we are in this wagon a week. It is heavenly not to have to stand Zählappell hours on end after a long hard day's work."

It was evident from the beginning the guards had little stomach for the task before them, being locked in with us for the trip.

"Silence, dirty Jew dogs. Silence or I'll kill you, you Jew swine. It is because of you that I have to be here and smell your stink. It is because of you there is a war. You will die like dogs in anguish and suffering. Soon there will be no more Jews in the world." And then the guard ate heartily, made a bed of blankets, and went to sleep.

All was quiet. We fell asleep from sheer exhaustion. Through the grill I saw the gray light of dawn. The train was moving.

Luyzi had a knife of which she was terribly proud. I think she smuggled it out of Canada. It was a possession, something she could call her own. A knife was especially precious. With it, one could cut a piece of bread into many small portions. If you tore the bread it was gone in a few bites. Luyzi gave to each (we were five including her) a small piece of bread and a dab of margarine.

"Eat slowly," we encouraged one another. "If you eat slowly you will be less hungry."

And so we chewed and chewed and slowly ate our ration. This was one of the most powerful examples of self-control I have ever witnessed.

The wagon contained only one tub to take care of our natural needs. The guards forbade bowel movements. Only voiding was permitted. When the tub was filled, we threw the contents through the grill. Being high it was difficult to access, resulting in splashes on those adjacent. Those who could not restrain their bowel movements had it under themselves. The stench from one hundred and fifty women was overpowering and sickening. The guard cursed and berated us for the vile stench. This was typical of the German mentality. He felt himself blameless even though it was his order which prevented us from using the tub and disposing of the contents. Anyone who whispered was beaten ruthlessly with his rifle.

Then came the second night. While we slept someone reached out and stole our margarine from Luyzi. This was the ration of five of us, actually ten portions.

The full significance of this blow cannot be understood by anyone whose life has not hung by a piece of bread or a portion of margarine. We had to face not only hunger but the fear of hunger, the haunting fear that tomorrow perhaps there would be no ration. The pain of hunger is endurable; it is the fear of starving to death tomorrow that makes the flesh crawl.

Anger surged in me like a mighty stream. "Luyzi, give me all my bread. I will eat it now. It may be stolen." Then the voice of reason prevailed, and I ate slowly. But I ate all of it.

On the third day I had no bread. That afternoon the train came to a stop. The doors were opened. "Heraus! Out!" I tried to stand. I couldn't move my legs. Edging along on my buttocks I reached the doorway, pushed myself through, and fell to the ground. Rubbing brought sensation and life back to my legs. The depot was small. Bergen-Belsen was its name.

Aranka (left) and William Riederman (right) holding their children Mythieu (left) and Magda (right), 1922

Magda and her siblings circa 1925
Left to right: Magda, Mythieu, Susan

Magda and her siblings circa 1927
Left to right: Susan, Magda, Mythieu

Magda wearing a new suit in Uzhhorod, 1938

Left to right: Gustave, Aranka Riederman,
and Magda, May 1938

Magda and Gustave in Liptovský Mikuláš, May 3, 1938

Magda in Uzhhorod, March 1938

Magda and her mother, Aranka Riederman, 1938

Who is Afraid of Bombs?

T owering hills and mountains frowned down all about us. I'd never heard of this place. There was a continuous sound of shooting. Guards, both men and women, hovered about.

"Do not fear the shooting, girls. It is not intended for you. This is a training camp for soldiers."

Their gallantry and politeness were not lost on me. The Auschwitz guards had been gallant and polite, too, when we arrived. Again, long lines in rows of five. Up hill and down we trudged. We came upon hundreds of soldiers. I recognized the Hungarian uniform. It must have been Sunday for they were sauntering about.

"Lanyok magyarok vagytok?" they asked us. "Girls, are you Hungarian?"

"Yes," we answered in Hungarian. "What are you do-ing here?"

"We are Hungarian soldiers. Don't be afraid. The Russians are coming. You are going to be free. You are going back to your homes. We should like to go home, too."

185

They threw cigarettes for which we scrambled. This seemed to anger the guards and they urged us on. We never saw the Hungarian soldiers again.

We came to a thick forest in the depths of which were wooden barracks similar to those at Auschwitz. We were among the first slave laborers to arrive. A guard addressed us.

"You are going to sleep in tents for a few days. The barracks aren't ready. We have no work for you yet. Above all you must be obedient, and you must behave."

Our first food came from the soldiers' kitchen. It was delicious; hot, thick, black bread soup. Each woman was given her own bowl. No count of ten on the bowl as in Auschwitz. After three days of thirst, hot liquid put life and warmth into our frames. To each they gave a hand towel and a blanket. This was beyond our wildest dreams. A bowl of my own and a hand towel.

The towel I used as a bandana.

I was not conscious of any discomfort while sitting on the damp ground and eating. In the tents there were no cots, only straw on the bare ground. The guard was a fine man for he did not force us to stand three or four hours waiting for Zählappell.

"I don't care what you do now," he said, "but in the morning you must go outside and shower. And I mean everyone."

This was different from Auschwitz where we could shower only once a month. The weather was cold, and the prospect of an outdoor shower was not inviting. The mere thought made me shudder. In the evening we lay down; Klari, Luyzi, Suzi, Anci, the Dietelbaums, Pira, and I. We decided to put one blanket under us and the remainder over us and if we huddled together, we might keep warm.

Knowing Pira was a rich and rewarding experience I shall always cherish. Not because she is highly educated and a woman of culture; there were countless thousands of such. Not because she was a fine, gracious lady; there were countless thousands of such. What impressed me then and still does was her great, unwavering faith in God. As slave laborers under a cruel and barbaric heel in a Dominion of Evil, many no longer thought of God or spiritual matters. Many had become atheists.

"Children, I will pray," said Pira that first night in Bergen-Belsen, "and God will surely help us." Then she prayed in Hebrew. She said it was the 121st Psalm.

"I will lift up mine eyes unto the mountains..."

Mountains were all about me. There were nothing but mountains to lift up my eyes to.

"From whence shall my help come?"

I had asked that of myself a million times.

"My help cometh from the Lord, who made heaven

and earth."

Yes, but would He help me?

"He will not suffer thy foot to be moved; He that keepeth thee will not slumber."

This was hard to believe, but I would try to have faith. Maybe God wasn't sleeping after all, but was he growing old?

"Behold, He that keepeth Israel shall neither slumber nor sleep."

Then why were we here?

"The Lord is thy keeper; the Lord is thy shade upon thy right hand. The sun shall not smite thee by day, nor the moon by night. The Lord shall keep thee from all evil."

Was this a promise?

"He shall keep thy soul."

But that was in the future. I know all souls are God's, but I wanted to keep my own soul in my own body until I was old.

"The Lord shall guard thy going out and thy coming in, from this time forth and forever."

"Amen," I whispered softly, and comforted that God was personally protecting me, my eyes closed. Pira had prayed me to sleep.

A mighty cannonade of thunder and blue flashes of lightning woke me with a start. The wind whined and roared.

Torrents of rain soaked us to the skin. Without warning the huge tent collapsed on five thousand screaming women. They crawled and thrashed about. At length guards rescued us. The rest of the night was spent in the barracks. In the morning women guards ordered us to undress and shower outdoors in the biting cold. I didn't blame them.

Seeing others hide, Klari said, "Magda, let us hide in the woods. It is too cold to shower."

"Klari, I will make you take a shower. Being clean will help us live. Our bodies are dehydrated. Water is medicine." And so, I dragged her to the shower, chattering teeth and all.

Breakfast consisted of a bowlful of thick black soup, very palatable, and a portion of bread. I pondered on this. Why were the rations at Auschwitz so meager? Was the personnel, both Jewish and Christian, "organized?" Had the Germans really intended our daily ration at Auschwitz to be only a count of ten on the soup bowl and a crust of ersatz bread? Surely, they must have known that on this starvation diet slave laborers could not possibly be productive. I wonder.

Sitting on the cold hard ground the whole day, we had nothing to do but talk. We talked of our families, our home life, our weddings, confirmations, yearned for those who were lost, talked of everything but our plight. The Dietelbaums never ceased weeping for their dear mother.

We Were Strangers

On the next day we were assigned to barracks. It was a clean, spacious place and in our eyes now unaccustomed to comforts, delightfully cozy. There were real beds, bunks in tiers of three.

"Luyzi," I thrilled, "how wonderful. How very, very wonderful. I had forgotten what a real bed looks like."

Klari was stunned. "I don't believe it. I don't believe it. It's a mirage. I won't even put out my hand to touch it."

"You don't believe what your eyes see," I said. "Climb up on the mirage, then, we are taking a bunk in the top tier."

The commodious, ample washrooms were indoors. This luxury overwhelmed us. We were like youngsters in a toy shop. The water while not warm was not freezing and we were permitted to shower every day. Guards pleaded with us not to drink it, but as it had been so many months since we had access to drinking water, I drank until I thought I would burst. Water, just plain water but I could not bear to tear myself away. Again, and again I showered. I don't know why. The longing for water was an addiction.

"Until additional transports arrive," the guards told us, "the Kommando schedule will not be worked out. You have no duties for the present."

Life's values are relative. We were content. A bed for only two, a real straw mattress, one blanket beneath me, another on top, and my georgette coat on top of that—I was lucky.

Day after day we lay in bed. Mrs. Bardos, the lovely Budapest lady whose daughter entertained us with poetry in Auschwitz, soothed us as always.

"Ladies let us forget our surroundings," she said. "Let us forget why we are here. Let us discuss music, literature, and the arts. Let us plan the lovely things we shall do when we are free. When I return to Budapest, I shall build a new life, a life of beauty and courage and hope."

Her words were inspiring and set us on fire. Gone for the moment at least was our apathy. Gone were our torpor and lethargy. In our imaginations we were human beings once more, human beings with dignity and pride and decency. She breathed life into dead souls. Hungry, yes. Happy, very. No one whipped us. No one cursed us. No one threatened us. We began to feel rested. Agonizing pain subsided, and I was at peace. Mrs. Bardos's daughter recited poetry, not only the Hungarian poets but Shakespeare, and Russian, German, and Hebrew poetry.

One evening I shall never forget. There in the dark, for we never had light, I began to sing. The sound of my voice startled me. It was so utterly involuntary. Hungarian gypsy songs poured from my throat, songs of love and yearning, of wild desire, poignant and tender, impassioned and untamed. Women cried, many sobbed convulsively. For months the fierce urge to survive the daily struggle had smothered thoughts of self and of life's enchanting raptures.

"Magda, sing, don't stop. Please. You bring thoughts of my husband, my children, my mother."

And so I sang in several languages and tried to make everyone happy. A beautiful blonde, Rozey Dub, from Maramaros, Sziget, tapdanced and sang modern songs in English and Hungarian. Later she was to marry an English soldier who was with the troops that liberated Bergen-Belsen. Miriam who also came from Maramaros, Sziget and taught Hebrew in a girls' school, sang in Hebrew. Olga, tall, stately and dark turned over a metal margarine tub and with her fingers tapped out rhythm, whistling beautifully. Rozey Dub danced to this accompaniment. We put on a show almost every evening. An Aufseherin who enjoyed it said, "Girls, this is what I like to see. The singing is lovely and so is the dancing and whistling. And best of all you are quiet and well-behaved."

The guards drifted in, too, and were most generous in their applause and thanked us for the entertainment. One day a guard said, "Your singing and dancing have given us great pleasure. For their whistling, Olga will be the Block Elsterer, Rozey the assistant, and Miriam the bread cutter and dealer. There will be four Stuben Diensten of whom

Magda, because of her gypsy songs, will be one."

Me, a Stuben Diensten? My God, what is to become of me? Will I become a cruel beast like the Stuben Diensten in Auschwitz? Will I become a fiend like Roozia? My heart sank within me. Luyzi, Klari, and the others were delighted, thrilled, crowding around me in joyful anticipation.

"What great good fortune has befallen us. Now we shall eat. Magda, it is Providence that you are a Stuben Dienst and will provide for us."

I felt a million crawling things under my skin. "I'm not happy. I fear the girls will kill me if I don't deal out the soup to please them."

Oddly enough it was Klari who gave me trouble. One of my duties was to make certain the girls showered daily. Klari hated water. Pleas, threats, bribes, everything failed to move her. She was filthy, crusty with dirt.

"I like it this way," she screamed.

"Oh, you do, do you?" And grabbing her by the head with what little hair she had I forcibly dragged her to the showers and held her there. I got drenched, too, but I slept with Klari and she smelled.

My compensation for being Stuben Dienst was double rations. I scrubbed and cleaned the barracks while the others lay abed. As I shared my bonus with Klari, Luyzi, Anci, and Pira, actually the deal netted me very little food.

We Were Strangers

Each morning when I carried in the soup, two hundred and fifty pairs of eyes followed every movement. Reclining in their bunks, the two hundred and fifty ravening wolves were more animal than human. When one screamed, "My bowl is not full," I gave her an additional spoonful. Instantly howls, curses, and imprecations rent the air. Some pounced on me, shaking their fists in my face. The soup having been measured in the kitchen, my lot was not a happy one. Whatever soup remained was brought to Olga and she doled out a bowl to each Stuben Dienst. This was the bonus I shared with the others.

When I thought I was not being watched I gave slightly larger portions to my close friends. What howls, shrieks, and screams, what raucous, devilish yelps split the ear drums. They were maddened for food. Fear of the Germans did not enter into it. Fear of starving to death and dropping in their tracks, as they had seen others drop, made maniacs of them.

Transports of women began to pour in. From Ravensbrück came countless Hungarian gypsies. They were put to work without an hour's rest. Nights while we slept the sleep of the dead, thieving gypsy hands groped over us searching for bits of food or anything that wasn't tied down.

Having heard that a Holzkommando, a wood chopping detail, was soon to be formed, I was thankful to be a Stuben Dienst despite its drawbacks. The girls, we were told, were to go out into the forest, chop down trees, and drag in loads of wood on their backs. The cold was bitter. With only a thin dress, torn shoes, and a georgette crepe coat to protect me from the weather, I was grateful that a kind Providence was watching over me.

Our group was fortunate. The Blockführer was fond of Olga. When she pleaded, "Herr Blockführer, please don't send my thinly clad girls out into the deep snow," he spared us.

Evidently, I did not have the qualities that make a successful Stuben Dienst. One day Olga descended upon me.

"Magda, the girls have been complaining about you for weeks. I can no longer endure their grumbling. I don't want you. You are through."

I was almost too relieved to reply. A few days later Olga followed me into the washroom.

"Magda," she said, "for some time I have been attracted to your medal. I want it. If you give it to me, you may be Stuben Dienst again."

It was an oval medal of yellow gold with a cloisonné medallion of Moses holding aloft the Ten Commandments. This was my shield, my guardian that kept me out of harm's way. I had found it in the pocket of a garment in Canada and smuggled it in my groin past Drexler. Without a word I removed it and handed it over, knowing how overjoyed my friends would be at my reinstatement. For myself, I had no ambitions to be a Stuben Dienst.

One morning the Blockführer said, "Girls, from now on you must all go into the woods, chop down trees, and bring in wood. And you must work quickly."

To me fell the unhappy task of arousing the two hundred and fifty slaves at 4am. We had begun to have Zählappell. They refused to stir out of their bunks. Olga beat them, then handed me a board and ordered me to do the same. I lost my voice urging, pleading, ordering but I could not bring myself to inflict pain. In her panic Olga turned on me.

"You good for nothing nobody," she shouted. "Can't you do anything right? You don't get the women up in time for Zählappell. You stupid, dull cow."

When the workers returned in the evening, freezing, starving, weary unto death, they begged for soup. Only workers were given soup and it was cold. Non-workers received cold coffee.

One evening, goaded beyond human limits, the girls rebelled. "We will not go into the deep snow tomorrow and chop down trees. Do what you will. We won't go."

"If you don't go," threatened Olga, "Magda will get a beating from the Blockführer and that will be the end of her. It is her responsibility to get you out of here on time."

I crawled into Luyzi's bunk and cried from sheer fatigue. "I'd rather not be the Stuben Dienst. Surely I shall not work so hard in the Holzkommando as I do now."

In the morning confusion reigned. Discipline was shattered. Half of the women barricaded themselves in the toilets. Scores ran into other Blocks. Only a handful stood Zählappell. The Blockführer who at times was pleasant and amiable frequently went berserk, running among the women with a club and swinging it indiscriminately. This morning he was uncontrollable. Olga ran about screaming, why I don't know. What did it accomplish?

"You, Magda," she cried, "this is all your fault. I don't want you for my Stuben Dienst. The Blockführer is going to kill you."

"He'll kill you first. You are the Block Elsterer. I never wanted to be Stuben Dienst. Who cares?"

A few women were rounded up and sent out into the woods. I made the rounds of other Blocks hoping to find relatives or friends. A woman approached me.

"Aren't you Magda Riederman of Uzhhorod?"

"Yes I am," I answered, "or rather I was. Who are you?"

"I am Mrs. Farkas of Michalovce, your Aunt Malvine's

best friend."

"Where is Aunt Malvine? Do you know what has become of her?"

"Malvine went up the chimney in Auschwitz. She was too weak from starvation to be a slave laborer. The Germans captured your Uncle Martin in the Slovakian mountains and he, too, went up the chimney."

My God, what fine upstanding people they had been.

"What of their children, Mrs. Farkas. What happened to them?"

"Mityu and Hedy were hidden by Christians. Perhaps they are safe."

Later I was to learn they were saved and are living in Liberec. Hedy is engaged, and she and her fiancé wish to come to America. They have an uncle in New York who has sent them affidavits.

Mrs. Farkas introduced me to the Block Elsterer, Edith Hartman, a Slovakian from Žilina which is two hours by train from Mikuláš.

"You are from Mikuláš?" asked Edith. "Do you know the Wenetianer family?"

"Of course. My mother-in-law is a Wenetianer."

"Oh, then you must be Gustave's wife. And Valli Milch of Považská Bystrica must be your aunt." She surveyed the Block as if she owned it. "I knew your aunt, Valli Milch and her whole family. My father owned a large department store in Žilina and Valli Milch was not only a good customer but a very close friend."

When it was established that we had mutual friends she became friendly and expansive.

"I am an old-timer. I've been in Auschwitz since 1942. Bergen-Belsen is like a sanitarium for me. Let me introduce you to a girlfriend. She, too, came in 1942.

Wonder of wonders: she was a fat girl! I stared at her fat body and fat face. Then the light dawned. She had been a Block Elsterer in Auschwitz, and so she ate. She was a Slovakian, Magda Cohen. They introduced me to other Slovakians. They seemed to have a tight little clique.

"What Kommando are you in?" asked Edith. "Are you satisfied?"

"I certainly am not. Olga, my Block Elsterer, no longer wants me as a Stuben Dienst. My dress is in shreds, my shoes are torn, and I have no underwear. I don't want to be in the Holzkommando."

"I have been here only one week," said Edith. "The Russians are getting close to Auschwitz and it is being emptied one way or another. I came with my Block and am still Block Elsterer. The Blockführer told me we are going to leave here soon. He is organizing a large transport. He wouldn't tell me its destination, but those who wish to join may do so. Why not come with us, Magda? Ask your Slovakian friends to come along. We shall have a Block of Slovakian girls and get along fine."

I was delighted and enthusiastically agreed. That evening when the girls returned from the woods, I told them of my adventure. Pira was pleased and agreed at once. The Dietelbaums refused, saying they would wait for their mother. Luyzi, Klari, and Suzi said, "Magda, we will go where you go. We will follow you."

The next morning at Zählappell the Blockführer announced, "A new transport is being formed. Those wishing to join will gather in the field opposite the barracks."

It was still dark. The snow was waist deep. For several freezing hours one thousand women stood in that deep snow, their teeth chattering, their flesh numb and dead. At long last four civilians appeared, looked us over, and selected eight hundred for the transport. All my friends were among the lucky ones and for that I was happy.

To stand for a transport in an open field with snow to the waist; hungry, freezing, almost naked, waiting hours, waiting while the statistics were being taken—that is an experience, an unforgettable memory etched on the heart in blood. What is your name? Your number? Where were you born? It was almost dark. We had been in that field since before daylight. How close to freezing can a human being come, and yet not die?

We begged the Blockführer, "Please may we have a bandana for our heads? Our hair is short, and the snow and ice are torturing us." He assented and sent the Lager Elsterer, a Polish Jewish girl into the warehouse for them.

Grudgingly, as though she were giving her life's blood, she handed out bandanas. Woe to those like myself whose hair had grown out a few inches.

"You are not going to get a bandana," she snarled. "Your hair is long. You won't freeze to death." And so about half of the women did not get bandanas.

Running to the Block Elsterer, she babbled ecstatically, "Herr Commandant, see how many bandanas I have leftover." What did she expect for it, a reserved seat in the crematorium?

Shaking our fists at her we screamed, "A curse on you, you pestilence!"

Despite our curses she went indoors, and we stayed out. I fooled her. Between my legs was hidden a hand towel and I used it for a bandana.

Marching to the station the way we had come, I saw no Hungarian soldiers. Wagons were already strung out on the tracks. Each woman received one piece of bread. This was the only food given us that day despite our ordeal in the deep snow. Guards warned us to save the bread as the trip would take either one or two days, depending on American bombardments. This was December of 1944. Pira tore hers in two and swallowed each piece in one gulp. Asking Luyzi for her knife I cut mine into small pieces, eating slowly to make it seem like more. They locked us in, eight women to a wagon. Without guards to curse and beat us I envisaged a quiet, restful trip.

Soon pandemonium broke out. One fought tigerishly for more room. Another screamed she could not stretch her legs. One started to cry, another to talk. One was laughing hysterically. Another began to sing. Some wished to sleep. Others with no sleep in them deliberately disturbed the sleepers. For once I would have welcomed guards. At least it would have been quiet. Squabbling led to fighting. When blows rained on me I fought back, striking it matter not whom. It seems we had all gone crazy. A night of hell dragged on. In the darkness was committed the most heinous crime of all. They began to steal each other's bread. Toward morning the ghostly whining of sirens knifed our ears. The train came to a stop. From overhead came the droning sound of planes. Instinctively we knew they were American bombers. Bombs exploded all about us.

"Luyzi," I screamed, "the Americans are trying to bomb this train. They think it is an ammunition train."

The earth trembled. The loudest noise in the world

seemed to be inside of me. I was bursting. Anti-aircraft barked an angry reply.

In the gray light of dawn that came through the bars I looked about me. Of fear, I saw not the slightest indication. We were defiant. There seemed to be no feeling about the bombardment one way or another. Let a bomb hit us, or let it not hit us. Too emaciated and wasted, too far gone physically, emotionally, and nervously for fear, only one woman hoped a bomb would destroy us then and there.

"Are you crazy?" I screamed. "Why do you want a bomb to kill us? Why don't you pray for American paratroopers to jump right on this train and set us free? I *will* be free—do you hear? If you want to die, then don't eat your bread and die for yourself."

Luyzi soothed me. "Of course, you are going to be free, Magda. No bomb is going to hit you."

"Bombs? Who is afraid of bombs? No bomb can hit me. I am going to be free."

The bombardment stopped. Sirens shrieked the "all clear" signal.

"Klari, I think we are close to a city." The train started and after an hour's ride we came to a station. Guards opened the wagons. Before us lay a horribly bombed city. This was Braunschweig.

Stalin's Candles

"**I** 've heard of Braunschweig," said Mrs. Bardos. "I believe it is a German university city."

Out we climbed, ravening, freezing, filthy, and tired. This was the first time we saw civilians in a depot. They stared in open-mouthed amazement, refusing to believe the evidence of their own eyes. They simply could not grasp what we were, whence we came, and what this was all about. German women thinking themselves unobserved sidled over to us and whispered, "From where have you come? Who are you? Why are you so dirty and ragged?"

Were they really unaware of German murder camps, crematoria, and gas chambers?

Forming long lines in rows of five we marched through the town. I did not see a home or building which had not been hit by bombs or damaged by bombing or fire. The windows of every structure were broken. Half-razed residences were still occupied. Churches, museums, and public buildings were all destroyed. Whole streets were pulverized. Through gaping holes, I saw block after block, as many as ten and twelve blocks at a time. Suddenly three sharp unearthly whines pierced the air. People jerkily galvanized into life. They ran into houses, into basements, into anything that offered protection of a sort. Everyone seemed to have a child's wagon in which was heaped what they considered their most precious possessions. In one, food. In another, blankets or a child. We were indifferent, marching along blithely. Having no choice, we couldn't seek shelter from the bombs if we had wished to.

And then we saw them, Stalin's Candles. I counted ten Russian planes. It was an unforgettable sight of rare and awesome beauty, the falling bombs that glowed against the sky. Instead of trembling we were delighted and prayed for their success. Although the Russians seemed to be directly overhead their bombs did not fall as closely as those which fell near the train. The earth trembled, buildings shook, and the few remaining windows fell out from the strong drafts. But I did not have the sensation of bursting from the insides as on the train.

Then came the German fighters. They mixed with the Russians and when two planes tangled, they fell in an embrace of death. It was an awesome sight, like watching a pageant in a dream. We kept on marching. The streets were deserted. After a while we heard the "all clear." It was over.

Germans, dazed and numb, crawled from their hiding

places. In every street, I saw bomb shelters; bunkers, they were called. Thick concrete shelters with tiny windows.

At long last we reached our new "home." It was an indoor riding rink and horse stable. All the windows were broken. It was windy and strong cold drafts rushed through the building. It was a huge concrete structure. Four men, city police, addressed us.

"You have been brought to Braunschweig to work. You have seen the condition of our streets. You are going to shovel the rubble and debris from the thoroughfares. You will receive the same food from community kitchens as the townspeople. You will get bread but you will have to work hard for it. Above all, we demand obedience. You will have it good. You are going to live here in the riding stable. We have no other place for you. In fact, we are pressed to find living quarters for our own people. Later we shall try to find better quarters for you. Tomorrow, you start working."

We were pleased with this arrangement and said to one another, "We are going to live among people. Perhaps we shall even receive more food. Let us thank God it is not a camp. There are no crematoria here." I think what pleased us most was living among people. I felt it was a step on the road back.

The vast high-ceilinged rink was dead cold. On the floor was straw that had been slept on. Later we learned that as the Germans retreated from Russia they took hundreds of thousands of Russians with them, slave laborers. This had been a Russian prisoners' camp, and they had been removed the day before our arrival. Only God in heaven knows what happened to them.

At the entrance each woman was handed a cup of soup, Hungarian goulash. It was delicious. I hadn't eaten anything so delectable since I could not recall when. We only got a few teaspoonfuls, but the taste and flavor were excellent. I believe it really came from the community kitchen.

An Aufseherin barked, "Each one will keep her cup. In the morning you will be given coffee. Now lie down, five women under one blanket, and silence."

The straw was filthy and hard and I used my georgette coat as a sheet. The cold was intense. It froze the marrow. Five of us shivered and trembled under one blanket. Many believed themselves to be freezing to death. I looked at them in their anguish: slave laborers who had once been women and known the feeling of beds and clean sheets and blankets; women who had loved and been loved, who once knew the feeling of hot water and soup, perfume and silk underwear, and food in their bellies. Cold and stiff they closed their eyes not knowing if they would awaken in the morning.

Five had comfort. Edith Hartman and her clique appointed themselves to the positions they held in Auschwitz and Bergen-Belsen. Edith was Block Elsterer, Fat Magda Cohen was the assistant, Katka was the Stuben Dienst, and the other Magda and her mother were bread dealers. They took much of our straw, many blankets, and retired to a private room, a horse stall.

In the early morning before daylight six guards unlocked the doors and woke us up in a mad rush. No water, no opportunity to take care of our natural needs, and the hated Zählappell; this was our first morning. Edith made herself important and ordered us to form lines in rows of five. Elderly civilians armed with rifles were to be our guards. They were called Posten.

"If anyone attempts to run away, she will be shot," we were warned. They separated us into groups of one hundred and assigned two Posten to a group. There were eight groups or Kommandos.

En route the Posten questioned us. "Where is your home? Where have you come from? What happened to you? What brought you to Braunschweig? Are you criminals?"

"We are not criminals. Our only crime is that we are Jews. We come from good homes in Hungary, Czechoslovakia, and Poland. We are slave laborers."

"This is schrecklich. I heard some talk of women slaves

but could not believe it."

When I told one of the Posten of Auschwitz and the crematoria and gas chambers, he refused to believe it. His mind could not grasp and comprehend what I was saying. He had difficulty enough in believing the evidence of his eyes. He saw us in thin rags, ravening and starving, and that his mind must accept. Farther than that he could not go.

He was a short, slight man and wore glasses through which empathetic eyes shone with unshed tears. "Don't worry, girls. It is not going to be too rigorous. I won't force you to work hard. You think I like being a Poste? I am a poor working man with a large family of children. I prefer working in a factory. I could earn more. And even then what would I be getting out of the war? The leaders told us we would prosper. But I guess they are the only ones who are prosperous and safe. I am hoping the war will soon be over. We suffer already for eight years. Look at the people about you. Look at the cripples without hands or feet. Look about you at the blind and the paralyzed. God, how we suffer."

"I cannot understand why you should be poor. Germany stole billions from other countries, billions in gold and agricultural and industrial products. Germany has stolen billions in industrial equipment and even whole railroads. The war has cost Germany nothing in dollars and cents."

"But think of our manpower."

"Think of the manpower of the ravaged nations. Germany will come out of the war strongest in manpower even if she loses."

He flared, "Germany cannot lose." He is right, I thought. No matter what the outcome militarily, Germany cannot lose.

He was kind but, German-like, his sympathy and pity were only for Germans. I wondered how he was so utterly unaware, so utterly incapable of understanding that the German people themselves were responsible. He must have known that in the past eighty years Germany invaded friendly neighbors and started five wars. The murdering, looting, torturing, and enslavement of other peoples was simply a matter of indifference to him. He was congenitally incapable of understanding German guilt. He was a kindly man, but his overwhelming emotions were self-pity and apathy for Germany's crimes. He whined about poor Germany's sufferings and privations until we reached the storage building.

We were given large, heavy shovels which we swung across our shoulders. Again we marched, I should judge a distance of several miles, but I can never be absolutely sure of distances. Our little Poste said, "This is the street where you are to work. I don't care what you do. I shall walk among you and pretend to supervise your work. When you see a guard coming, start working."

Having learned at Auschwitz how to handle a shovel, I began to clear away debris and rubble. The shovel was cumbersome and heavy, and it took great effort to make even a little headway. It was cold, the bitter, clawing cold that stiffened our bodies and made movement torturous.

"Herr Poste, there is much kindling here. May we build a fire?"

"Of course, children. Build a fire. Make yourselves warm." With good will and alacrity, he himself gathered kindling and with his own matches started a roaring fire. One hundred freezing creatures huddled about and soon life returned to our bodies.

The little Poste cautioned, "Some of you should make a pretense of working because if you are seen the fire will be put out." He suggested that groups of ten warm themselves for ten minutes, the ninety remaining to spread out, shovels in hand. This was a logical arrangement and he offered to be our lookout. This went on for several hours.

One of the girls came across what looked like the entrance to a cellar. Clambering down she found a fortune: potatoes, half burned and half frozen. This was manna from heaven. We ate them raw until our Poste suggested that we roast them in the fire.

"But take care that an Aufseherin does not catch you.

You will note signs all about: 'Plünderer werden getötet.' Looters will be put to death. I have seen prisoners shot for less. Now, into the cellar quickly and bring up all the potatoes you can carry. I will warn you if the guards are coming."

There was great activity. Rushing into the cellar we carried out all the potatoes we could hold in our flimsy skirts. Into the fire they went. We roasted, and we ate, and we were warm.

It was too good to last. The Poste shouted, "Aufseherinnen kommen!" It was a routine inspection. We began to shovel feverishly. The Aufseherinnen were wearing the usual guard uniform of gray skirt, Death's Head insignia, and high boots. They stamped out the fire, and when they saw the potatoes, they became apoplectic.

Shaking their fists at us they shouted, "There will be no more fires. No one may have a fire. And you have stolen potatoes from a cellar? The first Jew dog found in a cellar will be shot on sight." They left. We dared not build another fire. Our little Poste was afraid, too.

No longer freezing and starving, we began to shovel. The Poste talked to us encouragingly, urging us not to lift too much at a time. His teeth chattered, and he suggested that we post our own lookouts and discontinue working. He then crawled into the cellar which offered some protection from the bitter cold. We stood about talking until dusk. With shovels over shoulders we headed for the storage building.

To our utter astonishment we saw a queue of Germans standing in front of a theater.

"My God, can this be real? Do people still go to theaters?" we asked one another.

Entertainment and recreation seemed like ghosts of a dream, like something on Mars and entirely disconnected from this planet. In the next street there was a bakeshop with one whole loaf of bread in the window.

"Dear God," sobbed Klari, "if only once more in my life, I could have a whole loaf of bread for myself, I would eat until it hurt."

People stared at us in wide-eyed bewilderment when they dared. Guards observing their curiosity threatened them and they scurried away.

Next to the storage building was a narrow brick residence with a gabled roof. It was very quaint like something in a fairy tale. I noticed a little old lady peering through a small ground floor window. Tears were streaming down her cheeks and her hands were folded across her breast in an attitude of prayer. It gave me a warm feeling to know someone felt for us in our travail.

Standing there one evening cold and hungry and

tired, I heard her door quietly open. She beckoned me to her. Thrusting a bag into my hands she slid back into the house and closed her door. I opened the bag: bread! It was old and dry with hard crusts, but it was bread. Dividing equally with Klari and Luyzi I put the balance into my bosom, happy and excited. Tonight, I am going to sleep with the knowledge that tomorrow morning I shall have bread for breakfast.

Reaching "home" we stood Zählappell by the door, forming one long line to receive our bowls which were handed to us by the Stuben Dienst. It was the duty of Fat Magda Cohen to deal out each portion from a large tub. For our group of eight hundred there were thirty-eight tubs of thick soup. As a matter of easy computation I believe our allotment must have been forty tubs. Two must have gone astray en route from the community kitchen. We regarded the thickness of the soup as a criterion as that meant solids. If an Aufseherin were present, Fat Magda had to stir the soup and serve the thick as well as the liquid. In the absence of an Aufseherin she served from the top which was watery, keeping the balance for herself and her friends.

A very tiny girl pleaded, "Please give me a little more. You have given me only water."

"Oh, you ask for a little more. I'll give you a little more. I'll give you all you have coming." And so saying she gave her a terrible blow across the face. A blow like this coming from the horse, Magda, was enough to kill any one of us.

From that moment the women hated her. She was no better than the Polish Christians in Auschwitz. Sitting on the floor tailor-fashion we ate our precious soup. Only a few had spoons and they were mostly half-spoons which had been found in the streets. Borrowing a spoon cost a piece of bread. I ate without a spoon.

Feeling uncomfortable that night, I opened my dress. My whole body was red. That meant lice. Others looked to themselves. They, too, were red. To us lice meant typhus. There had been no lice at Auschwitz. In a flash I recalled the night the entire Gypsy Lager had been cremated because lice had been discovered on them. Others had the same thought. A panic ensued. Fat Magda stormed in like a guard. "What is this," she demanded. "Be quiet, you choleras, you pests, or you will get no food tomorrow. How dare you disturb us."

"We have found lice on ourselves. We are afraid. You know why. The Germans will burn us."

"Lice. That's nothing. You will find more. Be quiet."

The crying continued. She found a club and began to beat us, striking right and left in the dark. "Quiet," she snarled. Women cried hysterically. Fat Magda waded through us stepping on bony bodies and clubbed and clubbed until exhaustion stayed her hand. To be trod on or clubbed by that heavy brute was murderous. At last we were quiet. She went to her own room, a horse stall which she shared with her satellites, two Polish Jewish sisters, Brona and Gena, and four others.

An Aufseherin called us before dawn. Everyone began to scratch herself. My arm pits were alive with lice. They were eating my flesh. I was to learn lice are dormant in the cold but once indoors they tortured us unmercifully.

Magda Cohen dashed in screaming, "Heraus! Get out!" The Posten were waiting. We waved to our little Poste. The commandant who came every morning to count us observed this friendly greeting but said nothing. Breakfast consisted of black coffee only. And many mornings not even that. Water was never available for any purposes and we learned later that Magda and Edith used our coffee for bathing and shampooing. They never worked outdoors, remaining in the rink all day and eating the bread held back from our portions. It was simple. They cut eight slices to a loaf instead of six.

Our little Poste said, "It's too cold to care about work or anything else. Do what you wish, I don't care. If you want a fire, I'll build one. If an Aufseherin catches you, remember I don't know a thing about it. Just keep me out of it."

We Were Strangers

We went through the motions of working. Our Poste gathered wood and started a fire, and soon we were warm.

One girl found a cellar in a bombed-out house. Now we had two cellars of food, potatoes, and carrots. Carrots were a great delicacy. Digging them from the dirt in which they were buried, we did not even pause to wipe them on our dresses. In a few minutes one hundred ravening wolves had consumed them all. Our stomachs were full, and we were indifferent to what was going to happen that day. The fire was blazing, and we were happy.

Suddenly from nowhere an Aufseherin appeared, flamed into anger and began beating the unfortunates nearest her. Savagely, again and again and again with her gummi knueppel until she could no longer raise her arm. The poor things cried and moaned like dogs. They had not the strength to cry aloud. And to our Poste she stormed, "If you permit them to have a fire, you will get yourself in trouble."

He was really alarmed. He trembled and shook and there were no fires that day. Dejected, we wandered about aimlessly. No one touched a shovel. Creeping into a base-ment because down there it was not freezing, we sat and ate raw potatoes.

And then we began to speak of home. The lives we lived, when we were human beings and part of a family group; the devotion of dear ones and friends; the luxury of beds and regular meals, and bathrooms and toilets. Some cried, "What is to become of us? How long can we endure these hardships?"

Another cried, "Why should I live? What have I to live for? My parents were burned alive by the Germans."

"My children, too, were killed by the Germans."

"My husband was a famous surgeon. The intellectuals were the first to be murdered."

"My husband was a rabbi and a scholar and my four sons..."

I was the only one who could say my parents are living. "I am suffering, yes," I admitted, "but I am happy it is I rather than my parents or sisters or Mythieu. In my heart there is a good feeling because my dear ones are safe. I hope my husband is alive and that he is not suffering. He is strong, and I hope to see him some day. With all my heart I pray for this. Come what may, I *know* I am going to live."

One girl said, "I hear the Russians are in Auschwitz and all the slaves have been freed." We moaned in chorus, "If only we had stayed in Auschwitz we would be free now."

My greatest hope and ambition was to be liberated by the American army. Rumors were flying. Each day brought a new one. I sensed the Americans were near, getting closer all the time. This must have been January of 1945. All about us we saw block after block of bombed out homes. I did not see a business establishment; rarely a grocery or bakeshop. And they were empty. The war will be over soon, I thought. People cannot live this way. This was the hope that kept me alive.

We drifted off. In the midst of our dreams the lookout screamed, "An Aufseherin is coming." Out we scrambled and started to work. Seeing there were no fires blazing and the women were quietly and diligently shoveling, she soon left us to our own devices.

One evening marching home we heard the whining signals of the "alert." From all directions came Germans, their small wagons loaded with children, food, or blankets, running to the bunkers. We kept marching. Our Poste could have gone into a bunker if he wished. He said, "Girls, I'm not going in. Perhaps I shall be saved with you. I don't think *anything* can kill you." We were strangely quiet, at peace and unafraid, feeling almost as detached and objective as spirits from another world.

Clouds of smoke blacked out the skies. The Poste said, "The smoke is to conceal the bombers. Russian bombers, they are. I can tell by the bombs. You see they are long and tubular and lighted at one end; Stalin's Candles." The explosions were ear-splitting. Huge fires roared. What was left in Braunschweig to feed these fires, I wondered.

It was wondrously beautiful and breathtaking to watch the gracefully falling "candles" with brilliant blue and white lights at the end. There was no one but us on the streets. After a half hour, sirens shrieked the "all clear." It was over. People poured out from everywhere and we marched "home."

One morning our little Poste was not waiting as usual. Evidently it had been noticed that we were on friendly terms. The commandant addressed us. "Today," he said, "you are going to have a new Poste." The new Poste did not talk, he didn't even look at us. He just marched along until we reached our work area. He permitted no fire. No one could enter a cellar to forage. The weather was cold, bitter, and the work grueling. We were outdoors from dawn to dusk with never a moment's respite. Evenings the chief topic of conversation was the merit of our Posten. "Oh, you have a good Poste? How lucky you are."

One evening at Zählappell, the Aufseherin called out numbers, the numbers tattooed on our arms. Ten girls stepped forward. They were unknown to me, not being in my group. "What is it," I asked, "a new Kommando?"

"Yes," someone answered, "the Trouble Kommando." They had been caught in cellars.

Each received five murderous blows across the back and buttocks with a wooden club and had to remain standing with her face to the wall all night outdoors. In the morning we were told they had been shot. I did not see the shooting myself but the girls were never seen again. The tragedy of it was they were not given their suppers and had to starve all night as well as freeze.

This did not dampen Klari's spirits. "I don't care if they shoot me," she said. "Tomorrow I will go into the cellars and I will eat." And she did. The next evening the numbers were called again, and several girls stepped forward to receive the same beating as the previous group. They, too, were never seen again. Hunger knows no deterrent. I felt the same as Klari. Every evening a few unfortunates were "selected." But what of that? Every day I crawled into cellars and foraged.

To take care of our natural needs, we dug a trench, deep and wide. A narrow board was placed across the length about two feet above the ground. One night a woman slipped and fell in. The night Poste certainly must have heard her cries for help. In the morning she was found, one hand protruding above the excrement.

One day we saw hundreds of men working in the streets. Some of the girls recognized them by their uniforms as fellow nationals. I spotted Czechs. I called to them, "Are you Czech?"

"Yes, we are," they called back. "We are prisoners of

war. We work like slave laborers even if we aren't Jews. We refused to fight for the Germans."

"I am coming by this way toward evening. Have good news for me."

"Good news. I can give that to you now. We are going to be free in a few weeks. The Russians are even now in Czechoslovakia. Try to hold on a little longer."

That evening marching back, a Czech boy dashed into our lines, recognized me as a Czech, and gave me a whole loaf of bread. He had risked his life for me, this Christian Czech boy. A Christian risked his life for me. I stood like a stone holding the bread to my breast. A Christian had risked his life for me. Something within me sang. Luyzi reached out for the loaf. I clutched it involuntarily.

"Don't be alarmed," she said. "You know it must be cut into pieces. I'm not trying to take it away from you."

I must explain that we frequently tried to smuggle raw potatoes to those suffering from diarrhea. Unable to eat their bread or soup they begged for raw potatoes which seemed to help them. And so, we traded potatoes for bread. When caught we were beaten but that didn't stop us. I was determined to smuggle in a piece of this bread. It could be done. If one portion were found on me the Germans would think I had not eaten my last ration of bread and thus I would not be suspected. Luyzi was the richest among us. She had a knife, a comb, a spoon, and a small broken mirror. I never looked in the mirror. Once only I saw myself and swore never to look again. I couldn't bear the sight of my dirty, skinny face crawling with lice.

Luyzi cut the loaf into six portions, two for me and one for herself, Suzi, Klari, and Pira. I swallowed one piece then and there in one big gulp. Nothing was said when the Germans saw the other piece. I was given my ration of soup and was no longer hungry. The next morning, I had two whole pieces of bread.

Day followed day and fewer and fewer were going to work. One morning less than six hundred stood Zählappell. About two hundred were lying on the concrete floor. They couldn't talk. They couldn't move. They couldn't get up to take care of their natural needs. They lay there in their own excrement. The stench was nauseating.

The commandant was summoned. "You cannot walk or move? You cannot work? Very well. Tomorrow a truck is coming. You will be taken to a hospital. There you will receive medicine and medical care and will be cured. Today, remain indoors."

In my group was Mrs. Roth of Beregszász, Czechoslovakia, and her three daughters. The middle daughter was sick.

"I don't want you to go to the hospital and leave us here," Mrs. Roth pleaded with her daughter. "We must try not to be separated. If you feel ill, you may stay here and rest today. But, remember, tomorrow you must work."

That evening when we returned the place was empty. The bereaved began to cry. One wept for a dear mother and for the tender love that watched over her like a guardian angel and sobbed the prayer, "Thou has gone from me but the bond which united our souls can never be severed." Another mournfully sobbed for the young sister whose bodily and mental unfolding she had lovingly watched and for whose future she had fostered beautiful hopes. And still another moaned agonizingly for her child, the child she had conceived in the image of God and brought forth to be a blessing, a symbol, and a fulfillment of her own happiness and love. God, where were you that day?

The commandant tried to quiet them. "Believe me, on my word of honor, they were taken to a hospital. The Aufseherin who accompanied them is coming back later tonight. She will tell you where the girls are." We lay in the dark—waiting.

She came. "I have returned," she said. "I bring you greetings and happy messages. Your dear ones and friends have clean clothes, clean beds, medical care and they will soon be well. On my word of honor as a German."

The word of honor of a German? With one anguished accord we struggled to our knees and feet and from every throat came the lamentation: …'yamlich malchusey, be-chayeychon uv'youmaychon uvchayey d'chol beys Yisroel, baagolo uvizman koriv, ve'imroo amen.

This is the Kaddish, the Mourner's Prayer, the prayer which does not acknowledge death but promises resurrection. It is a prayer of immortal hope, that though the body returns to the earth, the spirit which is of God, returns to God, to live forever. The Kaddish is a prayer of adoration for God and thanks for his manifold mercies.

We learned they had been taken to Ravensbrück and burned alive. Now we were less than six hundred.

Four weeks had passed since our arrival. There were fewer cellars to forage. We had eaten them up. Every morning before daylight we marched to work, but nothing was accomplished. We stood around. The Posten didn't care. They were freezing, too. Bombardments were frequent, five and six daily. The earth trembled. Time and again I had the sensation of bursting from the inside out. The Posten dashed for the bunkers and we were left unguarded. These were our best times. Dashing for newly discovered cellars we searched for food. Klari was tiny and could crawl into every niche and cranny. With bombs falling about us, she jumped into a hole and I after her.

One day we found dusty, cobwebbed bottles of wine and began to drink. It must have been very old wine. I was soon tipsy. "Klari," I mumbled, "I've had enough. Let us leave the wine. I'm afraid I cannot find my way back." And we couldn't. We crawled through a dark maze of cellars until we saw daylight and climbed out. Here was a strange street. This was not my group. Where were we? I was scared. A Poste seeing that we were not of his group inquired, "What are you doing here? Why aren't you with your own group?"

"Herr Poste, we hid ourselves from the bombs and cannot find our own group."

"Really?" You hid yourselves from the bombs? Since when are you Jews afraid? I smell wine. You have been drinking. I have been thirsting for wine for three years and you find it. Tell me where the wine is—I want it."

What could I say? If I admitted I had been in a cellar I could be shot.

Just then Papa Meyer appeared. I must tell you about Papa Meyer. He was a fine man. A war casualty with a crippled hand, he had a civilian position, Supervisor of Posten. At a time when food was so scarce it was more precious than diamonds or rubies, every day he gave his lunch to the girls. He said he could not bear to eat when those about him were hungrier than he. It was apparent his heart felt for us. Yet when we cried, "Papa Meyer, we cannot work. It is cold, we need a fire," he said sympathetically. "I cannot help you, children. The Führer says you must die out. You yourselves see the signs all over: 'Jude Verreck!' Jews must perish."

When the Poste repeated his demand that we tell him the location of the wine, Papa Meyer told us not to be afraid to tell as no harm would come to us. We did and never saw him again.

"Girls," asked Papa Meyer. "What Kommando are you in?"

"We are in Number Three Hundred and we are lost."

He directed us and Klari and I ran all the way back to our own group. Our Poste was infuriated by the delay.

"I will give your numbers to the Aufseherin," he raged, "and tell her you have been in cellars."

Klari and I trembled in terror the whole way. "I don't care about the beating and the shooting," I said, "because I know I am not going to die. But it kills me to think of missing my soup and bread."

Lined up for Zählappell, I awaited my doom. When the numbers of the unfortunate ones were called, Klari's and mine were not among them.

One day when the bombs were raining, we ran into what looked like the cellar of a bombed-out store. We found a large vat containing a thick white liquid with an oily fat surface. I stuck in my fingers and tasted it.

"What can it be," I asked.

"It is cream, real cream," said someone.

"Cream?" we shouted in unison. Oh, delirious delight! Cupping it in the palms of our hands we lapped it with lighting speed. It tasted fine. I thought my stomach would burst. I was full at last. Papa Meyer came down looking for us. The "all clear" had been sounded.

"My God, what are you eating?"

"Cream, Papa Meyer, wonderful cream."

"You know what you have eaten? Paint. Tomorrow you will die."

It was a game. Every day we found treasure troves but never encountered a German civilian in the cellars. Perhaps they were afraid of the signs, "Looting cellars punishable by death."

One day a girl scrambled into a cellar and we waited and waited and she didn't come out. Fearing the bombardment would be over before we learned what she found, her sister went down to fetch her. There she was, a bottle of whisky in her hand and laughing and singing at the top of her voice. She was drunk. Just then the overkommandant came for inspection. Noticing a group of girls laughing hilariously and peering into the cellar his curiosity was aroused. She now had a bottle in each hand, waving and swinging them about and still singing. We tried to carry her up but weak from laughter and fear couldn't make it. The commandant himself went down and filled his pockets. Germans were hungry for liquor. That evening at Zählappell he commented, "The liquor was good, wasn't it?" How would I know?

Sundays we worked until noon. Then was the time for the weekly police inspection to determine how the work was progressing. One Sunday morning I went to work in a blinding ice storm. It was a combination of wet snow and rain and froze as it fell. I was so tired. The endless hours of walking to and from work, the bombardments, the hardships of labor, shoveling mountains of debris and rubble, starvation, lack of water, millions of lice which had eaten every square inch of skin from my body and were eating my flesh, the cold and filthy concrete floor on which I slept...I was tired.

Papa Meyer warned, "Girls, be careful. Don't go into the cellars today. We are going to have an important inspection. Remember no cellars today."

The cold numbed me. I wanted to lie down and sleep. I crawled into a cellar. I knew it held no food. We had already eaten it. There was a straw sack. I was cold beyond endurance and sleepy as I had never been sleepy in my whole life. I cannot recall lying down. I must have fallen asleep on my feet and toppled over. Suddenly I was awake, a powerful light in my eyes. The policeman stood over me.

He wore a yellow shirt. I struggled to my feet. He struck me full across the face. I fell down in a heap at his feet.

"What is your number, Jew dog?" He grabbed my arm and wrote the number in a notebook.

"Tomorrow, Jew dog, you will be shot and there will be one less Jew in the world."

Sobbing and moaning I reached the street. "Magda," my friends tried to console me. "What has happened? Try to control yourself. For God's sake, what has happened to you? Tell us. Don't tremble so."

"I am not going to get my supper tonight. How can I live without my supper?"

The thought of being shot on the morrow held no terror. But God, how I wanted my supper.

I ran to Papa Meyer. He was like a father. "Papa Meyer," I sobbed pointing to the retreating Yellow Shirt, "he said I am going to be shot tomorrow because he found me in a cellar. Believe me, I wasn't eating, there was no food there. I was too sleepy to stay awake. And now I shall not get my supper."

Without a word, Papa Meyer ran after the Yellow Shirt. Girls working nearby told me he said to him, "If you will give me the numbers, I shall take care of the shooting for you tomorrow."

Papa Meyer showed me my number in the notebook

231

and tore it to bits before my eyes. He had courage and a heart. That evening I received my usual ration, no one questioned, and the incident was closed. Eight unfortunate girls were "selected" and we never saw them again.

My friends said to me, "You don't know how lucky you are. You were found in a cellar by a Yellow Shirt. You were going to be shot like a dog. Papa Meyer saved your life." Unable to appreciate it at the time, I now know luck was with me always and everywhere.

Day followed day. Every day a few died. Perhaps someone sleeping or sitting next to me. We had no feeling about it one way or another. The bodies were thrown on the ground near the latrine and when a sufficient number had accumulated, they were carried away. The guards said, "When there are thirty corpses we send for the truck and not sooner." We never knew who was going to be next.

Book of Life

Christmas in Braunschweig was just an ordinary day, unmarked by any evidence of its observance as far as I could see. No throngs of churchgoers walked the streets; no happy greetings gladdened the air; no bells tolled; no Christmas carols rang out; no Christmas greens or lights smiled and twinkled. The people themselves gave no indication that this was the anniversary of the birth of Jesus of Nazareth. Could it be because Jesus was a Jew? Or was it because the sight of us, the blood kin of Jesus, slaving in their streets, filthy and starving and dying, was too much for their stomachs? I studied them. They seemed sad and depressed or angry and enraged. Each one went about his own business, hating the world. No one smiled. They rarely exchanged a word with one another. They didn't have newspapers, only placards as far as I could see. I wondered if we would be bombed on Christmas Eve. We were. An Aufseherin remarked, "They must be Russian bombers. Americans are tender-hearted fools and would not bombard us on Christmas Eve."

It was just another working day. When we came home that evening Fat Magda Cohen was waiting at the door. We smelled potatoes, a wonderful fragrance.

"Tonight you will feast like an animal." Her taunting sarcasm made our hearts sink.

The Germans observed Christmas after all. Each girl received one teaspoonful of potato with a speck of gravy, and on each piece of bread a dab of marmalade and a dab of margarine.

My thoughts went back to Yom Kippur in Auschwitz and how we Jews observed our Holy Day. On the morning of the Day of Atonement no one touched their black coffee. No one. This was a fast day, a day of silent devotion and prayer. We were working a full twelve-hour shift besides standing hours for Zählappell. I was uplifted, exalted, filled with love and reverence for my brethren. We are not beasts. We are not clods of flesh. We are God's children. People of the Book. I prayed for peace and blessedness for mankind, that the mighty shall be just and the just shall be mighty. I prayed that I might continue to love God and put my trust in His infinite mercy. I prayed for the forgiveness of my sins, and I prayed to be inscribed in the Book of Life. I prayed all the prayers I could remember and then I recalled the following lines. I think they are from the Book of Job.

> Behold, happy is the man whom God correcteth;
> Therefore despise not thou the chastening of The Almighty.
> For He maketh sore, and bindeth up;
> He woundeth, and His hands make whole.

234

He will deliver thee in six troubles;
Yea, in seven there shall no evil touch thee,
In famine He will redeem thee from death;
And in war from the power of the sword.
Thou shalt be hid from the scourge of the tongue;
Neither shalt thou be afraid of destruction when it cometh.
At destruction and famine thou shalt laugh;
Neither shalt thou be afraid of the beasts of the earth.
And thou shalt know that thy tent is in peace;
And thou shalt visit thy habitation, and shalt miss nothing.
Thou shalt know also that thy seed shall be great.
And thine offspring as the grass of the earth.
Thou shalt come to thy grave in ripe age,
Like as a shock of corn cometh in its season.
Lo this, we have searched it, so it is;
Hear it and know thou it for thy good.

Our fast was longer than anticipated. Standing Zählappell I thought I'd drop. The Aufseherin who counted us said, "Jews, this is a work camp. Here there is to be no religious observance. If you can fast all day, you can fast all night. No supper, Jews." Had we known this in advance it would not have made any difference. We would have observed Yom Kippur at any cost.

During bombardments we ran wild and unguarded through Braunschweig cellars. One day we were given orders to seek shelter in the nearest structure when the bombs were falling. I suppose they assumed it would keep us out of the cellars. Nearby was a large Catholic church.

235

That very afternoon we ran in. The bombardment was ear-splitting. I looked about me. It was a huge edifice. We numbered four hundred and we were lost in its vast expanse. Putting down the shovels we walked about idly. The church had been badly damaged. Gorgeous stained-glass windows had once ornamented the partly empty frames and added beauty and grandeur. Just as I was admiring the few remaining fragments, powerful drafts from the bombardments shattered them. Pews and benches were smashed. Breaking them into kindling with shovels, we started a fire. The smoke attracted the Poste.

"Put it out," he warned. "If guards learn you have started a fire you will be punished. I know you are freezing in your thin rags, but the fire must be put out at once."

On the high windows hung velour draperies, dark green, heavy, and beautiful. We ripped them down and tore them into scarves and shawls. We found prayer books, the first paper we had seen in ages. Ripping out the pages, we placed them under our dresses for warmth.

On the wall hung a huge oil painting of some Pope Pius, beautifully framed in gold leaf. A girl from Maramaros, a tall blonde she was and very coarse, stood in front of the picture, and shaking her fist at it screamed, "You! Because of you we are here. Because of you we are suffering. We slave, and we starve and we die. Why don't you excommunicate Hitler and Von Papen and Mussolini and France and Henlein and Pétain and Laval and Tiso and Pavelich? If you think they are doing evil things, why don't you excommunicate them?"

We were more animal than human. Yet when she lifted her shovel to slash the beautiful oil painting, that superb work of art, we fell on her, our flailing arms beating her to the floor.

"Shame on you," we cried. "Do you wish to bring us down to the level of our persecutors?" She lay sobbing. "But he is responsible for the Concordat with Germany and the Lateran Pact with Italy." What could we say to that? It was, unfortunately, true.

I found a stairway leading to the apartment of the sacristan. He had a bed and a cupboard. We found bread, conserves, and marmalade. We devoured them and not even a crumb was left.

The poor sacristan on discovering his plundered apartment reported it to the police. In the morning the commandant addressed us. "Your work does not warrant the food you consume. We have no use for you. You are to be bathed and deloused."

We understood. He meant inspection and "selection." Not being able to bathe, wash, or clean ourselves in ten weeks, few expected to pass. In the afternoon we marched to the soldiers' barracks, the Kaserne. I think the word is international. At least the song, written about Lili Marleen and the Kaserne, is.

The Kaserne was outside town. It was a beautiful day, sunny and cold. We noticed garbage cans. Darting out of line, we lifted covers in search of food. I made a haul, potato peelings, and thought they were luscious. I ate everything in the garbage cans and so did the others. We cleaned them out. The Posten scurried about, beating us with a gummi knueppel, but so what? He couldn't whip everyone. And a beating was nothing when food was at stake.

On the ground I saw a rotten apple. "Oh, girls," I screamed in joy, "an apple, a real apple!" This was a mistake. I ran for the apple. The girls ran after me. Just as I was about to scoop it up about thirty girls fell on me. I fell on the apple. A mammoth dog being walked by a woman heard the screams and becoming excited jumped on the girls. Fortunately, he wore a muzzle. The girls were frightened, picked themselves up and ran back into line. I lay there on top of the apple too winded to move. The dog licked my face through his muzzle. His mistress pulled him away. A guard beat me across the back and I got to my feet. The apple, now squashed to a pulp, remained where it lay.

The Kaserne was frightening. It reminded us of the shower room in Auschwitz. We thought we were being prepared for gas chambers or crematoria. When we balked and refused to enter, soldiers beat us. Reluctantly we went in, one hundred at a time, and I in the first group. The soap was like stone, no suds. I rubbed vigorously. The dirt did not come off. When hot water flowed over me, I knew perfect bliss. After ten weeks of filth and dehydration I wanted to remain in the showers forever. In the end the soldiers had to beat us to make us leave. When we came out the others gasped in amazement. "You are still alive? No one has been selected?" No one could believe her eyes. It is a miracle I thought. We have actually come out of the showers alive.

As we passed through the door, an attendant with a large spray supposedly deloused us. The Braunschweig lice did not retreat so easily. Our clothing was burned, and we were given new "outfits." One got a pair of man's pants, another a pair of long white drawers. I got a pair of black shoes. This was kindness beyond words. And a gray cotton dress. Nothing else. This was January of 1945. I walked out of Braunschweig with an uplifted, exhilarated feeling; lice weren't eating me alive. Gratefully we marched to the depot.

I consider Braunschweig the most evil, the most foul camp in my whole experience as a German slave laborer. To review: four hundred or half our numbers died in ten weeks; at no time was water available for drinking or bathing; we were forced to sleep on a cold concrete floor on lice-infested pulverized straw. When we asked for fresh straw the commandant said, "Straw? In all of Germany there is no straw. We have no straw for our horses." Mornings I felt I was dying. Lice had eaten my whole body to a mass of inflamed flesh. It is beyond belief that creatures so small as lice can cause so much anguish and pain, can eat the skin and then slowly but inexorably feast on the raw flesh. Sunny days we sat in the streets, opened our dresses and tried to pick off the lice. We knew it was futile, but I felt I had to keep trying. German civilians regarded the spectacle as a sideshow and looked upon us as shameless freaks. I wasn't ashamed when they stared and jeered. Was the shame not theirs?

As I marched through the streets of Braunschweig the day of departure, I was exhilarated. I had attained another goal. I had lived to survive the hardships and cold and typhus and lice. At the depot I observed German civilians closely. Some laughed and shouted insults. Others felt sorry. You could see it in their eyes. And a few brave souls whispered, "Try to live. It can't be much longer. The end is near. The Russians are coming."

Our commandant, the same German gentleman under whose authority starving girls had been shot for foraging in cellars, bade us a courteous farewell and turned us over to our new commandant. The latter said, "Girls, you are going to work in a factory. You will have it good. You will be provided with beds and food. In return you are expected to work hard and behave."

The same old German theme song: "Girls, you are going to have it good." Why were they always pleading with us to be good? They held machine guns.

We were assigned one hundred to a wagon. I began to breathe freely. I feared inspection; my lice-infested, inflamed body would not pass. "Thank God," I said, "No inspection and no selection."

"Don't be so sure. We are going to have them when we reach our new camp." I shook with fright. I don't know why. A few said, "The best thing that can happen to us is that we die now. To what end do we suffer another day or another month?"

To what end? To live, of course. As long as one breathes, one wishes to live. Even had I known that the worst was yet to come, I doubt that I would have preferred death. My urge to live was stronger than I, and drove me on. I lived in hope. There were occasional black moments but always the thought of what life could hold for me kept me driving, ever driving.

Sitting in the darkness I thought of Gustave. Someday, darling, I shall tell you of my experiences and you will know the real heart and soul of me. My God, how good it would be if only I were with Mama. She would know how to heal my wounds.

Starvation and brutality had crazed us. Painfully crowded for space, the girls began to push one another. Guards rode in an open wagon. I wished they were in with us. When we were alone, women tried to kill one another. Again, there was a tub to take care of our natural needs but only voiding was permitted; no bowel movements. We rode through a night of continuous squabbling and fighting.

In the morning the doors were opened. "Get out!" Hungry and weak I edged along on my buttocks to the door and fell to the ground. My legs were wobbly. I was too weak to stand. Two of the sitting women were dead. No one gave them a second glance. We had been wedged in so tightly no one knew when they died. The bodies were thrown out. It was commonplace. So many times, a woman sitting near me died, sometimes during a conversation. It was dark and I didn't know the difference. It was all very casual.

I looked about. We were in a rural area with only a few scattered dwellings in sight. The depot was small. A sign read Beendorf. Where was I?

Salt Mines

For some reason the girls were in a jubilant, hopeful mood. Rumors were flying. "Have you heard? The commandant said we are going to work in a canning factory." By the time the rumor made the rounds and returned to the originator, it sounded like this: "Have you heard? The commandant said we are going to work in a canning factory and have all we wish to eat."

Klari said, "We'll be lucky if they don't eat us. Jews have been made into fertilizer for German cabbage fields. How much farther do they have to go?"

Poor women. They indulged themselves in fond dreams and went on building castles in Spain. Everyone was buoyant and walked on air for several miles.

The new camp looked like an ammunitions depot. All the buildings were concrete. I was surprised to see civilians. I learned they were non-Jewish slave laborers. I was never able to learn the nature of their offense.

Beendorf was a small town. It had been so thoroughly bombed there was little left, only a few scattered houses. An Aufseherin counted us. We were less than four hundred.

The beast hunger was clawing at my insides. I was almost too weak to stand Zählappell. And then they led us into a Block. We called it that. It was really a vast cement building. It consisted of a cement hall so large the Aufseherin said we could stand Zählappell indoors. Adjoining it was another large hall of equal size, furnished with a long table and chairs.

This was the first time a table and chairs had been provided. Strength flowed into me. Now I would eat like a human being and not like an animal on the floor or in the Koya. Doors in the dining hall gave access to two dormitories. My heart almost burst with joy. Real bunks instead of Koyan. Real bunks, three tiers high and two in a bed. I touched one reverently.

The Aufseherin warned, "I hope you have come here clean. We are very careful and have no lice in Beendorf. They are not permitted." No one said a word. The Braunschweig lice were even now eating me. Klari and Luyzi shared a bed and so did Pira and I. Edith Hartman was the Block Elsterer, Fat Magda Cohen the assistant, and Katka the bread dealer. They had a room to themselves.

For the first time we had artificial lights, electricity. Klari rubbed her eyes. "Look, Magda, a straw mattress and two blankets on every bed." There was no food for us. The kitchen was closed. We hadn't eaten since the morning of the previous day. I was used to it. The Aufseherin promised, "Tomorrow morning you will get a full meal, not just black coffee." German promises don't fill the belly. We were not permitted to use the outdoor toilets. There were no charged fences and they feared we would run away.

I climbed into the bunk and slept like the dead. In the morning I could hardly move. My lice wounds were festering. Wherever I touched myself it hurt agonizingly. My flesh was a mass of inflammation. We got up at dawn and waited for the commandant to assign us to our new Kommandos. First, we were ordered into the washroom. There were neither towels nor soap, so we wiped our faces with our dresses. I'm afraid I didn't get very clean. Magda Cohen and Edith were giving the orders. They lined us up before the Aufseherin came to count us. Fat Magda ordered ten girls to carry out the slop tubs. When they hesitated she screamed. "So? You don't want to do it. I'll make you, you lazy choleras." And she beat the poor things with her wooden club. Either she found wooden clubs in every camp or she carried the same one from Auschwitz to Sweden. I am happy to report that she was eventually arrested in Sweden for her brutality.

The Aufseherin came after we'd been standing for an hour and counted us. This was the first indoor Zählappell and we were thankful not to be standing outdoors in the freezing cold. "You are going to work today," she told us. "The commandant will come later and assign your work." The kitchen was manned by Russian prisoners and located just beyond our door. Ten girls carried in tubs of black coffee. Five women to a bowl, five swallows a woman. We watched each other like vultures. The coffee was bitter, but it was hot and gave us life. Whenever Fat Magda and Edith wished to bathe, we got no coffee. Several times I saw them washing the long table and chair with our coffee.

Crawling back into our bunks we lay there sick and hungry. Many were suffering from diarrhea and lack of kidney control. All were covered with festering and inflamed lice sores. Shortly before noon they brought our first food. I barely had the strength to crawl out of bed and stand another Zählappell. But we were dying for food and staggered to the dining hall. Fat Magda stood at the entrance like a guard, supercilious and arrogant. A girl handed me a bowl, another filled it. It was a carrot and potato soup, thick and hot. A bowl to myself meant I was an individual above the level of swine and cattle feeding at a common trough. It meant I had a chance to be human again. Something stirred within me. I willed to survive. Life was sweet.

An hour later there was an air of excitement and Magda was screaming, "Zählappell!" This was the third time. An Oberscharführer accompanied by two officers came in. They asked, "What kind of work can you do? Are any of you tailoresses? Can you do fine embroidery work? Are there any pianists among you?" I raised my hand.

He continued, "We are going to classify you according to your training and ability for special work. Will pianists raise their hands first?" Mine went up high. Am I going to play the piano, I wondered? Officers examined my hands. What kind of work would I do? Common sense told me the Germans were not expecting me to entertain them. The chosen ones, including about twenty pianists, lined up in another room and again they examined our hands. We were given extra rations: a slice of bread, a slice of wurst, and a dab of margarine. I noticed Fat Magda was not cutting each portion of wurst in two portions. No wonder she was fat. We lay on our bunks for the rest of the day. I was elated and thrilled. No one was beating me and I was resting.

The following morning at four, shouts awoke us. "Zählappell! Aufstehen! Roll call! Get up!" The Aufseherin assigned the women to their various Kommandos in groups of one hundred. Here as in Auschwitz the Kapos were diseased German prostitutes. There was a whole Block of them. One was a lovely blonde with evidence of good breeding. I felt sorry for her. My Kapo, Lillian, was a real tough whore with long black unkempt hair. Her speech was vulgar and coarse.

We followed Lillian to the main gate where we were counted once more. Then out we marched into the dark cold morning guarded by Lillian and two Posten. They set a brisk pace. I could hardly walk. Every step was agony. I had to keep up with them. The snow was deep, the weather freezing, and all about us thick forests looked dark and sinister. The cotton dress and shoes, all I had on my body, were no protection from the cold. In one hand I held a piece of bread and in the other the piece of wurst I'd saved from the previous evening. This was my tie to life, literally; a piece of bread and a half slice of wurst.

About thirty minutes later we neared a spacious residence. It must have been a private villa but now was headquarters for German officers. Beyond was another building, not very large, that looked like a factory. Its interior was one large room, crudely built and dirty. We entered an elevator. Down we went, down, down, down into the dark earth. My heart sank with the elevator. I trembled like an aspen. Down, down, down; were we going into the bowels of the earth? Did the Germans have a direct route to hell? I couldn't have stood it another second and then we stopped. I looked about me. I was deep in the bowels of the earth and for me it was hell. I was in the salt mines.

Brilliant lights illuminated the solid white salt walls.

The ceilings were salt. The floors were salt. The walls were salt. The elevator shaft was dug in solid salt. I was in a block of salt, I don't know how many miles deep or long or wide. A network of narrow tunnels led in all directions. Posten with lamps like coal miners led us through dark tunnels. The passages were just wide enough for one. Loose salt got into the open wounds of my sore, infested body and feet. I began to itch. It seemed we walked through the network for about five miles. Perhaps it just seemed like five miles. At last we came to a bright opening and here was another elevator. I saw hundreds of civilians of many nationalities: French, Polish, Russian, Italian, Spanish, and German. They were Christian prisoners permitted to live "free" in Beendorf but forced to work. We entered the second elevator and seemed to be going up but were still underground.

I got out in a brilliantly lit hall. It was lined with dozens of doors leading to other halls. The lights were dazzling. The hall in which I was to work was the size of a square city block. Thousands of girls and men were working on machines under the supervision of civilian German engineers. I was in a munitions factory.

An Aufseherin led us to a corner where about two hundred slaves were working and said to the three engineers in charge, "I have brought the pianists. Divide them among yourselves as you wish."

The engineer who selected me was tall, handsome, and had thick black hair which shone under the brilliant lights. "Girls," he said, "I understand your plight and how you have reached your tragic situation. I am sorry for you. Don't be afraid. I'll do what I can for you." He was a gentleman; fine, intelligent, generous, and considerate. Leading me to a machine, he offered me a chair.

"You poor girl. Don't you get enough to eat? You look sick. Don't work hard. Take it easy and do your work slowly." He sat down and instructed me, and I wonder now that he did not shrink from my lice and sores and smell. No one was supposed to know the nature of her work, and precisely what she was doing. My work was obvious. I worked on the interior of bullet cartridges. As I put one on the machine it turned and made spirals on the inside of the case. I examined it through a loupe and if I saw rainbow colors that meant it was perfect. The colors were lovely.

Air was brought in by ventilators. I pinched myself. Was this I sitting at a table in a warm room under bright lights? Not freezing and not clawed by hunger? At noon when we were given soup, I was almost sure Germany had won the war. This is the first time we were given food during the day. Six workers sat in a row and in back of us the three engineers studied piles of papers. I hated to leave. I dreaded walking through the tunnels and the salt sifting into my open sores.

As each Kommando marched into the Block at the end of the day they were ordered into the washroom. The water, cold of course, was turned on for only a few minutes daily; until the sinks were filled. Woe to the girls who were a few minutes late. They had to wash in dirty water. The "toilets" were actually garbage cans. Privacy was out of the question.

An Aufseherin appointed two girls as caretakers. One was Hainal from Tizsa Ujlak, Carpatho-Russia. She was a handsome blond. She gave the impression of being a fine, amiable person but I soon found out she was base and cruel. The other was a coarse creature from Beregszász, tall and ugly. It was their duty to keep the washroom clean and see that no one entered for any purpose except during the designated periods, mornings and evenings when the water was turned on.

The evening of my first day in the salt mine, Katka dealt the bread and a Stuben Dienst from Košice handed each woman a small onion. "Mine is so small. Please give me a larger one," I begged. "If you don't shut up," she snarled in Hungarian, "you'll get nothing." Every woman was supposed to get three onions, we found out. They had bushels of onions left over and ate them all week.

The next morning my feet and legs were swollen to elephantine proportions. I couldn't walk. I tried. I tried to put on my shoes. I finally forced my sore feet in but couldn't lace the shoes. Among us were slaves who were doctors and nurses. "It is water, an edema," said one. "Your end is near." Edema or no, I walked to work and into the salt mines I went.

The Revir clinic was run by a slave doctor, a French Jewish woman. "Girls," she warned, "don't come into this Revir. It means death. Three girls are dying in one bed. I have no medicine, no instruments, no gauze or bandages. I have nothing for you but a bed with a dirty straw mattress. If you want to die, come to the Revir. If you want to live, keep on working."

I kept on working, swollen legs and all. I think it was the thirst which was more agonizing than my inflamed body. My thirst was a burning, searing scorpion. I was dying for water and we were not permitted to drink in the salt mines. The water was polluted, they told us. I could see it was dirty. There was a tap in the hall and when I thought an Aufseherin wasn't looking I drank. There were so many Aufseherin walking about I knew I would be caught. It was well worth the beatings they gave me. Not that they cared if I died, they told me, but I must not contract a disease which might become epidemic. I found another way of getting water. We were permitted to go to the washroom once a day to take care of our natural needs. There was a wash basin with very dirty water. I drank that. Nothing happened.

The engineers begged us not to drink the dirty water. "We'll make coffee for you," they said. "Drink it when no one is looking. But for God's sake, don't drink the water in here." They prepared ersatz black coffee on an electric plate. Kusa, a Polish Jewish girl, sat in the corner. They told her to divide it among the six of us. But what did she do? She kept it for herself. No one else got a drop. I continued drinking in the washroom. One day Kusa caught me. She dashed out and called an Aufseherin. I was trapped. She struck me savagely across the face with her gummi knueppel. I thought I'd die on the spot.

One evening I was too weary to go to the washroom. Taking my portion of bread, I crawled into my bunk almost too exhausted to eat. From the bunk above came a stream of water, right in my face. I was nauseated and enraged.

"What are you doing?" I screamed to the one above. "You have urinated on me!"

"I'm sorry. I didn't know what was happening. I didn't feel it." I was angry and berated her. How was I to clean myself? Pira soothed me and said, "It's quiet. Perhaps the washroom girls are sleeping. Go in and wash yourself, they won't know."

Tiptoeing in, quiet as a mouse, I began to wash my face. Without warning someone struck me with a stave, again and again. It knocked the breath out of me. I couldn't raise my hands to defend myself. It was Hainal, the wash-room girl. "You just wait, you dirty cholera," she screamed. "Tomorrow I will tell the Block Elsterer, and you won't get your supper. You came in here when it was not permitted? You will suffer."

I tried to explain but she wouldn't listen. "May I *please* use the tub," I begged her.

"No! You know it is not allowed." I went back to Pira crying. "Pira, I have to pee. I can't stand it."

"Don't be silly. Do what the others do. Go on the floor." And I did.

When the Stuben Dienst came to call us in the morning the floor was pretty wet. She screamed, "You dogs. You bandits. I will tell Magda Cohen and she will report you to the Aufseherin."

Thinking it was an idle threat we didn't take her seriously. That evening when we returned from work an Aufseherin with a gummi knueppel stood at the entrance. She raged, "Now I am going to show you what it means to use the dormitory as a toilet. Bring a chair." This was unreasonable. She was the one who originally gave the order which prevented us from taking care of our needs decently during the night. As each in turn leaned over the chair she was given five hard blows across the buttocks with the gummi knueppel.

There was no supper that night. Not even a piece of bread. Fat Magda hid herself in a little room. "God will punish you," we screamed at her through the locked door. "You fat devil. You swine who eats our food." To her mother we said, "Shame on you that you have so vicious a daughter."

"I can't help it," the poor woman cried. "I'm afraid of her, too."

It was not the beating that made us frantic. It was the loss of one day's bread and soup, a loss which could mean the difference between life and death. The next morning, I was grotesquely swollen and could not sit down all day.

One day the engineer said, "Starting tomorrow, we work nights. You are going to be on the night shift." A Block Aufseherin told us, "When you come in from work at 7am you will get black coffee. At 2pm when you get up you will get your meal here instead of at the factory." Unfortunately the food was brought at noon while I was still asleep and Edith Hartman, Fat Magda, and the Stuben Dienst gorged themselves on the vegetables and left thin soup for the sleepers.

Sundays I occasionally found a bit of meat in the soup.

I called out, "Who wants to buy my meat?" The very ill could no longer eat bread and traded it for meat. I complained, "I wish I did not feel like eating bread. I'm sick, too, but I'm hungrier than ever." I was always hungry. I reached the point where I would have done anything to fill my belly.

One morning the Stuben Dienst approached me. "Magda," she asked, "would you like a bowl of soup at twelve o'clock?"

"Would I? There isn't anything I wouldn't do for a bowl of soup."

"Well, if you are willing to wash the chairs and tables and clean the dining hall every day, I'll give you a bowl of soup."

I was beside myself with happiness. Instead of going to sleep and resting, I worked. "Stuben Dienst," I said, "my hands are swollen. I am sorry, but I cannot put them in cold water. It's very painful."

"I'll give you a tub of hot coffee," she said, "use that."

I kept it up for one week, getting an extra portion as promised. My only rest in twenty-four hours was from noon to 2pm. My wasted body was unequal to the demands. One night at work, watching my finger on the machine go back and forth, back and forth, I fell sound asleep. No one realized I was sleeping until an Aufseherin happened along. She struck me across the head. "Give me your number, Jew dog."

I knew this called for punishment. I didn't care. I hadn't the strength to take it to heart. In the morning the Block Elsterer told me to report to Block Fourteen. The Aufseherin was waiting for me. A German prostitute cut off my hair close to the scalp. It was a matter of indifference to me. I was so lousy, it was a relief not to have hair. I didn't have a comb, anyhow.

When I got back to my own Block the girls gasped. Pira was shocked.

"Magda. God how you look; the worst of the worst."

I, of course, was spared the awful sight, but I can imagine what I looked like. Klari had once told me my head is large and with my shriveled skeleton-like body, I guess I frightened Pira. She pitied me, too.

"You cannot go to work with a bare head, out in the freezing ice and snow," she said. "A woman found a man's hair net. She wants to sell it. Give her a piece of bread and you can cover your head."

"Are you crazy, Pira? A piece of bread for a hair net? Never. My Gustave isn't here."

Pira was determined and offered me half of her portion. I agreed and "bought" the hair net. Pira rejoiced, "Oh, Magda. You look so different now." She was happy that my head was covered.

We Were Strangers

She, too, worked in the salt mine but we were not together. Her superior was humane and Pira could do many things. On her machine she made combs from strips of metal. These she smuggled in her shoes into the Block. Now I had a comb, but no hair. However, I used the comb for scraping lice off my scalp.

On the night shift, hot soup was served to the Christian personnel. Jews received a cup of black coffee. Our engineer gave his soup to his six workers, each night to another girl. He showed no favoritism. Pretending to be showing me the work, he'd say, "There is soup for you. Take it when no one is looking. Don't let anyone catch you." Watching and waiting for my chance, which sometimes took more than an hour, I ate the soup. It was delicious. The engineer must have known how nourishing it was. He unselfishly denied himself. It was usually bean or split pea soup and sometimes there was a pudding. It was always a source of wonder that such food still remained in the world.

Frequently on the pretext of teaching me a new operation, he talked. "The war will soon be over. I am glad. The Americans are coming on one side, the Russians on the other. If the Russians get here first, my wife and I will be sent to Siberia." He was in deadly fear of the Russians. It was a complex, I thought.

"Herr Engineer," I asked, "aren't you afraid the Americans will punish you if they get here first?" He laughed.

"Ach, Americans are fools when it comes to understanding. They forgive and forget too easily. I'm not afraid of Americans. I pray they will capture me."

"I don't think Americans are fools. My parents and family are in America. They think it is the best country in the world."

"I am only speaking of the American gullibility. If Germany loses, instead of our paying reparations, America will give us millions, hundreds of millions. We won't suffer."

"I don't call that losing. Unless you are punished how will you ever know the wickedness of the crimes you are committing?"

He laughed. "It's human nature. Germany goes to war because she knows she has nothing to lose. Either she wins and then it is her conquest, or she loses, and America floods us with food and money and pity. And in the meantime, we keep what we have taken."

"Like the billions in gold and material from Czechoslovakia?"

He smiled good-naturedly, "Yes. Why not?" And he was a fine gentleman even as he said it. He only knew fear of Russia, not remorse for Germany.

Once he told me about his life in Berlin. "We aren't far from Berlin. The bombardments drove me mad. Day and night. Night and day. I could never sleep. I came here to the country with my wife. I haven't a radio. I don't hear bombardments. I don't know what is going on. I am happy."

"How can you be happy if Germany loses the war?"

"We'll win the next one."

It really was a blessed relief not to hear the bombardments. That was one advantage of working in the bowels of the earth. The guards told us openly that if the Americans or Russians located the factory they planned to flood it. "We will open the water pipes and, Jew dogs, you will drown like rats." This made no impression on me. My mind was benumbed. I felt I was going on until the end of time down in the salt mine. I said to the engineer, "I feel now that I shall never be free. I shall live but I shall never be free."

"Listen to me," he said. "You will soon be free. You are better off than I. You don't have to fear the Russians. Can't you see our production has dropped to almost nothing? We have no oil. We have no benzine. Why have I told you to work slowly? I have no work for you."

My daily quota was eighty bullet cases. I made it the first day. After that I kept dropping. The engineer had a hidden reserve. Everyday he put about twenty-five on my bench saying, "I'll leave some everyday and it will appear that you are making your quota." An Aufseherin asked, "How are they working, Herr Engineer? Are you satisfied?"

"I am very satisfied. They make their quota every day."

Luyzi was suffering from diarrhea. Her whole body, like mine, was one festering inflammation.

"Magda," she wept, "I am going to the Revir to die. I can no longer work. I am too sick and too weak to help myself. With my last breath, I beg you, try to live. Live, my child. And sometimes think of me."

Klari was working. Dirty and covered with festering sores, she kept on working. As she was on another shift we met only when our lines passed. Invariably I whispered, "Was ist heute abend die Zulage?" I meant what do we get this evening besides bread? Perhaps a slice of wurst or cheese or an onion? And she answered running past. Then she was no longer with her Kommando. And I knew it was all over with Klari. Either she was in the Revir dying or had already died. I asked no questions and no one asked me about her.

A very charming, lovely girl from Vienna had a warm woolen dress. She told me she was studying to be a concert violinist. I can never forget her because she carried herself like a princess. Now she was sick and too weak to lift her hands. She always looked at them as if they were her children.

She was going to the Revir to die she said.

"You have a warm woolen dress," I said. "May I have it?

Mine is only cotton."

"You are welcome to my dress if you can get it off."

Pira helped me. Now I had a warm woolen dress. She whispered to Pira. "You are good, Pira. You love God and He will listen to you. I am dying. Please pray for me."

"Hear, O Israel, the Lord is our God, the Lord is one." Pira stroked her brow. She bade us goodbye and the Stuben Diensten carried her to the Revir to die.

One awful night I felt the cramping pains of diarrhea. I couldn't work. I begged the Aufseherin for permission to go to the toilet. She arrogantly refused. "You know it is permitted to go only one time during the night." I told the engineer of my plight. He couldn't help me. It came through involuntarily, running down my legs like water. It soiled my dress. He saw it. I had no feeling of shame or embarrassment—just pain. He pointed to a cabinet and whispered that I step behind it. He brought me a bowl of water and a rag. I cleaned myself as best I could and went back to work.

When the Aufseherin stopped at his desk for a friendly chat, he said, "With a woman who has no feeling for another woman, I do not care to talk." She turned red.

"It is the regulation," she said. "What can I do?"

My dress was filthy and stank. In the morning a group of German prostitutes standing in line behind me kicked me in the buttocks and jeered, "Phooo. You stink, dirty Jew."

I couldn't answer. My heart was crying. My eyes had no more tears.

An Aufseherin who had been transferred from Braunschweig recognized me. Her friendliness and amiability had always been puzzling. She had never badgered or plagued us. I instinctively recognized she was trying to help me. I saw it in her eyes. When no one was looking she smiled. And then she did a daring thing. She asked civilians for their supper and brought the food to the six of us. Quite by chance I thanked her in Czech. She whispered, "I thought you are Czech. I am, too. I was born in Prague of German parents. When the Germans occupied Czechoslovakia, I had no choice but to come to Germany." That explained her humaneness. She was a Czech Aufseherin. And she had dared to bring me food under the very noses of the guards.

One morning as I was leaving I met Pira in the elevator landing. We had to wait our turn. There were hundreds milling about.

"I can't go on, Pira. I cannot take another step. My arms and legs are swollen. Lice are eating every inch of my body. I am inflamed. I am festering. They can do with me what they wish. I am not coming back to the salt mines." And I cried and cried for the agony.

The Czech Aufseherin was on duty and came over. "What is it? What is wrong?" she asked in a kindly voice.

"Aufseherin," said Pira, "she wants to die and be free of her torture and pain. Look, her whole body is one sore."

She soothed me. "You dumb goose. The war will soon be over. Very soon. And you will be free. But me, they will send to Siberia. The Russians will make me their prisoner." She, too, was in fear of the Russians. Like an angel of mercy, she helped Pira lift me from the salt floor.

Pira helped me back to the Block. I crawled into my bunk. My arm was swollen and painful and I prayed for Luyzi's knife that I might cut it off. I cried and moaned. Edith Hartman heard me. Quietly she led me to the Revir.

"Don't leave me in the Revir, Block Elsterer. I beg you. She who stays in the Revir dies."

The French Jewish woman doctor looked at my arm. She had no chair on which to seat me. I stood against the wall. The doctor cut my arm and pus squirted out, a lot of it. I think I might have fainted for a moment, but Edith held me up. Immediately, I felt easier. The awful throbbing pain seemed relieved. The doctor had only toilet tissue with which to bandage my arm. Edith helped me back to my bunk and I fell asleep.

The next morning, I begged Edith Hartman, "Don't send me to work in the factory today. I am sick. I can't move my arm."

"You cannot remain in your bunk. If you are seen by

an Aufseherin, you know it means the Revir for you." She considered for a moment. "Today, Magda, you may remain in the Block. However, you know you must work. Help the Stuben Dienst with the cleaning. I'll try to place you in the paring kitchen."

With one good hand I helped the Stuben Dienst and cleaned the dormitories, dining hall, and the main hall. Always like a pestilence there was Fat Magda. She pointed to a window high up near the ceiling.

"Listen, you filth," she commanded, "you wash that window from the outside." In an ordinary building it would have been a third-floor window. She brought an extension ladder and set it up. Carrying a ladder was nothing for her.

"Go," she ordered.

I looked up and said, "My God, how can I climb up so high? I can't even move my legs. They are like wood. I'll fall."

"I will hold the ladder, cholera. Nothing will happen to you. God doesn't want you and the Devil won't have you."

She is right, I thought. If I fall nothing will happen. I will die, and that is better than suffering from inflammation and lice. Up I climbed and washed the window with my good hand, holding the ladder with the other. I was afraid to look down. I was dizzy and sick. Suddenly an Aufseherin was scolding my tormentor. "Listen, Jew. If she falls it will be your fault, not ours. Don't you see that she cannot even move her legs?" And she called up to me, "Come down. Leave the window as it is." Magda looked daggers and I knew it boded no good.

The chores completed, Edith Hartman sent me to the Revir to have the "bandage" on my arm changed. Suzi was lying on a plain wooden table, naked. The woman doctor was cutting away the poisoned flesh without anesthesia or narcotics. Her buttocks had been eaten away by lice and sores, and the exposed bones protruded. It reminded me of slicing beef on the butcher's block. Suzi was weak and haltingly said, "Look, Magda. Look what is being done to me."

I quietly asked her, "Where is Luyzi?"

"Luyzi is dead."

I had no feeling or reaction. It was simply a fact. She is no longer here. Everyday so many thousands were dying. I was insensate. The doctor's assistant, a nurse, removed my paper bandage. It was crawling with lice. She washed it with plain water and gave me a piece of toilet paper which I wrapped around my arm myself. A long line was waiting for her attention.

When I returned to the Block the Stuben Dienst said, "You must do whatever we order you to. The Block Elsterer has done you a big favor by permitting you to work here. Get going. Carry out the garbage cans."

They were large and heavy and using both hands I dragged them to the rear of the kitchen. I noticed I was being watched by a boy in a prisoner's uniform. No one was around, and he asked in Polish, "Czy jestes głodny?"

"Yes, I am hungry and sick."

"Come back in a few minutes and you'll find carrots hidden near the wall." I was happy at the thought of carrots but doubted that he would give them to me. Out of curiosity I went back in a few minutes and looked. And lo and behold, like three beautiful blessings from heaven, were three of the largest carrots I have ever seen. Putting them in my bosom I ran back to the Block. When no one was looking I put them in the straw mattress. Pira and I were in transports of delight and for a whole week we nibbled on carrots at night. It wasn't the actual eating that made us joyful. It was the security of having food in reserve.

Food

The next day Edith took me to the paring kitchen. They gave me a knife and my job was to peel potatoes. The Kapo, a primitive, dictatorial German woman, threatened, "If I catch you eating a potato, or if you try to smuggle a potato out of here, I'll beat you to death, Jew swine." She was the only person I was truly afraid of. She was a killer, depraved and bestial.

The first day I didn't eat even a sliver of a potato. I was grateful just to be sitting there. Others ate. I didn't dare.

Pira was now on the day shift in the salt mines. That evening she pleaded, "Magda, I have diarrhea. I am so sick. I beg you, please, bring me a potato. Just one?"

"Pira, I'll do it. I don't know how, but I will."

The following evening, I hid a potato in my groin and slowly walked out of the kitchen. I had only to go through the door. The Kapo grabbed me by my hurt arm, tapped me all over and then pulled my legs apart. The potato dropped down. She struck me across the head, I don't how many times. I was blinded.

She screamed, "You can't come back to this kitchen. You are lucky I don't kill you, Jew thief."

We Were Strangers

Running into the Block I sobbed and screamed at Pira, "I hate you. You are my undoing. Because of you I can't return to the paring kitchen. On account of stealing a potato for you I have lost my good job. I am unable to work in the salt mines. They will put me in the Revir and I will die. You are my death. I hate you. I hate you. I never want to lay eyes on you. I won't sleep with you. Get out of my bunk." At my hysterical outburst, Pira cried like a baby. "Magda, darling, don't be angry with me. I am so sick."

When I told the sorry story to the Block Elsterer, she was sympathetic. "I'll try for you in the morning. Maybe the Kapo will take you back." Edith begged for me and I was reinstated.

As I peeled, Pira was on my mind. I truly loved her. She was the finest, noblest soul I have ever known. Every night she prayed me to sleep. I loved her Hebrew prayers and chants. She was the one slave who never showed vulgarity, vindictiveness, selfishness, or ugliness of character, no matter what the provocation. She was an angel. It must have taken generations of quality breeding to produce a lady like Pira. And besides I had no one else to love. Luyzi and Suzi were dead. I wanted Pira to have a potato.

"God, please help me to help Pira. She has diarrhea. She needs a potato." Then what does God do? At the exact instant the Kapo stepped out of the kitchen for a moment, my Stuben Dienst came in to return a knife. I gave her five potatoes and begged her to slip one to Pira.

"We are not on speaking terms," I said, "and she needs it desperately. She has diarrhea."

In the evening Pira put her arms around me and said, "Magda, you saved my life. I know you are good. We are all nervous. Please forgive me." We kissed and cried. I loved her so. And she came back and slept with me.

Pira was better and I was happy. The raw potato never failed. In the morning she was able to go to the factory. She was making tweezers which she hid in her shoes and smuggled into the Block. The Block Elsterer and the German prostitutes wanted them for their eyebrows and facial hair. She "sold" them for a piece of bread. Occasionally we were given a half beet. The girls colored their cheeks and lips. I was not one for vanity. I thought if I live through, I shall buy cosmetics. Those who had men friends tried desperately to keep up their appearance. Me, I ate all the beets I could get hold of.

One person I shall never forget. Her name was Joly, an attractive brunette from Beregszász, Carpatho-Russia. She was a Stuben Dienst. One evening a few kindred souls were gathered in Edith Hartman's room. Through the open door I saw the kitchen Kapo among them. They were feasting on wurst, cheese, and other delicacies, and threw bread crusts on the floor. Joly was boasting of her affair with a Hitler-loving German. She was proud of the fact that he was not a prisoner. He had given her a whole wurst and she came into the main hall and waved it at us.

"My God," I said to Pira, "I'd be willing to give my whole life, everything, even myself for that wurst." We sneeringly called her a whore, but I knew every woman in that Block would willingly be a whore for a whole wurst. However, he liked her. With the wurst he gave her a whole loaf of bread, and a kilogram of butter. She ate in front of us and smacked her lips. Her lover gave her powder, lipstick, and cologne and she had a wonderful life.

One morning in the kitchen my Kapo said to another German prostitute, "You know what the Aufseherin told me? She said the Russians are coming on one side and the Americans on the other. We may have to run away any moment." She lifted her skirts and revealed three sets of underwear and three dresses. She was filling a basket with bread, potatoes, and margarine.

The prostitute asked her, "What are you doing?"

"I am fixing this basket of provisions because we may leave at a moment's notice."

I listened and looked at the other girls and saw the happiness on their faces. We tried to hide our feelings. That evening Pira told me the factory was being closed. She wasn't going back to the salt mines. She couldn't believe it.

"I'll know in the morning," she said. "If we have Zählappell it means work."

Morning came. No one called us. We woke up by ourselves. All was quiet. No Zählappell. No breakfast. It was daylight and we were still in our bunks.

"The Germans have run away," I said. "Maybe the Americans are coming today."

"Maybe the Russians are coming to free us," said one woman. "I think the Germans are so scared of the Russians they have fled for their lives to the Americans for protection."

An Aufseherin dashed in screaming excitedly, "Get up! Roll call!"

The day was bitterly cold. About five thousand slaves stood Zählappell outdoors. We waited hours. At noon the commandant addressed us. He was young and very pleasant.

"We have closed the factory and are leaving Beendorf," he said. "I don't know yet where we are going. And I don't know when. You must be prepared at a moment's notice. You must be ready when I give the order. If anyone tries to run away, she will be shot. We have hundreds of Posten to guard you. That is all I have to say."

The Stuben Diensten brought in the soup and little did

I realize it was to be the last. All afternoon we lay in our bunks thinking and talking.

"None of us has coats," I mused. "We have only dresses to cover our nakedness. From the top bunk I have looked over the partition. In the next Block are thousands of coats."

I was on fire. Weren't the Americans coming—maybe today?

"Let's get coats for ourselves. What difference does it make now? We are leaving soon." I jumped.

You would think a tornado had struck. With one uncontrollable impulse, hundreds climbed up to the top bunks and started jumping over the partitions, landing on the garments below. Other hundreds followed and fell on them. Fighting broke out. Wildly we struggled and fought for desirable garments, pulling and tearing and ripping clothing from each other's grasp. It was bedlam. I threw a coat up to Pira who was afraid to jump, a gray woolen coat. And for myself a beautiful beige camel hair. God alone knows to whom it had belonged. We screamed, and we fought. When I tried to climb out, clawing hands dragged me down. We had jumped in by the hundred but how we were to get out never occurred to me. It was a frenzied hysteria. I punched, and I kicked, and I scratched, and I pulled garments from clutching hands.

A woman guard evidently startled by the raucous

screams and profane outcries burst in. She was furious.

"You need coats, you dogs. I will give you coats. I will give you poison. Because of you the Russians are coming. Because of you I will be sent to Siberia."

She was flourishing a stout wooden club. They always carried weapons of some sort. We tried to escape through the door. As we crowded through, she struck us. I caught it right on the head. I thought I'd drop dead. My head was bleeding freely. I washed the wound and covered it with a rag I found on the floor. Pira and I dashed into bed, put the coats under the straw mattress and pretended to be asleep.

I scolded Pira. "You are always afraid. You pray. You think if you pray you will get a coat, food, and everything. And I take the beatings. See how my head is bleeding. You are to blame."

I am ashamed to recall how shrewish I was. My head hurt horribly. The next morning it was swollen but the bleeding had stopped. Fearing I would be detected as one of the coat-raiders, I tore a square of lining from my coat and made a head scarf. Yet at Zählappell I wore my coat. What a feeling of pride and well-being it gave me to be wearing a warm attractive garment.

A guard barked, "We are leaving Beendorf now. You must take as many garments as you can carry." There was a mad scramble. We filled our arms with coats, suits, dresses, and soiled slips. Who had the strength to carry them? Not even a horse if he had lice.

We formed lines, five to a row, about five thousand slaves. Men and women in separate groups. The kitchen being a men's Kommando, they carried all the equipment and food. Longingly I gazed at the piles of abandoned carrots and I all but devoured them with my eyes. Marching along, I wondered why I had to carry these garments. For whom? Not for us. Others had the same idea and one by one we dropped them.

The Germans were driven by an awful urgency to get away. They were scared to death and made no attempt to hide it. They roared and whipped and ordered us to march faster—faster! We had no wish to run. We were hoping for liberation. I glanced over my shoulder from time to time expecting to see the American flag.

When the commandant was informed that garments had been discarded he ordered the last hundred women in line to walk back and pick them up. It was a distance of two or three miles. I never saw them again.

Suddenly we saw a whole field of carrots, heaped up in piles. In a flash, as if driven by the same impulse, hundreds dashed frantically into the field. We snatched them up and hid them in our pockets, our bosoms, wherever we could. Girls grabbed carrots from each other's hands. I don't know why. There were thousands of piles of carrots. Posten came running and beat us with their rifles. We ran back to the road. Someone told me two girls had been shot to death. I, myself, did not see it. Another few miles and we reached the Beendorf depot.

Wagons were sitting. Only now it was one hundred and twenty to a wagon. There was no room to stand, to sit, to lie down. It was dark. Only one tiny grilled window admitted air. Soon the tightly packed bodies created heat and it became warm and ill-smelling. The revived lice were eating me alive.

A voice cried out, "My carrots have been stolen." Another cried, "You are stepping on my wounds." I was dazed. So were the others. We could not determine if we were moving or standing still. We were delirious, crazed animals, unable to draw the line between reality and imagination. Pira crouched in a nearby corner. Next to me sat a lady from Žilina. Mrs. Spitzer was a real lady and with her two sweet and gentle teenage daughters. Madness seemed to have come upon her. She accused her beloved daughter, the one who was sick, of stealing her bread. We had no bread. She cursed and beat her cruelly. I gave her a carrot which she divided among them. It was their evening meal. Pira and I each ate one carrot. We were in hopes of receiving bread in the morning from the kitchen

Kommando. However, in the morning when they opened the doors to permit us to take care of our natural needs on the ground, it broke our hearts to see that the train had not moved. We had not received food for forty-eight hours, but they locked us in. Hours later we began moving and no one knew the destination.

The train came to a stop and they let us out once more to take care of our natural needs. Across the fields we saw civilians digging potatoes. What do starving, half-crazed animals do? With one shriek we dashed for the fields. They couldn't stop us. The startled workers gave one look and fled for their lives. They were terrified as who wouldn't be before the onslaught of a pack of screaming, wild animals running them down. We filled our bosoms, our pockets, the linings of our coats. All too soon the Posten were upon us, smashing with their rifles and kicking exposed buttocks. Helplessly, I lay there. Another kick, another blow with the rifle, and another. I couldn't move a finger. A Russian Christian girl, seeing my defenselessness, and noting that the Posten were pursuing others, robbed me of my hard-earned potatoes. She left me only two. Bruised and bloody I limped back to the wagons. Others had sufficient potatoes to live on for the whole trip.

In the dimness of the wagon I recognized her. She and a friend were eating my potatoes.

"Russian swine," I snarled, "you are eating my potatoes. You stole them. Give me a potato. I'm hungry. I was kicked and beaten for them, Russian thief."

"I will not, Jew dog. Die and you won't be hungry." She wore heavy wooden shoes and with all her strength kicked me in the ribs. This was the most excruciating of all the pain I had suffered. Drawing breath was an agony for weeks.

I screamed, "Pira. Pira."

Alas. Pira was beyond understanding. In her quiet voice she soothingly asked, "What is it, darling? What is it, honey?" She was in a world of her own. She cried, and she prayed, and she talked with God. She was delirious. Then she said, "I wish to go for a walk."

Somehow, she managed to stand and began to walk right over the women. In the dark they couldn't see her. But they felt her walking on them. They cursed and beat her and cried in their pain. Pira heeded them not. She neither heard their cries nor felt their blows. I couldn't help her. I couldn't move. I couldn't breathe.

In the morning light I saw Pira at the other end of the wagon. Her eyes were swollen and black. I thought she had lost one eye. She looked worse than the dead. She was praying and singing, utterly unaware of her injuries. The women laughed at Pira. In the midst of their agony they thought Pira was funny and were laughing at her.

This was the Transport of Death. Every morning about twenty dead were removed from each wagon and thrown on the ground. Guards left the corpses where they threw them.

The fourth day dawned. Outside of one carrot and one potato I had neither food nor water. I looked about me. Lips were swollen and black. No one had the strength to talk, not even the mad. Mrs. Spitzer's daughter was sitting there dead. It hurt me. She had always been so sweet, so considerate, so fine. And now she was sitting there dead. I turned to the mother. "Mrs. Spitzer, she is dead. Your daughter is dead." The poor deranged creature merely shrugged her shoulders and elevated her eyebrows in unconcern. At the next stop, the poor child was thrown on the ground with the other corpses.

Word came that the men were becoming enraged and maddened by hunger and thirst. They were screaming, cursing, and pounding on the floors and sides of the wagons. Guards finally opened the doors and let us out. The commandant ordered that each slave be given his share of whatever food remained in the kitchen. All that was left was sugar which I hadn't seen in a year and raw noodles. I tried to swallow but the noodles hurt my swollen throat. My sense of taste was gone. We crushed the noodles in the sugar and tried to lick it with our swollen tongues. I find it difficult to believe that creature was I. The commandant announced he had nothing else, not even water. We lacked the strength to raise our voices and were content to lick the noodles and sugar. Many drank their own urine.

We were too weak to climb back into the wagons and the guards helped us. And the lice—the lice were eating us. We never saw a town, nothing but fields, flat country. I don't know where we were. Toward dusk the train came to a stop. I heard the wagons being opened. I missed the sound of voices; the sounds people usually make when pouring out of wagons. Then the staccato rhythm of machine guns rang out. The Germans are battling with Americans or Russians, I thought. We are in the midst of an engagement. I was wrong. It soon became apparent they were shooting the prisoners in the wagons ahead. That is, it, I thought. Soon it will be our turn. We sat there quietly, quietly waiting for our own end. The quiet. During the night the train moved on. The men had been punished for their outburst of the afternoon. I heard guards shouting, "Who dares question German authority will die the same way." We found out half the men had been murdered.

Morning found us in a forest. From afar I saw barracks and men working. Some were cooking in an outdoor kitchen. This was a concentration camp. We hoped it would be our new "home." The commandant addressed us. "Be quiet. You are going to get bread and soup."

We Were Strangers

Too weak to stand we lay on the ground, breathing fresh air. Hundreds were never to get up. They died like flies all about me. Time passed, perhaps an hour or two. A train pulled in on the tracks parallel with ours and stopped. It was a long civilian train jammed with German soldiers. The doors were opened, and they swarmed out, staring at us in amazement. I think the majority didn't know who we were and what we were. They brought with them water, coffee, and food. They washed themselves and began to eat. We sat on the ground watching them intently, watching the movement of their hands from the plates to their mouths. I could not tear my eyes away from their food. Our stares must have made them uncomfortable, if possible. They fidgeted and began to talk.

"Who are you?" they asked. "Where do you come from? Why are you so filthy and lousy and covered in sores?"

"We are dirty and lousy and filthy because of you and Germany; because of your ambition and your brutality."

Pira tried to silence me, but I was past caring. And I told them the whole story from Auschwitz to the very spot we stood on. They listened without interrupting me. But they showed no emotion one way or another. We grabbed their empty, discarded cans and held them up to the soldiers, imploringly. When guards weren't looking, they gave us a little water or a little hot coffee. My God, how it tasted. I cannot describe how good. I can only say it put life into me. Pira and I walked along the tracks hoping to pick up leavings they might have thrown away. The last cars in their train were wagons. I climbed in and found a few kernels of rice, onion skins, and bean skins. A soldier poured a little water in my can and I made soup. I made a fire from wood shavings I picked up. I shared with Pira, half and half. I climbed into another wagon. Here I found a large marmalade can. It was empty but sticky. With our dirty hands we scraped the sides and licked our fingers. It was sweet. It was heaven. Being liberated or being killed were now matters of indifference. My only thought was food.

Whenever we had the opportunity we talked about the food we used to cook and eat. Chicken paprikash, stuffed cabbage, roast beef, strudel, hot coffee; Hungarian cuisine, Russian, German—these were all fascinating topics of conversation. When I talked about food it was almost like eating. The mere thought was nourishing and filling. We planned menus. We promised ourselves that when we were liberated we would have the best food. Such non-essentials as furs, jewelry, cars, costly furniture and pleasure trips would never interest us. But food...

I always said, "Girls, if ever I have a home again, I

shall fill the basement with hanging wursts, potatoes, marmalade, sugar, milk—everything the best. And I shall eat whenever I wish, even in the middle of the night." Food was the most fascinating topic of conversation in the world.

I can't forget how Pira looked. She wore the gray coat I stole for her in Beendorf. It swept the ground. It must have belonged to a two-hundred-pound woman. The pockets had torn linings and whatever Pira put in them fell down to the hem. Soldiers were loading trains with cases of food to prevent their falling into the hands of the oncoming Russians and Americans. Pira spied a small barrel of herring in sauce.

She screamed ecstatically, "Look, Magda. Herring." There were three herring in the brine. She put them in her pocket. They fell into the lining and the coat was wet. Just then the whistle was blown, and we formed lines for soup.

Guards barked, "Form lines. You will be dealt soup. Who does not have a bowl gets no soup." They didn't care. The hundreds of dead lying around were merely part of the scenery. Girls tried to steal each other's cans, the cans German soldiers had just thrown away.

Pira gloated, "I have a marmalade can. I shall get a large portion." Into the marmalade can she poured the herring brine. "I shall sell it for bread. Everyone is thirsty. Everyone is dying for a drink." It was so salty no one bought it. Pira and I drank the brine and became deathly sick. It brought on diarrhea.

The sun was shining, a March sun with a vague promise of spring. Several thousands stood in line waiting for soup, the soup which was to keep us alive for this day at least. Soon we were tearing each other to pieces because we had neither the strength nor the patience to stand in line. Maddened beyond endurance we broke lines and dashed for the food. Those in front fought tigerishly to hold their places. And I? I, too, was maddened by diarrhea pain, by hunger and thirst and the aroma of soup. They couldn't hold us back. We ran wildly. I remember going down under trampling, stampeding feet and then I knew no more.

A woman guard was lifting me up. There was pity in her eyes. As long as God gives me life, I will never forget her compassion. Her humanity was a balm which healed the hurt of my bleeding heart. Half dragging and half carrying me she got to the head of the line. I was among the first to get soup. Each portion was a half-liter of soup and a piece of bread. I sat on the ground eating. The soup was warm. I don't know what was in it. I could not taste. I only knew it was warm and the heat felt good. Pira found me. Poor Pira. Her half-liter of soup was lost in the five-gallon marmalade can and she had to tilt the can to drink it. She salvaged very little. We slept on the ground that night. Each saved her bread for the morrow. It was a wise precaution as they gave us no food at all. Walking idly about we conversed with German soldiers. When guards weren't looking, they gave us a few swallows of water.

Our Beendorf commandant was still in charge. I noticed his interest in a Hollander Jewess, a girl of outstanding beauty. Her hair was flaxen like that of the Belgium camp messenger who had slashed her wrists in Auschwitz. Her eyes were large and intensely blue. The short straight nose was almost childlike. She looked like Melozzo da Forlì's "Angel with Violin." Where had she come from? I wondered.

"The Hollander Jewess? Oh, don't you know? She was in Beendorf when we got there. She stayed with the young commandant in his quarters."

Now I understood why she was well-nourished and clean and well-groomed. On the third day she flaunted a handsome, clean woman's guard uniform, complete with hat and boots. No attempt was made to conceal the romance. She was living in the first wagon with the commandant. On the fourth day she accompanied him and helped count us. You would think she was an empress. His gallantry and courtesy to her were in marked contrast to her disdain for us. She was cruel and arrogant. She was an anti-Semitic Jew. She seemed to forget that in the eyes of the German government and people she was the same as we and that it was only by a stroke of luck she was not starving and lousy. The commandant didn't hate us personally. But she did. Maybe she had a guilty conscience. A more non-Jewish face you never saw. I expressed doubt that she was a Jew. However, another Hollander Jewess who knew her background assured me that she was indeed a full-blooded Jew. I am sorry to report it. Proudly flaunting her guard accouterments, she insolently addressed us, and her voice dripped with scorn.

"Be quiet, you. Into the wagons, quickly. You are going to a camp where you won't have to work. Be grateful for our considerateness."

On the fourth day the count revealed hundreds were missing, including most of the men who had survived the machine gun massacre the previous week. They were mostly Christian prisoners of Beendorf who worked in the factor and lived "free." The cook said his entire staff, all Russian prisoners, had fled too. And they took the kitchen equipment with them. The German prostitutes had also vanished. As far as I could learn no Jews ran away. We had no place to run to.

Their disappearance enraged the young commandant and he went berserk. The unfortunates who crossed his path during his rages were beaten inhumanely with a rubber truncheon. I, with my own eyes, saw men and women beaten to death. He ranted, and he stormed, and reason was gone from him. I was happy for the Christians who had escaped. With our last strength we tried to climb back into the wagons. One helped the other. The train started, and by morning we were in a city.

I was in a roofless wagon, the only one in the train. I climbed up the slatted sides and saw before me a great city, a city which had been bombed with a vengeance. I was in the upper level of a huge railroad station. The windows were smashed. The station was a shambles. This was Hamburg.

Below me was a market. Women were selling cabbages, beets, and carrots. I saw women doing menial chores and shoveling debris. Others were doing porter work. Later I learned they were Russian women slaves. I shouted to them in German, "Please throw me some vegetables. I am starving." I hoisted myself to the top and leaned over. Pira held my feet so I would not fall out.

They began throwing vegetables with a will, but we were so high only a few reached us. I was lucky and got a few carrots. They called in Russian, "Do you understand Russian?"

"Yes. Yes, I do," I called back to them.

Hearing their own tongue, they became excited and began throwing everything up to us. In my eagerness I almost fell out once or twice but Pira hung on to my feet for dear life.

The commandant must have heard our shrill and excited voices and our good fortune ceased as suddenly as it had started.

"Pira," I said, "let's save our carrots. We don't know what's in store for us." We counted them like misers—six whole carrots. Now I could face the world again. Pira's lining was the vault. The train backed up and we were on our way. Where next?

It began to rain, to pour. The open wagon afforded us no protection. Pira repeated from memory the story of Noah and the Flood in Hebrew. And she said, "This is the flood, and the windows of heaven are opened." They were, indeed. Volumes of water beat upon us. I cried, "Pira, the very heavens are drowning us."

That rain just had to stop, it had spent itself. I was in a forest. The women were silent and motionless. I wondered if they were all dead and if I, too, were to join their ghostly ranks. A sweet peace permeated my soul. I lay and looked at the sky studded with glowing stars, and I drank in its beauty. Physically I seemed to have no existence, but my mind was alert and consciously noted every detail of those about me and the heavens above.

Suddenly the skies were filled with lights and color.

It was a fairy tale come to life, illuminated with red and blue and white lights. In triangle formation, so high they looked like birds, came the bombers. There must have been hundreds, but perhaps this is a figment of my imagination. It was a bombardment of indescribable beauty. Stalin's Candles, those long tubular white candles with red and blue wicks, were gracefully wafting earthward. German searchlights were sweeping the skies. German tracer bullets etched radiant patterns on the darkness. They were thick enough to walk on. Planes with pierced hearts turned over and over and over and crashed. The noise was deafening. It filled the world and split the head. A bomb exploded so close I was blinded. Our bodies, which seemed to be only waiting for coffins, jerked and spasmed involuntarily. Several wagons in our train were on fire.

Some cried, "Oh, God. Why didn't it hit us? What a blessed relief from our suffering."

All about us the forest was on fire. We were too spent emotionally and physically to be concerned. I was numb. Frantic guards dashed about and at last succeeded in uncoupling the burning wagons. The train was moving. I looked back. The whole forest was going up in flames.

Death March

In the morning the train stopped at a small railroad station: Oxenzohl. Who knew what Oxenzohl was? In my whole life I had never heard of it. The commandant stormed up and down shouting, "Everyone out of the wagons!"

Many, too sick and weak to move, remained. Among them was Mrs. Spitzer's second daughter and she left her there. She clung to Pira and me for she was a Slovak and we spoke her tongue. At times she was a bother. In long lines, five to a row, we marched. Perhaps a distance of ten miles, I don't know. I removed my shoes because the wooden soles had fallen off. And I trudged along barefooted with swollen legs and bleeding feet. Pira dragged me and when she faltered, I dragged her. It took hours, grueling hours. Women dropped and that was the end of them. It was a death march.

Our new camp was small, and the amiable, young commandant bade us goodbye. Every commandant bade us a formal goodbye. I cannot understand it. With his own hands he had beaten human beings to death. Yet he felt impelled to bid us a civil and even courteous farewell.

We Were Strangers

The new commandant remarked the amenities the first day. He greeted us and said, "You do not have to work. There is nothing for you to do. The bread is sliced twelve to a loaf instead of six, but you will be given soup twice a day, morning and evening." Who got bread sliced six to the loaf? Not we. It was always eight to the loaf or more. We listened attentively and were delighted.

At once the Lady Caesars, Edith Hartman and Fat Magda, imperiously herded us into the Block, but what a surprise awaited them. Assuming they were to be Block Elsterer and assistant, they began to dictate and curse us like tyrants.

However, this Block had its own Block Elsterer, a Polish Jewish girl, a holdover. And she was not one to let her position and power be usurped by upstarts. She strode over to Edith and Fat Magda like a general and thundered, "Me, I am the master here. If you want to live, shut up and take orders from me." She shook her fist. "You are nothing, you are nobodies, you two. You are prisoners like all the others, and don't you forget it."

They sputtered and fumed in confusion and it was like dousing fire with water. They wilted before our eyes. Their halcyon days were over. We were assigned fifty women to a room, two to a bunk. A table gave me courage and hope. Painfully we crawled into the bunks thankful to have a place to lie on. But the lice. Millions of lice. Not only the lice we brought but the lice which infested the place. I was unable to sleep with my face upturned. All through the night a stream of lice fell from the upper bunk. I'd wake up and brush them from my face, waves of them.

Our new Block Elsterer spoke to us in Yiddish, the first time in my life I'd heard it spoken.

"Girls," she said, "I feel it is my duty to tell you the commandant is insane; stark, raving, mad, crazy, insane. One day he is gallant and friendly. He will promise you anything. Without warning he goes mad and will make you stand Zählappell from dawn to dusk. Or he might be taken with a fit of cruelty and beat someone to death with his gummi knueppel. I tell you, I've seen it happen. Otherwise it isn't too unbearable. You will get very little food. They don't have much here. But you don't have to work. Keep the rooms clean. You wash yourselves every day. If you find wood, you may make a fire and heat water. For those who are sick there is a Revir." She noticed our fright.

"You don't have to fear our Revir. It is run by a competent Jewish woman doctor. There is no crematorium here, so you don't have to worry about being burned alive."

She told us horse drawn carts had been sent to the trains to bring in the sick. Mrs. Spitzer who seemed to have recovered her senses sobbed convulsively, "My daughter is sick. Take me to her. I am a mother. Help me."

The Block Elsterer soothed her and promised to get the daughter into the Revir. We were not called for Zählappell and we stayed in the bunks. This was our dream of heaven. About 7am the Block Elsterer and two assistants carried in the soup and served us in bed. She beamed, "This is milk soup. It is nourishing, and your strength will return." Only Edith Hartman and Fat Magda were unhappy and frustrated. When the Block Elsterer looked at them and muttered under her breath, they quaked. I don't understand it.

"Milk?" we gasped in unison. It was really ersatz silk powder and warm water. As we lay in bed, we discussed the only subject that had any interest for us: food. There was nothing else to do but talk about food.

In the next bunk was an ugly, cruel, unpleasant creature, Mrs. Grossman. She was about forty and came from Hungary. She had more stamina and life than her two daughters. Their home was really in Eredely, Yugoslavia, but it had been incorporated into Hungary. She told us she had been a wealthy woman and the owner of several farms. She grew grapes, fed fat cattle, and bred fine horses. She was possessed of more determination and the will to survive than the two daughters put together.

She repeated over and over, "We must be free. We will

be free. I will get my farms back. The land is mine."

She loved the land. Food and its growing and preparation and breeding horses and feeding cattle were her constant topics of conversation. She talked only of what she cooked and baked and raised. She spoke only in Hungarian which bored and annoyed Pira who didn't understand a word of it.

"I'm not going to listen when you speak Hungarian," said Pira. "I don't understand it. I don't know what you are saying. I'm going outdoors to look around. Come, Magda."

I, too, would have enjoyed looking around. Mrs. Grossman's endless boasting was tiresome. But I hadn't the strength to move my feet. "Go away, Pira," I said. "I just want to lie here and rest."

Pira returned soon and I could see at once she was overjoyed. "Look, Magda, look. See what I have for you." From the lining of her coat she brought to light, carrot peelings, potato peelings and cabbage leaves.

"They are awfully dirty, I know. I'll wash them." And she fed me like a baby.

Others crowded about and begged, "Give me a little. Please give me just one little peeling."

"These are for Magda," said Pira. "I'll tell you where the garbage is, but you must get it for yourself. The kitchen is small, and the garbage cans are behind it. No one is

295

around and you, too, can get peelings." The girls dashed out shouting and jabbering for joy.

But alas, in they limped, beaten and bloody. Pira ran over to help them.

"What happened to you?" Pira asked. Poor Pira, she felt it was her fault.

"The kitchen Kapo, that German prostitute, heard us. We begged but she wouldn't let us have the garbage. She beat us with a club and threatened to tell the commandant."

She did. The next morning, they got us up for Zählappell before dawn. We were stunned.

"This is one of his days," warned the Block Elsterer. "He is crazy. Be careful."

He was indeed in his usual state of drunkenness. He stood in our midst and raged, "Jew dogs, if you move, if you just move your head, I will kill you with this whip." And he swung the gummi knueppel and slashed the air with it. With us were a few hundred gypsy women. I don't know where they came from.

"You dogs. I give you more to eat than I should. You do not have to work for your food. And then you steal garbage? I will show you what happens to the next dog who even touches a potato peeling."

He reached into the line with his big red paw and grabbed a gypsy and began to whip her with the gummi knueppel. She screamed in agony and gasped. He whipped her with all his insane strength. Reason was gone from him and he was mad, like a maniac. His face turned red and then purple. She fell to the ground. His arm went up and down, up and down. I followed every movement with my eyes; again, and again, and again. Time stood still. At last, and only when he was too exhausted to raise his arm, he stopped. He turned away without a backward glance. Lightly as if nothing had happened, he said, "Aus Zählappell. Everyone back to her room."

Her friends tried to pick up the broken, pulpy mass of what had once been a woman. At that moment I didn't care if they gave me food or not. I was sick to my stomach.

Our daily quota of bread was one tiny piece, about a mouthful. I cut mine into tiny pieces and ate slowly. Pira snatched hers and swallowed it in one gulp. For the rest of the day we were like ravening wolves. I lay in the bunk most of the time, too weary to move. Pira offered to help the Stuben Dienst and her two assistants carry tubs back to the kitchen, thus passing the garbage cans. At the risk of her life she stole potato and carrot peelings and cabbage leaves. Nothing else was there, only dirty pieces of peelings and cabbage leaves. She washed them and tried to feed me like an infant as I lay in the bunk.

"Go away, Pira. Leave me alone. My throat and tongue

are swollen. I cannot swallow. It hurts me."

Pira was no longer normal. She was always happy and smiling. "Magda, darling, you must eat," she said like a mother talking to a child. "You must be strong and happy. The war is coming to an end very soon and we will be free. Free, Magda, my sweet child. We are going to be free. Do you realize what that means?"

I didn't want to eat. I wanted to die. Pira made me eat. She broke the peelings into small pieces and forced them into my mouth. When I pushed her away and scolded her, she smiled and talked to me soothingly, sweetly like a mother. I begged her to leave me alone. "Just one more little piece, Magda, darling. It will make you strong."

Afternoons, women took their blankets and went outdoors to lie in the sun. The fresh air made me hungrier and actually made me sick. Pira pleaded with me. I begged her, "Pira leave me alone. I cannot eat peelings. I don't want to lie in the sun. It makes me sick. I want to stay here and die. Please go away."

Pira was not one to be deterred by pleadings or scoldings. Lovingly she brought me peelings and begged me again and again to eat them. Women said to me, "You don't know how lucky you are. You don't appreciate Pira's courage. We are starving yet not one of us dares to steal peelings for ourselves, but she steals them for you. And she eats only what remains after you have eaten."

One day I said to Mrs. Grossman, she who had the strong urge to live and return to her farms, "I would like to repay Pira for her kindness to me. She fed me against my will and gave me strength at the risk of her life. I am going to steal peelings tonight for her. Will you come with me?"

I asked her because she had a small water keg, which was her fortune. It was something to put peelings in. I was both quiet and excited. Mrs. Grossman and I spoke in whispers making our plans. My shoes I gave to Helenka, the self-appointed shoe repair woman. She was a short, dark, crude creature, an old maid from a backward village in Maramaros. I doubt if she could read or write but she was shrewd and had native wisdom. I was obliged to share the momentous secret with her otherwise she would have not repaired my shoes that day. And I had to promise her a share of the bounty. A French Jewess sitting nearby overheard the conversation, which was in Yiddish, and now four knew the secret. So, we four decided to raid the garbage cans together.

"As this was my idea originally," I announced, "I am going to carry the keg." When Mrs. Grossman offered strong objections, I said, "Either I carry the keg, or I go alone. You are going to steal for yourselves, but I must steal for two."

We Were Strangers

In the night when all were sound asleep, I put on my shoes with the wooden soles. I'll never know why I considered them necessary for this venture. They were large and clumsy and having no lacings thumped when I walked. It had rained all day and the ground was muddy and slippery. Hardly daring to breathe, step by step, slowly and agonizingly we four reached the kitchen. Garbage was strewn on the ground. My heart leapt for joy. Just as I was about to scoop the first handful into Mrs. Grossman's keg—on flashed the lights in the commandant's room. A guard saw us through the window and came dashing out. We fled. He ran after us. I dropped the keg. My three conspirators got away, but my shoes stuck in the mud and he caught me by the back of the neck.

Noticing the keg, he scolded, "You dirty pig. Do you want to die? If you eat this filthy garbage you will die. You know the commandant will kill anyone who touches a peeling."

"I don't care if I die. I don't want to be hungry. I want something in my stomach, no matter what."

He kicked me in the buttocks and I fell down. "This time I will let you go," he said. "But remember, dirty pig, the next time I must shoot."

I got up slowly and limped into the Block. The others had given the alarm. The whole Block was aroused, wondering and questioning. I stumbled in and crawled into my bunk. Women crowded about wanting to know all the details. I couldn't cry to save my life. I couldn't cry if they killed me. The disappointment was too bitter for tears.

Mrs. Grossman attacked me like a mad beast. She wanted her keg and she wanted it right away. She insisted furiously that I go out and find it and return it to her without a moment's delay.

There was nothing to do but crawl into the night and search for it. Leaving my shoes indoors, I crept on my hands and knees over the muddy ground, feeling and groping but the keg seemed to have been sucked into the earth. Suddenly a guard with a rifle shouted, "What are you doing? If you don't go in, I'll have to shoot you. Those are my orders."

"Herr Guard," I pleaded, "please don't shoot me. I have lost a keg which belongs to someone else and I must find it. The owner has threatened to tell the Block Elsterer and I will be punished. Maybe even miss my bread."

"Return to the Block quickly before I have to shoot if we are overheard. I'll return the keg to you in the morning if I can find it."

Mrs. Grossman was like an enraged monster. She was not one to yield an advantage. She insisted I go into the night once more, that she must have her keg. "I cannot go,"

I said. "I will be shot. You are going to get your keg in the morning. The guard promised."

"I don't care what happens to you. I want my keg." She kept up the tirade until the Block Elsterer ordered silence. I promised her my bread ration on the morrow and that was the day I started to eat grass.

From that night no one stole potato peelings. As the women lay outdoors in the sun they began to nibble on the grass. The choicest tidbits were leaves which grew on a climbing vine.

"Almond leaves," said one to another. "They are almond leaves and delicious."

Pira brought me a skirt-full of grass and leaves. I still refused to lie in the sun. It made me both hungry and sick. Every day we ate grass, even Edith Hartman and Fat Magda Cohen. Only now she wasn't fat. In the two weeks that we lived on grass, she lost her full face and her red cheeks. They were both thin and suffering. The women taunted them.

"Now you know what it means to be hungry. Now you know what it means to starve." They couldn't answer.

One warm spring day when Pira had finally gotten me to lie outdoors in the sun there was a sudden Zählappell. We were amazed. I tried to get to my feet. I couldn't get up. Pira pulled me and I managed to get to my feet. She helped me to the Zählappell Plaza.

This was a small camp, not more than two thousand slaves. The commandant addressed us. "You will return to your Blocks, get your blankets, and form lines in rows of five."

Depressed and unhappy we began to roll the blankets. One cried her legs hurt and she cannot walk; another cried she is too weak to march cruel miles and will surely drop in this death march. Mrs. Spitzer cried that she must leave her one remaining daughter to die alone. We didn't know where we were going or how many miles we would have to walk. I only knew I was desperately afraid I, too, would drop dead. With rolled blankets on our shoulders we formed lines in rows of five again. I had reached a point where I no longer talked. I didn't want to talk with anyone and I didn't want anyone to talk with me. When Pira tagged after me and said, "Magdaushka, I want to be with you, don't slip away from me," it made me nervous.

"I don't want to talk with anyone," I said. "Just pretend you don't know me and leave me alone." I don't understand it now, but it was nerve-racking for me to even talk. Her very solicitousness was irritating. I screamed, "My God, can't you leave me alone? I don't want to know you."

Standing there unhappy and terrified, we awaited the commandant's announcement. "You will start walking to the depot. And I warn you about the blankets. Don't drop them if you wish to live."

I thought to myself, everyone is dying of fear that she will drop dead along the way, and he worries about blankets. The Oxenzohl depot seemed to be a distance of ten miles away. It didn't seem to bother him that we had no bread. We were much weaker now. For many it was the end of the trail.

There were two guards for each group of one hundred women. The day had been fair and sunny but as we started to walk the very heavens opened up. Some cried, "Even God is against us." I thought perhaps the rain will keep me alive. It is cold, maybe it is also stimulating. The rain came in torrents. We could hardly move our legs. The weakest began to drop, one at a time. We tried to help them but when it was apparent they were unconscious or dead, we left them there. Soon it was dark. On we marched, on and on in the darkness and cold rain.

"Why are we forcing ourselves to walk," some asked. "For what purpose do we torture ourselves to the bitter end?"

Why? To live in spite of German people and their government. To live and bear children. To bring life where there has been so much death.

After stabbing, excruciating hours this march, like the others before it, came to an end at the depot.

Free

No food had been given us this day. Usually we were given at least a piece of bread when starting on a transport.

Lined up on the tracks were civilian trains. Guards tried to herd us in. We drew back in terror. We were accustomed to cattle cars, wagons. Civilian trains boded no good.

"Into the trains, dirty Jews," ordered the guards. "Yes, these trains are for you, you swine. We have no wagons or else you would never get into a German train. You devils, you will make our trains lousy."

They are German louse, I thought to myself.

The first thing I noticed was wooden benches. My God, I thought, benches. We do not have to sit on the floor. We crowded in on top of each other and for us it was heaven. We were protected from the rain and we were sitting on benches. Each woman clung to the soaking blanket across her shoulders. The authority of the commandant weighed upon us more heavily than the sodden blankets.

I wonder now why I don't have rheumatism. For so many countless hours I have stood Zählappell in the rain and snow, and then gone into a cold barracks and folded my dress under my nude body so it would dry from body heat.

Some women were in a hopeful, jovial mood. "This means something. You may be sure Germans would never permit us to ride civilian trains and sit on benches of their own free will. It isn't in their nature." And they were happy.

"Gossip and rumors," said others. "They are short of wagons, so they put us in civilian trains, that's all."

I, too, was puzzled. Germans would never of their own free will let us make their trains lousy. It would have been simpler to kill us. But what could it be?

In a few hours the train stopped. Out we stumbled; cold, weary unto death, wet blankets over our shoulders, with barely enough energy to draw breath. Guards gave us the usual orders, to form lines in rows of five. No one knew where she was or where she was going. Plodding along in the dark the night seemed endless. Just as a streak of gray was showing in the sky, we reached a new Lager: Zwickel Lager, we called it. Beet Camp.

Who should greet us but the beautiful Hollander Jewess from Beendorf, she who was the sweetheart of the young commandant? She seemed inwardly elated. Her lover stayed in the background, silent, mute, timorous. It was curious, but I was too exhausted to ponder on it.

"You have nothing to worry about," she said. "Go into the Block, go to sleep. In the morning I will have good news and you will be given food."

We dragged ourselves wearily into the Block. German promises don't fill the belly or stop hunger pangs. There were only a few beds. In the blink of an eye, hundreds of crazy, ravening wolves were fighting for them. We punched, and we kicked, and we scratched. Pira and I fought our way to a bed, a single size for one. Six more jumped in with us. We slept with knees drawn up under chins. Someone had her back against my legs. In five minutes, all was silent as the grave. We had no life left in us. I don't know what made me move or even live.

We awoke ourselves. No one called us. It was astonishing. It was a beautiful, sunny day. Because of the hundreds of tightly packed women lying on the floor we couldn't go outdoors to take care of our natural needs. How can one walk on a solid mass of bodies? We were obliged to take care of our natural needs where we sat or lay. No one can imagine what it was like: dirt, lice, excrement, and a nauseating stench.

One girl who had slept near the door and so could go to the toilets, came running in. "Girls," she said, "we are free. The Red Cross has taken us over."

We laughed and ridiculed her and weren't excited or impressed. "Free, are we?" we said. "In Auschwitz they said we are free a thousand times. But were we free? No."

"The Hollander Jewess said so and I overheard her."

"Stop this foolish gossip. We are too weak to laugh."

Pira whispered to me, "Magda, did you hear what she said? She said we are free. God has heard our prayers."

I screamed at her, "You are crazy. I don't believe it. I only know I am hungry unto death. My side hurts. I can't breathe. A bone is sticking out of my ribs through my skin. I can't even talk. Don't bother me with your crazy fantasies."

In a few minutes the Hollander Jewess came to the door and announced, "Girls, go outside. You will be given food." They never said breakfast or supper, just food.

For the first time we stood *one in a line*. The idea of freedom was beyond my ability to grasp. Suddenly I saw men in German uniforms.

"What did I tell you Pira, you with your wild talk of being free? If the Red Cross has taken us over why are German officers here?" Actually, they were Swedish officers of the Swedish Red Cross.

I saw a big tub of beet soup, steaming hot. My God, I can never forget it. Magda Cohen was the dealer. I was among the first in line. This was the supreme joy and proof of God's goodness. I had my own bowl and Magda filled it to the top. My God, I never in my life expected to see a full can of soup, and hot. I couldn't eat it. I was too stunned. It must be a mirage. Slowly I walked into the Block. Only two or three girls were inside.

Pira who had followed me said, "Hurry, hurry. Eat it fast. Quick. Quick."

"I am not going to eat it fast. I don't believe it is real. If it is, I'll eat slowly and enjoy it."

"Magda, you see even while you talk, I have eaten mine. Then I climbed through the window, got in line again, and got another bowl of soup."

Throwing all caution to the wind I gulped it down. As I stepped over the windowsill, I saw a Red Cross ambulance. Two men in uniform were getting out. I did not yet know they were Swedish Red Cross officers. I still thought they were Germans. My heart began to pound. I was paralyzed with fear.

I got in line. "Pira," I said. "This time I am lost. They saw me stepping through the window. Look, look, they are coming over."

And they did come over to me. "Are you getting soup?" they asked. "We hope it tastes good." My mouth fell open. I could only look at them in stunned silence.

"Pira? Did you hear them? Germans and they talk like human beings. Am I delirious, Pira?"

They talked with the young commandant, in German of course. We could not hear the conversation, but they were talking pleasantly and peacefully like gentlemen. As

I stood in line open-mouthed and marveling how German officers can actually conduct themselves so mannerly, Pira said, "They have no Death's Head on their hats. They aren't Germans. They are strangers."

They looked at us being dealt the food and smiled benignly. It was bewildering. No one had ever smiled at us in this fashion. Pira was charmed. I did not care about the smiles. All I wanted was another bowl of soup. Pira got hers and ran into the Block to enjoy it.

Fat Magda happened to look up from her dealing, right into my face. "You dirty thief," she said in Slovakish, "you've already had one bowl of soup. No more soup, I'll kill you first."

"Listen, you leprous swine, you see the American officers watching you. I speak English. I will tell them how you stole our food and they will kill you."

The words were vitriolic, but the tone of the voice was dripping with honey. The Swedish officers probably thought we were saying: "Darling, here is a nice hot bowl of soup. Eat it and come back for more. It is good for you." Then, "Thank you, honey. How sweet of you." But that's not what we were saying.

"Here, cholera," Magda sputtered in Slovakish, "take it and choke." And we smiled at each other like the best of friends, because the strange officers were watching.

Bursting with joy, I ran into the Block and began to eat slowly. I was unconcerned about the Red Cross or about freedom. It had no meaning for me. I only knew I began to feel life inside of me, a warm and good feeling. Food was life. Freedom, I thought, is something you cannot put in your stomach. I could not grasp ideas beyond my physical needs.

Suddenly a group of laughing hysterical women poured into the Block. They were laughing and crying and shouting.

"Free! Free! We are free. We have lived to be free."

"And we are going to hospitals and have clean beds and medicine and doctors."

"I am going to be free and go to my rich uncle in America. I am going to be an American."

"I am going back to Slovakia and kill the thieves who took my home and my furniture."

"I don't want to go back. Father Tiso's murderers cannot give me back my husband and my children."

"I am going home to Budapest and rest. Just rest and eat. I shall never stop eating."

"And I shall buy a trunkful of cosmetics and go to the hairdresser every day."

I had no feeling of elation. I had no feeling.

In the midst of their hysterical rapture two Red Cross

officers came into the Block. They spoke in German, sympathetically and tenderly. "You are free. The Red Cross is taking you away from this. The sick will travel in Red Cross automobiles, the others in wagons. We are sorry but only wagons are available."

They didn't state where they were taking us, and no one asked. Not a word was said about the war or its conclusion. No one knew their national origin. We only knew they couldn't be Germans.

They repeated, "The sick will please come into the Red Cross Ambulance."

No one, not one woman among the hundreds standing there ready to drop, admitted she was sick. Being sick meant only one thing, being put to death. Even now we'd rather die on our feet than admit illness. We had no faith in their offer, with one exception: Pira, of course.

She whispered, "Come, let us ride in the automobile. God has sent them. They are good men."

I poked her with my elbow and shrieked, "I don't care who sent them. Do you want to be burned alive? Do you want to be cremated? Yes? Then ride in the Red Cross automobile." I think they heard me. I hoped they understood.

No one with the exception of Pira believed them. Not in a million years.

The ambulance was backed up to the entrance of the

Revir. I looked in. The place was orderly, the beds plain but clean. I gasped. Who should be lying in a bed but Klari? My God, Klari. I thought she had died in Beendorf.

"Klari," I called, "Klari, it is I, Magda. Klari don't you know me? Klari Czetel, speak to me." She looked at me blankly and there was neither recognition nor intelligence on her face.

And then I saw them carry her into the ambulance. Poor Klari, she had almost made it but not quite. This was the end of Klari. The next to be carried out was Mrs. Spitzer's daughter. Poor children. May their souls rest in peace, I thought, they are going to heaven. When all the sick ones had been carried out of the Revir and placed in the ambulances, Pira said, "Sh'ma Yisrael Adonai Eloheinu Adonai Ehad."

We returned to the Block. The women were uneasy, uncertain, not daring to believe. Their joyous outbursts had consumed their physical and nervous energy.

For the first time in a year I had enough food in my stomach. Life surged within me. Suddenly, I don't know why, I began to sing; Hungarian songs, gypsy ballads. A hush fell, and they listened to me. I began to feel for a few seconds like a human being. Guards stood at the windows looking. A hush was upon them, too. I was coming out of a fog.

When they entered the Block, they were mild, almost gentle. "Outside. Form lines in rows of five." Our hearts and our hopes sank.

"Do you want to go in the Red Cross ambulance now, Pira?" I asked. "Five to a row. We are still slaves of the Germans."

And we marched back the way we had come less than twenty-four hours ago. But who should be at the station to greet us? The two Red Cross officers. They smiled so sympathetically and mercifully that our hopes rose once more. I shall never forget what their smiles meant to us.

They gave orders to the guards that only forty women were to travel in one wagon. For the first time steps were placed in front of wagon doors, and there was straw on the floor. We thought we were in heaven. No one had treated us with so much kindness. We sat down, forty women instead of one hundred or one hundred and twenty. I could stretch my legs or even lie down. One guard was assigned to a wagon. We were given a portion of bread. Two cans of meat were given to the guard for our morning ration.

The guard said with evident displeasure, "In the morning you will get food, even though you do not work for it." I could see he was nervous and irritable. "I don't want to hear a word out of you. I am tired and wish to sleep."

Near him was sitting a Hollander Jewess. It was not

she who was the young commandant's sweetheart. He turned to her and said, "I place you in charge of the women. You will see that they are quiet. Tomorrow morning you deal out the meat. I haven't the nerves for it." We were afraid to talk.

When darkness fell, we began to talk quietly. Pira, as always, was by my side. Nearby was a girl from Királyháza. Her name was Fanny Rosenberg and with her were her sisters Esther and Rozi. The fourth sister, Pitu, had been a patient in the Revir and was now in the Red Cross ambulance. She hoped that Pitu was alive but admitted it was highly improbable.

Despite their suffering and privation, they were comely, and I felt sorry for them. Fanny told us her mother had urged her to marry a fine boy for whom she did not care. She loved a boy who had tuberculosis. As he lay dying, he begged for her saying, "I want to see Fanny before I die." She went to his home and he kissed her hands and said, "Fanny, I love you. I must have you." And the next day he died. She said she feels he is calling to her. Even when we were in hospital beds in Sweden, she said, "All of you are going to be free. I am going to die. He is calling me." She regained her health and as far as I know is alive today.

The Hollander Jewess who spoke crude German announced with an air of importance, "I am going to deal the meat. You will learn how different Hollanders are from Hungarian and Czech witches who held back food and gave larger portions to their friends and ate themselves fat." On this note we fell asleep and the train roared through the night.

In the morning we stopped in a rural area, a very small village with a few scattered houses. Steps were placed in front of the doors and the Red Cross officers, we still did not know they were Swedish, asked us to step out and take care of our natural needs. This we did on the ground. A number of women including Pira ran into houses to ask for food. I was too enervated to join them. When the train was ready to leave, guards counted us and, realizing some were missing, dashed into the dwelling to round them up. The girls were ecstatic, entranced. They had bread and even milk. Pira had a whole bottle of milk. We gasped in amazement, almost unable to believe our eyes, a whole loaf of bread. My God, was there a whole loaf of bread left in the world? It was electrifying.

We clustered around her and asked, "Where did you get a whole loaf of bread? A whole loaf!"

"Oh, I went into a house. Bread was baking. On a table were six loaves. I took one." She hid it under the straw.

The guard said nothing, and the girls climbed in with their treasures. Milk, Pira had a whole bottle; my God, a whole bottle of milk. Reverently I touched it.

The guard began to search, shoving and pushing and cursing under his breath. He found the bread, found the milk, and found the eggs. Most of the food had been given to them. He threw the food out. He was seething with rage. "You dirty Jews," he screamed, "you won't live to eat German bread."

He had not dared open his mouth or show his hatred when the Swedish men were present, but now he was the Lord and Master.

"Dirty swines, now you are going to eat white bread, chocolate, and milk. Our enemies are going to feed you. We will do the same to them as to you. We will have the chance someday. We will make them suffer. Germany will never forget."

Some were terrified and said, "Oh, woe unto us. He means we are going to be killed."

I said, "Don't be afraid. He skulks when the Red Cross officers are near. I think he is more frightened than we."

Grudgingly the guard opened both cans of meat, and the Hollander began to deal one spoonful to each, first one side then the other. Just as she was about to serve me, a girl from the opposite side intruded and said, "You have not given me enough, the spoon wasn't full." And she gave her a little more. I was next.

She said to me. "You got yours, you have already eaten it."

"No. No. I want my portion. I am dying for the taste of meat." I began to cry.

"You'll get your portion. I'll tell the guard you are trying to steal and lie."

The girls backed me up. They pleaded, "Magda has not had her portion. Give her some meat."

"You'll get your portion, Czech liar." And she told the guard, pointing at me. "She wants two portions."

It was as though a fuse had touched off an explosion. His eyes turned in my direction. Like a demoniacal monster he advanced upon me step by step. I cowered in a corner too hypnotized to move. He reached out his hairy paw and raised me by my shoulder. He raised his bare fist and crashed it on my head. He beat me on the face, the head, the body, again and again. All the hatred and frustration and violence that was in his soul he took out in beating me. His fists rained on me, on and on and on and on. He was taking the German defeat out on me. This was his revenge. I fell down unconscious.

When I opened my eyes, I was alone in the train. My God, where am I? I was too weak to sit up. I heard voices, laughter, shouting, excitement. I looked out. Father in heaven—Red Cross ambulances, all kinds of automobiles full of food; people, children throwing candies, chocolate, bread, cookies; Danes, and they were delirious with joy. Everyone was smiling, elated, jubilant, buoyant, thrilled. Women in Red Cross uniforms were dealing milk. I was surrounded by food. Was I delirious? Was I normal? Was I dead? The world was suddenly full of food and kind-hearted people, and I was too weak to crawl out and get it. Someone, I don't know who, carried me out of the wagon. I have no recollection of that. I couldn't stand. I was leaning against something. I was too weak and dazed to reach out my hand for food. More dead than alive, I could not move my feet to bring myself to the food. The girls were running around exultingly among the wonderful, benevolent, good brave Danes. Hundreds of Danes were beside themselves with joy.

I seemed to be apart from it all. I was aloof, like a disembodied ghost. The girls were stuffing themselves. I had not the power to reach out for food even though my life depended on it. They were grabbing goodies, chocolates, cigarettes from the generous hands of the Danes. Cigarettes? My God, who could smoke?

Suddenly one of the girls noticed several cars of potatoes on the tracks. With wild, hysterical shouts which must have led the Danes to think they were mad, hundreds of screaming women including Pira, dashed for the cars and climbed aboard. Pira filled the lining of her coat with potatoes. The Danes looked puzzled. They wolfed them and put the potatoes in their pockets and bosoms.

It was all so unreal, like something in a dream. A man came over and put ten coins in my hand, crowns, I think. I thanked him quietly and just looked at the coins. They had no value for me. He must have come to the station without a food package and wished to participate in the Danish welcome. It would have meant far more to me at the time had he placed a piece of bread in my hand or a glass of milk. But I shall always be grateful for the kind heart which prompted his act of righteousness.

I said to a bystander in German, "Here is money. Will you please buy food for me?" I don't know why I didn't ask him to bring me something to eat. The Red Cross was distributing truckloads of food and Danes by the hundreds had brought their own food packages for us.

On the tracks headed for Germany I saw a train full of German officers. I believe they witnessed the entire scene: the loving welcome of the brave Danes, the joy, the generosity, the love.

As long as God gives me life, I shall never forget the venom and hatred in their eyes and on their stony faces. It was a threat and a promise.

Our train pulled in. Someone got me aboard. I don't know who. It was a civilian train with upholstered seats. I was sitting by a window. The man to whom I had given the ten crowns found me and said he was sorry, but the stores were closed and he could not buy food. Perhaps it was Sunday.

Suddenly I began to cry. Tears rolled down my cheeks. These were the first tears I shed in a year. I was crying because everyone was getting food; cheese and white bread and chocolates and I was too helpless and dazed to reach out my hand. Pira came in. She was my last hope. I was depending on her to bring me good food. And she brought me raw potatoes. It was a crushing disappointment.

I pushed away her hand. I didn't want them. They were nauseating. The others were eating white bread and drinking milk, and many had sandwiches and chocolates. Pira did not know what she was saying or doing. She was hysterical and delirious. I wasn't sobbing but the tears were flowing down my cheeks. All about me was happy laughter as they tasted good food. I sat there. I still didn't have anything to eat.

Pira was sorry. "Magda, darling here is a raw potato. You always liked them."

"I will not eat a raw potato while all about me are luscious food and milk."

Near us was sitting a young woman about twenty-six years of age, from Tisza Ujlak. Her name was Aranka. She had married a Hungarian from Budapest. He was called into the Hungarian army and taken to Russia. She had about twenty slices of white bread.

And then I did an unheard of thing for which I would have been almost torn to shreds a few days ago. I said, "Will you please give me a piece of bread, a small piece, just to taste it?"

She said, "Yes," so sweetly I couldn't believe my own ears and thought I was no longer normal. She gave me a whole slice of bread.

Her younger sister asked, "Will you please give me a potato?"

"A potato?" I said in astonishment. "You have white bread and you want a raw potato?"

"Yes, if you please," she said, "I have diarrhea."

She ate the potato and I the bread. Suddenly we were different, no longer hateful, snarling wolves; for the present at least. And Aranka gave me a slice of bread for Pira.

You who read this cannot realize, cannot understand the magnitude of her generosity, for a piece of bread could mean the difference between life and death. Pira was still not normal. She seemed to be on another plane. It was all so unnatural.

Toward evening Red Cross ladies boarded our train and gave us milk, sandwiches, and eggs. I think all the words in the world are inadequate to describe my feeling when I drank milk and ate an egg and the sandwich; a ham and cheese sandwich with real butter spread on the bread. Swedish and Danish sandwiches are made from thinly sliced bread, with all sorts of delicacies between and about five inches in thickness. I cannot describe the bliss, the ecstasy, the rapture when I put luscious food in my mouth. I hated to let it go down. We ate and ate. The Danish ladies were angels. The seats were soft and comfortable. My back pained agonizingly but I fell asleep.

Morning found us in Copenhagen although at the time we didn't know where we were. Gracious Red Cross ladies with baskets of food boarded the train. Between us was no common language of words, but their generous and noble service, the sweet tones of their voices, the motherly smiles, the compassion we saw in their eyes, spoke for them and their people, the Danes. Not shrinking from our stench and lice and sores, with their own hands they gave us food and milk; milk tinged pink with strawberry syrup. With the giving they gave of themselves, and I could see it brought them happiness to serve their fellowman.

How different are the races of mankind? One people, the Danes, finds happiness in healing; another, the Germans, an orgasmic rapture in inflicting agony.

We boarded a ship. Cold sea winds swept the decks.

We were given questionnaires. For the first time in more than a year I held a pencil. Hundreds were unable to write or even hold a pencil because of lack of muscular coordination. Sitting down on the deck I filled out the blue pasteboard forms. Pira and I had no food and I "sold" my writing services for an egg, a piece of bread, and a bit of cheese. She was the collector and the lining of her coat, our storehouse. The questions were in German and concerned the vital statistics: name, address, place of birth, and so on. Pira was grabbing food with enthusiastic ardor and soon we had a goodly supply of bread.

This can't be real, I thought to myself. I am dreaming that heaven has opened and the Horn of Plenty is overflowing. And I wrote faster and faster until Pira's lining was bulging and could hold no more.

Strolling about the deck, nibbling and happy in the knowledge that we had food, I peered through a window. My God. I saw a large dining room, long tables covered with white tablecloths, gleaming dishes, sparkling crystal, and silverware. It was dazzling. I had no idea it was for us. My face pressed against the glass as I tried to drink in the elegance of civilized life.

Suddenly I gasped, "Look, Pira. Look who is inside, our girls."

"My God," said Pira, "it must be for us, Magda. We are

dead, and this is heaven and we don't know it."

"Let us go in then," I said. "If it is heaven, who has a better right than you, with all your praying."

Frantically we darted about looking for the entrance. We tried door after door. Finally, one was unlocked. We were in a kitchen. On the stove, pots of delightfully smelling foods were bubbling. A silver platter was heaped high with golden biscuits. In the blink of an eyelash, Pira scooped them into the lining of her coat. We ran.

Gulping down the biscuits we tried desperately to find our way into the dining room. It was tantalizing. We implored the girls, but either they didn't know or wouldn't tell us. After much agitated searching, we found the entrance.

I believe we were about four thousand in number and it seemed they were all trying to storm the portals. Waiters and waitresses stunned by the impact of the ravening wolves were vainly attempting to maintain some semblance of order. They were roughly pushed aside, and the deluge inundated the dining room and overflowed. The women were served again and again and refused to leave their places at the table.

Pira and I, unable to enter with the first flood, remained outside, our mouths watering. When it became apparent they were glued to their seats, a gentleman who seemed to be in charge ordered everyone to leave and make room for the hungry. The sad part was that many had not yet been served.

With a mad scramble we rushed in like crazed animals. Pushing, shoving, punching, kicking, they fought like tigers for places. Pira and I clung to each other, and like woodchips on a wave, were swept along to a table. Never again in my life had I expected to be seated at a table and served food. The finest fish, vegetables, cookies, cakes, milk, and other delicacies were heaped before my eyes. We were starving for sweets. I knew I was dreaming. My mind could not grasp that it was anything more than a mirage. It isn't real, I told myself. When Pira and I finished, we found places at another table and ate a second meal.

And then a feeling of drowsiness was overpowering me. I was falling asleep against my will. I felt I was sinking, sinking. I looked at Pira. She was sound asleep. I shook her, "Pira, Pira. Wake up Piroschka." She came to.

"Oh, I am so sick, so sick." Her eyes turned upward, her face turned ghostly white, and she fainted. I called for help in German. A waitress understood and called a doctor.

When our group was requested to leave the dining room, Pira and I were permitted to remain. The waitress interpreted the doctor's orders that it was too cold and windy for us on the deck.

I sat there. Nothing was on my mind. I could not

think. I was incapable of thought or emotion. I was empty, drained.

Suddenly the awful driving forces, the desperate urgency which was stronger than I and had kept me battling, battling, was gone. I sat there and looked at the food, the silver, the crystal, the china, trying to grasp their significance. I only looked at the food. I never thought food would again be within my grasp and I'd not reach out for it. I had not dared to dream that an abundance of food existed in the whole world. It was too much for me to grasp. I was dazed, numb. It was an unrealistic fantasy.

We Were
Strangers

We entered the harbor of Malmö on the afternoon
of May 2, 1945. And what a welcome the people of
Sweden gave us. Thousands of all ages, from the very old
to the very young, cheering, "Welcome! Welcome!"

"Velkommen nå til Sverige!" They must mean us, I
marveled. We, who had shoveled debris in the streets
of Braunschweig and were never permitted to walk on
sidewalks but only in the gutters like beasts of burden,
raised our heads.

The people of Sweden were taking us into their
hearts as well as their land. They considered us people,
not debased animals. Even the most dazed among us
grasped the significance of their welcome. They really
wanted us. It was electrifying. A Christian people was
extending the hand of welcome. I mused they are like
the Evangelists of Slovakia, who did not participate in
the persecution and murder of Jews, but tried, although
unsuccessfully, to help them.

I walked off the ship in a halo of Swedish smiles. They

were showering us with chocolates. It was like a dream. Who on God's earth would be welcoming us? Our spirits had been crushed, ground into the dust. We felt we were the outcasts of the world. And here were the people of Sweden taking us into their homeland, into their hearts, happily and of their own accord. The realization was staggering.

They could not come near us because we had to be deloused and placed in quarantine. Awaiting us were representatives from the Red Cross, the Jewish Distribution Committee, the United Nations Relief and Rehabilitation Administration, and Hebrew Immigrant Aid Society.

We were grouped according to nationalities; Czechs, Poles, Hungarians, Hollanders, Greeks, Yugoslavs, French, and so on. The consul of each group warmly welcomed his nationals. It astonished me that anyone still cared. The Czech consul, Dr. Schutz said, "Girls, you are free. You need have no fear. You are going to be cared for and will receive clean clothing, food, shelter, and medical care. First you must be deloused and quarantined. Every week you will receive five crowns from the Czech government and five crowns from the Swedish government. I shall visit you tomorrow and tell you everything."

Czechs numbered about one thousand and Pira remained with me. We boarded buses. The city is beautiful. Everywhere one looked there were flowers. This was my first impression of Malmö: flowers and cleanliness. I have never seen so passionate a love of flowers. Flowers everywhere, in every nook and corner. Flowers whichever way one looked. Flowers beautifully tended.

In about a half hour we came to an open square which seemed to be near the outskirts of the city. It was filled with tents. We were directed to enter them in groups of ten. A nurse entirely swathed in white, her mouth covered, her hair covered, only the upper part of her face showing, greeted us. In Sweden everyone speaks so sweetly and politely. She knew a few words of German and spoke it awkwardly, but oh so motherly. "Please undress." The doctor, too, was swathed in white, only his eyes showing.

And there in front of the man who was a matter of indifference I threw off the lousy dress I had been wearing for months. I looked at myself. It was the first time I had really looked. I gasped. I was a living skeleton. No breasts, entirely covered with open running sores swimming with lice, months of dirt on top of dirt, my legs like sticks, my bare ribs exposed without skin or flesh, no skin or flesh on my buttocks, and there, too, the bare bones were exposed.

We all looked the same. If one girl were accidently touched by another, she screamed, "Don't touch me, it hurts." We ran into a larger tent, steam-filled. Men attendants, wearing only shorts, had their hair and mouths covered. We stepped into tubs and were given soap and brushes. They poured pails of hot water over us and we soaped and rubbed our bodies. It hurt but the feeling of hot water and soap was good. It took a long time and many pails of water but at last we were clean. Emerging from the steam tents we were sprayed all over, especially the head, armpits and groin. Those who had hair turned gray for twenty-four hours. I had no hair. In the third tent a Red Cross lady handed us towels and we were permitted to sit on benches and dry ourselves. This was the first towel since Budapest. I weighed seventy pounds; less than half the weight I started with.

In a fourth tent Red Cross ladies gave me a nightdress, a brown coat, and a pair of black shoes. Their charm and lovely refinement are stamped indelibly on my memory. Wearing leather shoes was exhilarating, even though my legs were wobbly sticks. With high-heeled shoes I was a woman again. I was regaining my sex, right there, because of a pair of high-heeled shoes.

At last, thank God, I was free of lice. The people of Sweden had conquered the lice of Germany. What a feeling of elation to be rid of lice; lice crawling over me day and night, eating me alive.

Pira got a black coat. She was never satisfied and later complained, "You are always lucky. You get a fine brown coat, and I, a grandmother's black one." I had not noticed what kind of coat I wore, since I was so happy to have a clean one.

A Red Cross officer conducted us to a bus. He was pleasant and courteous. We were grateful and at ease. He gave us chocolate bars and smilingly urged us to eat them.

Our destination was the tennis stadium, a spacious modern building with large windows where the King of Sweden had played tennis. We came into a large hall. On the floor were hundreds of mattresses, and paper partitions divided the place into cubicles for privacy. The beds were clean and comfortable. Hundreds were already asleep. It was quiet. Red Cross ladies were walking about quietly. When one noticed an uncovered girl, she tenderly drew the covers over here. It bewildered me. Was there still kindness and feeling in the world, one human being for another? With my own eyes I had seen her draw the covers over a stranger, just like a mother. I began to feel. My frozen emotions were beginning to thaw.

Pira's bed was beside mine. The second I lay down I was sound asleep. While we slept, hundreds of visitors walked among us; military officials, representatives of various governments, all kinds of people. They did not disturb me. The following afternoon about four, I was awakened by an agonizing pain: diarrhea. There had been previous attacks, but nothing like this. Every five minutes I had a seizure. Putting on my coat I ran out, unmindful of the hundreds of onlookers milling about.

There was a fine infirmary staffed around the clock with capable, devoted, untired doctors and nurses. Pira and I went in. Our doctor spoke German. His medicine helped me and arrested the seizures somewhat. He advised me to eat and eat and then eat more even though I had no appetite. My appetite was gone. I had lost the desire for food.

Dinner was prepared in the hospital, and the greatest care was exercised as to the amount and kind of food most healthful in our present state. On this, our first evening we sat at a long table laid with a sparkling white cloth. As I sat down, I realized this was the crucial moment which would reveal who was who. Well, here it was. A table with a clean white cloth, a plate, a knife, fork, and spoon. Those who had been accustomed to the amenities of refined living knew what was correct and proper. The others, ill at ease, watched us intently and patterned their table manners after ours. I believe we all began to feel like normal human beings. Our animal days were over.

Near me was seated Hainal, the girl who had beaten me in the washroom in Beendorf. She was smiling and Pira whispered, "Look at her, Magda. See how sweetly she is smiling at you. She is watching to see how you use your knife and fork and is doing the same as you."

After dinner, I tried to stand up and walk. Pira seemed strong but I could hardly move. I felt I was sinking. Pira was holding me up. Everything was so unreal and wavered before my eyes. I grabbed Pira for support. And then I saw a piano. With my last strength, weakly and painfully, step by step, inch by inch, I forced myself toward that piano. Slowly, I opened it. I ran my fingers across the keys. I cannot describe the feeling of rapture and awe. My eyes filled with tears and I began to play. And it all came back to me in a flood, as if I had never been away. I began to play Hungarian folk tunes. Crowding about the piano, the girls cried and sang. Hungarian songs have so much feeling and emotion. Everything was hazy, swaying before my eyes.

Hainal came over and said, "How is it that you play the piano? I didn't know that you play."

I looked her in the eye. "In Beendorf, I could not play. You were playing on me." After that she was afraid to come near me.

A photographer snapped us. The next day the picture was in the newspaper. One look, and it was too much for me. I looked worse than any corpse I had ever seen, and I had seen thousands.

During the evening an orchestra entertained us with classical music. It was truly lovely, nourishment for the soul.

It was heartening to know that somewhere in the world were people who thought we were worth playing for. I was too weary to hold my head up and crawled off to bed.

In the morning I had another seizure of diarrhea. My running sores made it necessary to change the sheets and blankets frequently. The Swedish doctor took care of me with loyal devotion. I shall never forget him. One would think I was a princess.

The bathroom was a source of wonderment to us. To have soap and towels and hot water and toilets away from the prying eyes of German men, I was never so entranced in my life.

Many were sufficiently strong to walk outdoors in the fenced-in yard. Surrounding the fence were hundreds of Swedish people, looking and smiling. The girls looked at them and smiled in return.

I state this now with all sincerity and earnestness, that only the Swedish of all people have that magnificent, heart-warming smile and high-principled character plainly visible on their faces. It is a national characteristic. It is as if God had put his stamp on the face of these people, the stamp of goodness and honor.

The next day they returned and brought with them dresses, shoes, lingerie, purses, cosmetics, and delicacies and threw them over the fence to the girls.

Being weak, I remained indoors; the sun made me sick. Pira stayed with me and hence we got none of the gifts. An elderly Red Cross lady noticing our plight brought me a large suitcase of clothes; dresses, blouses, all kinds of sweaters, shoes, and underwear. I swooned with joy. It was almost more than I could bear. It was not the gift itself that moved me—it was knowing that she cared. I shared equally with Pira.

A day or two later Pira came running. "Magda," she said excitedly, "the girls are being given money by the Swedish and are sending children to buy cigarettes and candy. Give me your ten Danish crowns and I'll send for cigarettes and candy, too." Alas, I had left them in the pocket of my old coat. I almost cried.

One afternoon Dr. Schutz visited us. He said, "You may remain in Sweden until you regain your health. Beyond that I do not know. We must try to learn if your families are alive. You will have to decide where you wish to go. Do you want to go home, or do you wish to go to a foreign land?"

For months I had forgotten I had a family. I suddenly remembered—and was startled. "Dr. Schutz," I said, "I have parents in the United States. I don't know where they are now, but the last time I heard from them about five years ago, they were living in Rock Island, Illinois."

I was so dull, so apathetic and lifeless. I assumed he

would communicate with my parents and left the details to him.

We were taken to a hospital for X-rays, and then to a school building where we were given clothing. I tied a scarf around my shaven head, put on lipstick and looked like a woman. And I began to feel like one, too. There is something revitalizing about cosmetics.

I had difficulty walking by myself, and Pira and I leaned on each other. I hated to look in a mirror. I hated having my picture taken. I covered my face when we were photographed.

The following day the results of the X-rays were made known. Many women had tuberculosis and were taken to a sanatorium. The lucky ones, about five hundred of us, were taken to a school in Landskrona, for a rest cure. It is not far from Malmö. Most of them were able to walk, but I was too weak and stayed in bed. My sores did not heal. Neither did Pira's.

We were operated on frequently under local anesthesia, but as fast as the old sores were cut away new ones appeared. Finally, when I could no longer walk, Pira and I were hospitalized. Dr. Lund, a superb surgeon, performed the operation, cutting away all the sores at one time.

When I awoke, I was in a clean, quiet room. Pira was lying in the other bed. I think what I needed most, besides the surgery and food, was quiet and privacy. For so long I had not known the luxury of quiet and privacy.

Pira whispered, "Are you in pain?"

What was physical pain? Nothing. My chief thought was that I have food and sleep. Sleep. I thought I would never get enough sleep.

Dr. Lund had left orders we were to be given food whenever we requested it. It seems we were always ringing for food. We slept intermittently, awoke, and rang for food, over and over again around the clock.

The prompt and loving response of the Swedish nurses, I will never forget. They brought us the finest foods: ham and eggs, cream, milk, ice cream, whatever we wished. We lay there for two weeks rarely speaking to each other. Dr. Lund came twice daily heading a parade of about ten assistants. He showed them our sores. He questioned us in German about our experiences, and we told him as much as we could in our weakened condition.

One day I began to cry. "Doctor, I want my parents. Shall I ever find them? Am I going to die now that I am free? And I have just recalled—I have a husband, too. I can no longer walk. I think I am going to die without ever seeing my family."

"No, child, I know now you are not going to die. When you came in and had your blood checked, I could not believe you were alive. But now it is all over. You must eat and get strong. Eat. Eat. Eat."

The nurses were the souls of kindness and goodness. We communicated only by signs, but they laughed and smiled and brought in trays heaped high with good Swedish food. The amount of food we consumed amazed them. Milk was always on the bedside tables.

The head nurse, Anna Marie, a beautiful woman who spoke perfect German, asked us about our life as German slave laborers. She listened attentively and said the patient in the next room, a little old lady, wished to present us with a gift of our own choice.

Pira and I decided on wool, hoping we would be strong enough to knit. I got turquoise, and Pira who has black hair, got red. Then a strange thing happened. As we began to knit, we began to talk. It was quiet and clean and peaceful.

Returning to Landskrona, I was assigned to the same room, fifteen to a room and a bed for each. When I was finally able to walk, I knew what was going on in every room and became the ringleader. I discovered a platter of leftover potatoes outside every door. The good Swedish were always amazed at our consumption of potatoes and I know they would gladly have given them to us, but somehow where food was concerned, we felt impelled to steal. We took turns.

Honesty is a national characteristic of the Swedish. I sincerely believe if one were dying of starvation, he would not steal a crust of bread. At that time their national honesty seemed so strange.

When Dr. Bergreen, a wonderful man, sweet and good, made his daily call, he stopped at my bed for I was the only one who spoke German.

"If there is anything you would like to have, please tell me." And he made every effort to please and help us.

"What is your problem today?" he asked. "What can I get for you?"

"Doctor," I said, "we live like hermits. We have no one but ourselves to talk with and nothing to do. May we have a radio?"

"A radio? I don't have one to give you, but I'll try."

Our request was published in the newspapers. And do you know how good the Swedish are? The very next day we had a radio. And before long there was one in every room. The Culture Hall was amply supplied with books in Swedish and German. I was yearning for a piano. I had only to ask and the following morning there it was.

We had a merry time playing and singing Hungarian, Czech, and other national folk tunes and ballads. When Dr. Bergreen observed the singing and dancing of so many national groups he was interested and suggested, "Why don't you arrange a program of the songs and dances of the various groups and invite the Swedish?"

The girls shouted, "Yes, doctor. We shall be glad to. Magda will arrange it."

And thus, I became the producer, the program director, and the pianist. As a child I had played and sung and danced in public as an amateur. I searched in every room for talent. I found singers and dancers in the Polish room, the Romanian, the Hollander, and others. The Hollander girls danced beautifully. Lili from Maramaros danced the Hungarian csarda with professional skill and was easily the star.

Swedish girls brought us colored paper and we made the national costumes. I am not an accomplished pianist. I am in fact not even a good one, but at rehearsals as the girls sang their selections, I was able to play the accompaniment satisfactorily. We had no written music, of course. Rehearsals took three weeks. Every day Dr. Bergreen eagerly inquired, "When will you be ready?"

When all was in readiness the public was invited.

It was a beautiful Sunday afternoon. The audience was so large that many were unable to enter the hall. The show was a great success and was enthusiastically applauded. I was dressed as a maid and sang in Hungarian, "How nice it would be to be a lady!"

The Swedish are so good. Coffee and cake were served in the garden and everyone was happy. Then surprise of surprises. Swedish boys and girls in their national costume danced for us. It was wonderful, and we were overjoyed. It was thrilling to be among fine, intelligent people.

To bring us happiness, Swedish artists, singers, musicians, and dancers entertained us. We were ecstatic. In the beginning we were not permitted to leave the premises and mingle with the public. It was feared we might spread disease, but every effort was made to keep us amused and happy.

At the end of these happy days, when we got into bed, we were haunted by our own thoughts.

God, where is my mother? My father? My sisters and brothers? My children? My husband? Each yearned and wept for her own.

Week followed week and grew into months. One day, like a bolt from the blue, it occurred to me to send a telegram to Slovakia. When I had enough crowns saved, I addressed a telegram to Gustave's friend, a Christian pharmacist. I felt there was a greater chance that he had survived. With a Jew, it was doubtful. "Send me word of Gustave." And I waited and waited.

Others were receiving telegrams and excitement swept us. One found her mother, another her husband or brother. Mornings we lined up in front of the building waiting for the postman. If one had good news, the others bowed their heads, their eyes filling with tears, and crept back to their room yearning for their own. If the news were tragic, they all cried with the bereaved one.

One day Pira received a telegram stating her mother and sister are alive but her husband is missing. When I saw with my own eyes that she had a reply from Slovakia and not I, I cried day and night for my Gustave. Every night someone woke up screaming hysterically for a dear one. Unsympathetically we snarled, "You have disturbed us. Go back to sleep. We have our own tragedies." It shames me when I think of our callousness.

I, too, was heavy-hearted. No word from my parents. No word from my husband. Whom would I love now and who would love me? I was crying the bitter tears of heart-hunger and loneliness.

The door opened. In walked a Red Cross officer with a telegram. Fifteen pairs of questioning eyes followed every movement. Walking over to my bed, he handed it to me. My heart palpitated. My hands shook. I was terrified to open it. Handing the telegram to Pira, I begged, "Pira, please. I have not the strength." With trembling hands, she opened it and read, "Happy to hear you are alive, Gustave." The girls crept into their beds and began to cry. No one expressed a word of felicitation. No word was spoken. I understood.

The good Swedish people came every day and stood at the fence for hours, smiling sweetly. We couldn't converse, but their goodwill radiated from them like a blessing. They never stopped throwing goodies and money. Walking over to the window I held up the telegram. They understood and were happy for me.

The news ran through the building like wildfire. Magda has found her husband. Magda has found her husband. No one but the Swedish were happy for me. Many thousands had lost their husbands and they loved them as much as I adored my Gustave. And so, I could understand their resentment.

One happy day Pira received a letter stating her husband is alive and we two hugged each other and wept for joy.

Late in the summer, lying outdoors in the sunshine, a girl said, "Magda, do you know you have received a letter postmarked Stockholm?"

"Stockholm? I don't know a soul there. Who could be writing me from Stockholm? It must be a mistake."

Opening it, I recognized the writing on the inner envelope. I was almost delirious with joy. It was from my Gustave. He wrote that while visiting in Prague he met a lady of the Czech consulate in Stockholm, and he asked her to mail his note from there. "I am the happiest man in the world knowing you are alive. Am counting the days until you return to me. My parents are dead. I have no one but you. I need you and love you. Gustave." In all Sweden no one was as happy as I.

I learned later that during the occupation, Gustave fought with the underground. Returning to Mikuláš after the liberation he found an empty house. His friends and family were dead.

He cabled my parents: "I am alive. Search for Magda."

Papa and Mama gave me up for dead and mourned and wept. Why not? More than six million Jews had been murdered.

However, when Gustave got word I was alive, he cabled them. This was the first information they had of my whereabouts.

One unforgettable day I was summoned to the office and there was a cablegram for me. When I saw United States, I was filled with a suffocating ecstasy. There are no words to describe the feeling. It read, "How are you? Do you need money?" My reply was, "I am well. Send money."

I was afraid to tell the girls. Entering the room quietly and in a subdued manner I said, "Girls, I have received a cablegram from my parents." One or two said, without enthusiasm or spirit, "Really? Isn't that fine." I understood.

Girls from camps in Germany began to pour in. Many were still sick and weak. Some were able to walk. Most had to be carried.

One day a girl bounced into our room and sang out, saucily and with a world of assurance. "Any Hungarians in this room?" I recognized the voice and looked up. My God, it was Klari.

"Klari! Klari," I screamed. She looked at me in amazement.

"I don't know you. Who...Magda!" She recognized my voice.

We flew into each other's arms and kissed and laughed and cried. To me she was risen from the dead. With my own eyes I had seen her carried into a Red Cross ambulance in the Zwickel Lager and though her eyes were wide open, she knew not what was happening. Did not a German Red Cross ambulance mean the crematorium?

And she climbed into my bed and told me it was not a German ambulance, and she had typhus and was taken to an American hospital in Germany and had been given good food and wonderful care by American doctors and nurses. And when they asked her if she would like to go to Sweden for a rest cure, she was delighted. Luyzi and Suzi were dead.

The same irrepressible Klari, she was soon boasting of her romance with American soldiers. "Americans are so direct. They say on meeting a girl, 'Chocolate? Promenade?

Come schlaffen?'" And she added with a toss of her head, "and you know, Magda, I am very fond of chocolates."

With the coming of September, the school in which we lived was needed for the children, and the women were distributed among other camps. About two hundred including the fifteen in my room and Klari were sent to Småland, Växjö. Our new home was a barracks about four miles from town.

The doctor, a Christian refugee from Finland, was handsome, and he liked the women. As he was the only man in camp, every woman was crazy about him. Now that we were regaining our health, we began to have the instincts and desires of women.

Most of our time was at our own disposal. Walking into town every day, no longer did we spend every penny for food. Girls began to save for cosmetics, for a dress, for a pair of shoes.

One thing wounded me deeply: the wolf whistle. It sounds the same in all languages. I had the uncomfortable feeling these men were disrespectful because they believed we had been at the will of German soldiers. True, there were those who permitted themselves to be picked up by the Swedish wolves. And this is how Klari met her husband. I, too, would have liked the companionship of an intelligent, interesting man, but I knew a worthwhile man would not pick up a girl in the first place, and the other kind who had evil thoughts and designs did not appeal to me. So, I had not even the companionship of a man with the exception of occasional discussions with Dr. Koiv.

Not functioning normally, I said to him, "Dr. Koiv, I am not menstruating." He smiled.

"Is that so strange?" he asked.

"What do you mean, doctor?"

"Well, after all you are a young healthy woman. It is not surprising. It is only natural for you to be pregnant."

I jumped to my feet. My heart pounded. Anger raged in me like a mighty torrent. I had not been so enraged in months.

"Pregnant? I haven't seen my husband in two years! What are you saying?"

It was evident he doubted my word. "Well, I'll examine you."

"Yes," I stormed, "I would not have it otherwise."

The examination over, he apologized. My temper flared again. "Now you have found out that I am telling the truth, and it is due to the German drug I was given in Auschwitz."

He was embarrassed and promised to remedy the condition, which he did successfully.

I poured out my heart to him. "Why is it that many

349

have the impression we are immoral, unprincipled women? When we walk in the street, men whistle, and smirk, and try to pick us up. We are the same as Swedish girls. We had good homes, loving parents, and were tenderly reared. Do you believe German soldiers would look at women who were dirty, covered with open running sores, crawling with millions of lice, skinny and sick, and suffering from diarrhea which made their bodies and the one lousy dress they wore month in and month out stink to the high heavens? Would any man take an unbathed creature covered with excrement? Those women who were taken for immoral purposes, and in the end, we envied them, were fed and deloused and kept clean and healthy. Yes, we would like to meet and associate with men but in the proper manner. We are not happy living like recluses in the forest cut off from all social life. Why do you not bring us together with good Swedish people? I am dying to dance and have fun."

"You are right, and I apologize. There is a men's chorus in town and I shall invite them for a Sunday song fest. Then, we'll have coffee and cake and dance." I was thrilled.

The girls could hardly believe it. We were floating on pink clouds of delight and enchantment. It had been so long, too long, since we had danced with a man.

Early Sunday morning the girls began their preparations. They fussed with their hair and nails. One cried,

"Oh, what shall I wear?" Another begged, "May I use your lipstick? The shade is just right for me." And still another, "Please let me take your comb. Mine is broken and I cannot do a thing with my hair."

And they were in a whirl of pleasurable anticipation and borrowed powder, rouge, and did everything to present an enticing appearance.

Early in the afternoon the men, about forty of them, came in a truck. We were enraptured. They sang, and it was really good. Conversing with them in our limited Swedish we had a fun time. And then we danced. I was the first to be asked by Dr. Koiv. My dress was turquoise wool which Pira made for me and I thought I was elegant. My high-heeled, toeless pumps, Mama had sent from America. Pira wore the alligator pumps I got from the United Nations Relief and Rehabilitation Administration (UNRRA). She yearned for them.

"Do you know what kind of pumps you have?" she asked. "Crocodile. They are elegant. How I would love to wear them when I return home. I am dying for crocodile shoes."

"Don't die. You may have them. The heels are too high for me, about four inches."

Most of the girls wore the striped wool dresses we got from UNRRA. But with the money Mama sent, I was the "rich one," the plutocrat. The affair was a huge success and I danced and danced, and it was heavenly.

Christmas in Sweden is like a fairy tale come to life. Weeks before the day itself, the spirit seems to embrace the Swedish and their preparations are wholehearted and elaborate. They garnished, they polished, they adorned, and they decorated. It reminded me of Mama's arduous preparations for Rosh Hashanah in Uzhhorod. The city was aglow with lights and flowers, and if a stranger from another planet had dropped in, he would have known the Swedish were observing Christmas. Every word, every gesture, every smile sang a paean of joy.

On Christmas we had a bountiful dinner, festive decorations, a large dazzling tree, and gifts for everyone. Who but the Swedish would welcome us to share in their festivities? The nurses sang in Swedish, "Angels from heaven came to us." The song is well-known in Hungary and I sang it for them, "Mennybol az angyal lejött hozzátok, pásztorok, pásztorok!"

The Swedish have a festival honoring Saint Lucy, about which we knew nothing. One night in our darkened room, we were suddenly awakened by the appearance of several nurses. One wore a long, flowing white robe and a crown of lighted candles. One carried coffee, another cake. They sang lovely Swedish songs as we lay there like dolts, too astounded to say a word.

There are no words to adequately describe the warmth, the friendliness, the sincerity, and integrity of these people. The Swedish people, I honor and love them. God must love them, too. For one hundred and fifty years, He has given Sweden men wise enough and strong enough and honorable enough to keep Sweden at peace. May God always bless and keep her and grant her that most precious gift, Peace. Amen.

Letters from Mama implored me to come to America.

"Come child, we haven't seen you in eight years."

Letters from Gustave implored me to return to Czechoslovakia. The decision was mine to make. I was torn.

What future was there in Europe? Men had died by the millions, but ideas can never be killed. On one side, there was communism; on the other, fascism. Between, nothing. In most of Europe there never would be, there never could be. I wanted to be free.

I wrote Gustave, "I have my visa. I am going to America."

He replied, "Your parents are right. Go to America. I will try to follow as quickly as possible."

When I saw the Statue of Liberty, I vowed, "To this my new homeland, I promise to give the best that is in me; my heart, my soul, my energy, my loyalty." My tears were tears of thanksgiving.

We Were Strangers

Papers were sent to Gustave. Having been born in Budapest, he came under the Hungarian quota and a two-year waiting period was indicated.

Reunited with my precious family, my heart nevertheless yearned and hungered for Gustave. Every instinct within me rebelled against further separation. I was love starved and sex starved. It was more than flesh could bear. I sailed back to Europe in May of 1947, having been in the United States for one year.

As the train was pulling into Prague, my desire for atonement was so strong that I gasped for breath. For three and a half years, I had not known the convulsive rapture of his embrace and the sweetness of his lips. I stumbled off the train.

There stood Gustave, my heart of hearts. I ran to him. He came to me. I looked at him. He looked at me.

We were strangers.

About the Type

ITC Veljovic was selected as the heading font because of its calligraphic heritage. The creator of the serif face, Jovica Veljovic, was influenced by Israeli typographer and book designer Henri Friedlaender, who developed the Hadassah Friedlaender Hebrew typeface and co-founded the Hadassah Printing School.

The body text is set in Dante, a typeface designed by Giovanni Mardersteig. Conceived as a private type for the Officina Bodoni in Verona, Italy, Dante was originally cut only for hand composition by Charles Malin, the famous Parisian punch cutter, between 1946 and 1952. Its first use was in an edition of Boccaccio's *Trattatello in Laude di Dante* that appeared in 1955.

Our Philosophy

We believe that life-writing is essential to living; that writing life is a privilege, right, and responsibility; that written words captivate the atmosphere of lived experience; that there are as many styles of life-writing as there are lives.

We are zealous preservers of memories and legacies. Preservation is not just the recollection of ancestors and origins, but also pre-serving: a proactive form of service for family, community, and posterity. Our mission is to create narratives that enlighten, entertain, and inspire while preserving stories that are vital to life.

bioGraphbook.com

9 781951 946005